Service with Character

Service with Character

THE DISNEY STUDIO AND WORLD WAR II

David Lesjak

Theme Park Press

© **2014 David Lesjak**

All rights reserved. No part of this book may be reproduced in any written, electronic, recording, or photocopying without written permission of the publisher, except in the case of brief quotations or excerpts embodied in critical articles or reviews provided to the general public free of charge and for non-commercial purposes.

Although every precaution has been taken to verify the accuracy of the information contained herein, no responsibility is assumed for any errors or omissions, and no liability is assumed for damages that may result from the use of this information.

The views expressed in this book are those of the author alone.

All of the collectibles referenced in this book are owned by the author, unless otherwise noted, and all of them reside in private collections located in Canada, the United States of America, Australia, and Europe.

Neither Theme Park Press nor the author is affiliated with, authorized or endorsed by, or in any way officially connected with The Walt Disney Company, or any of its affiliates, or with any other business or governmental entity referenced within.

This book is an independent publication. Any references to copyrighted or trademarked intellectual property of The Walt Disney Company, or of other rightsholders, are made strictly for editorial purposes, and no commercial claim upon that property is made by Theme Park Press or the author.

Theme Park Press publishes its books in a variety of print and electronic formats. Some content that appears in one format may not appear in another.

Editor: Bob McLain
Layout: Artisanal Text
Cover Design: Travis Getz

ISBN 978-1-941500-05-7
10 9 8 7 6 5 4 3 2 1
Printed in the United States of America

Theme Park Press | www.ThemeParkPress.com
Address queries to bob@themeparkpress.com

I dedicate this book to those who fought against tyranny during World War II. Many made the ultimate sacrifice to ensure that we have freedom—a gift that many people today take for granted.

And to Walt Disney and his staff of talented artists, who made innumerable contributions to those serving on both the home front and the front lines.

Contents

Foreword   ix

The Studio   1

Home Front   25

Gremlins and Friends   93

Insignia   109

Propaganda and Training Films   177

Epilog: Postwar   207

Walt Disney's Comics and Stories   211

Print Media: Magazines and Newspapers   215

Appendix I: Wartime and Military Short Films   227

Appendix II: Walt Disney Gremlins Letter   231

Appendix III: Gunther Lessing WASP Letter   233

Appendix IV: Matchbook Covers   235

Appendix V: Insignia Licensing Agreements   239

Appendix VI: Oskar Lebeck Letter: "Der Fuehrer's Face" Party Favor   241

Appendix VII: Community Singing Game: "Der Fuehrer's Face" Party Favor   243

Appendix VIII: A Message from Walt   245

Appendix IX: The World Is Our Marketplace   247

Appendix X: Mickey Mouse and the D-Day Password Puzzle   249

Acknowledgments   251

About the Author   255

About the Publisher   257

More Books from Theme Park Press   259

Foreword

When the World Trade Center was destroyed in an unprovoked attack in 2001, the citizens of North America suffered a widespread sense of vulnerability. But seventy years prior, there was a harsher time when a *universal* sense of fear gripped the peoples of the United States and Canada. It seemed that international foes might strike our national soils without contest. The civil rights of Japanese Americans were suspended. Food, gas, and clothing were rationed. Individuals purchased War Bonds to pay for the cost of a worldwide lethal conflict. Men and women joined in the sense of sacrifice that either placed them in military uniforms or immersed them in one of many home-front campaigns to protect freedom for themselves and others in distant lands.

During the hard years of World War II, people turned once again to symbols to make sense of the confusing world around them. The concepts of truth, honor, and heroism were essential, but as always, hard to grasp or even see in everyday life, or on the battlefield. As the ancient philosophers suggested, pictures were again "worth a thousand words" to soldiers, housewives working on assembly lines, and to boys and girls assisting with scrap drives. And one source for pictures stood out above many others for its ability to inspire, amuse, and train in so many necessary ways for the times.

The Walt Disney Studios compiled a service record that should never be forgotten. Well over one-thousand individualized insignia were designed for U.S., Canadian, and Allied forces, featuring famous and beloved characters, lesser-known supporting cast members from early classics, or a stable of newly invented cartoon heroes capable of achieving all tasks assigned to them. Clever critters with eight arms could repair any ship or truck, and Donald Duck was every bit the patriot we knew him to be.

But the Disney Studio went well past supplying cartoon symbols to boost morale. Studio personnel served in military units, produced training films for all branches of the Armed Forces, released epic cartoons that inspired and educated a worried public, and even suffered for a brief time the housing of military units on the studio's property.

Documenting the output and the influence of The Walt Disney Studios during World War II is no easy task. Categories of discussion need to include advertisements, articles, ink blotters, books, trading cards, certificates, Christmas items, decals, envelopes, flyers, films, heat transfers, labels, magazines, manuals, matchbook covers, menus, newsletters, insignia patches, photographs, pins and brooches, post cards, posters, programs, sheet music, stamps and stamp albums, stationery, ceramic tiles, war bonds, and yearbooks.

Each category, no matter how benign it may sound, plays an important part in the saga of how the Disney Studio faced up to the crushing economic challenges that could sink it, while delivering pamphlets about why airplanes ice up and why donating to the Red Cross was a good thing, booklets about what is propaganda and how civilian employees were expected to behave on military bases, and why the citizens of South America were our good friends and caballeros before Axis Powers could convince them otherwise.

No one understands the contributions of The Walt Disney Studios to the military men and women of World War II better than David Lesjak. He has compiled the single most comprehensive overview of the studio's accomplishments pertaining to the war effort. He sees the full merits of studio insignia drawings as well-crafted art, but he marries them effectively to the service records of the military units that used them. He's interviewed veterans that served in the units, including some who suffered as prisoners of war, and has their proxy to explain long after they are gone the meaning of displaying a Disney character on a uniform, or on the side of a truck, or on the nose of an airplane, whether sanctioned by The Walt Disney Studios or not. The subject of Disney militaria is alive on Lesjak's vigorous website, toonsatwar.blogspot.com; through his frequent contributions to today's military magazines and journals; and through his curatorial work with Army, Navy, and Air Force bases eager to display the artifacts he has identified and located.

Philosophers have been debating for centuries about the purpose that art plays in human life. Many agree that art delivers embodied symbolism so effectively that "a picture is worth a thousand words" hardly covers the truth of it. Read on via Lesjak's scholarship how The Walt Disney Studios led the way in a massive number of home-front campaigns, and how Disney's characters provided soldiers an invaluable anchor to home, and tangible reminders of the spirit of freedom they were defending against determined enemies in distant places.

And to my favorite war-time hero, Goofy, thanks for your bravery in whatever uniform you wore, in whatever scary place you endured, without even once saying "GOSH!"

Sam Grabarski

Sam Grabarski is an established collector of classic Disney Studio drawings and memorabilia. Grabarski credits David Lesjak for stirring and stoking his interest in Disney militaria as "the most authentic and reliable source of information on the subject". Grabarski resides in Saint Paul, Minnesota.

CHAPTER 1

The Studio

"...but fate had other plans for us. The war turned our Studio into a military reservation. All facilities were devoted to making films for the war effort...insignia for submarines, planes, ships and tanks... training films for the Army, Navy and Air Force."[1] —Walt Disney

Prior to the start of World War II, the Disney Studio had several films in production including *Peter Pan, Wind in the Willows, Bongo,* and *Cinderella*. The Studio was coming off a highpoint in its history. The 1938 release of *Snow White and the Seven Dwarfs* was a huge box office success, grossing an estimated $8.5 million. More Americans knew the names of Walt Disney's Seven Dwarfs than those of the President's cabinet.[2] Profits from *Snow White* and related merchandise enabled Disney to build his new, ultra-modern, three-million dollar studio on 51 acres in Burbank. The future looked promising.

While the mood at the Studio was upbeat, political relations around the world were strained. In the February 1933 issue of *College Humor*, Douglas Fairbanks Jr. interviewed Mickey Mouse. Answering one question, Mickey replied:

> Why do I follow the Hitler movement...why do I bother with Stalin? Simply because, my dear boy, the unrest prevailing in the world threatens my sales. Over 50% of my net income comes from so-called foreign sources. When a European president has been shot, or a bomb has been thrown into a group of Japanese generals, I know there will be a terrific drop in the French and Chinese attendance of my films.

This was a prophetic statement for a cartoon mouse. The outbreak of war in Europe in the fall of 1939 could not have come at a worst time for Disney. Just as a string of Disney's newest features were about to open in England, France, and Germany, European theaters closed their doors as blackouts were put into effect. The black side of Disney's ledger quickly flowed red.

---

1 Walt Disney quote is from a TV special on the making of *Peter and the Wolf*.
2 Estrin, Jack. *American History Made Simple*. NY: Doubleday, 1994. p. 262.

Walt Disney saw his gross income evaporate as overseas markets collapsed. Before the war, Disney films had been distributed to 55 countries. By 1944, 81 percent of the Studio's box office revenue was being generated by only three countries:

- United States and Canada: 56 percent
- England: 25 percent

The rest was generated by:

- Mexico and South America: 6 percent
- Australasia: 6 percent
- All other foreign: 7 percent[3]

The massive decrease in overseas revenue eventually forced Disney to scale back operations and abandon all feature production. The May 29, 1942, *Dunkirk Evening Observer* reported:

> After release of the completed *Bambi*, no more Walt Disney features will reach the screen until at least a year after the war's end. Production of shorts will continue, but 75 percent of Disney's output already is devoted to Army and Navy training films. All the service pictures are being made at cost.[4]

Motion Picture Daily also confirmed this percentage: "According to a statement released by RKO, the Walt Disney Studios are now devoting 75 per cent of their facilities to Government films."[5]

Two weeks later, a story appearing in the June 11, 1942, edition of *The Port Arthur News* reported, "Walt Disney halts production on three features to concentrate on government shorts." Roy Disney later remarked, "It was a bad decade for us; we really got into a tight bind around here."[6]

On June 14, 1941, Walt Disney (or a member of his publicity staff), penned a letter to preferred shareholders. Written on *Fantasia* stationery, the letter gave an indication as to how the two-year-old war in Europe was impacting the Studio's bottom line:

> Reduced income, due to the spread of the European War and its repercussions, and working capital requirements for producing and

---

3 Annual Report for Employees, September 30, 1944.

4 Harrison in Hollywood, *Dunkirk Evening Observer*, May 29, 1942.

5 *Motion Picture Daily*, May 14, 1942.

6 Thomas, Bob. *Building A Company*. NY: Hyperion, 1998. p. 150.

carrying our feature pictures for release in the most advantageous manner in the markets now available, have made necessary the omission of the Preferred Stock sinking fund payment due April 1, 1941, in the amount of $50,000, and deferment of the quarterly Preferred Stock dividend payable July 1, 1941.

Several weeks ago the company inaugurated a program of reduction in production designed to bring output in line with reasonable expectations of results from the distribution of its pictures in the United States and Canada.

The *Walt Disney Company Annual Report* for the year ending September 27, 1941, reported:

In our annual report to stockholders issued December 1940...we stated "the effect of the war in Europe upon the affairs of your company has been serious and the full measure thereof cannot be determined." It was evident that the loss of foreign markets necessitated a sharp lowering in production costs in order to assure a profit from the remaining markets...since the date of that report there has been a further deterioration in the foreign markets.

Long-time Disney animator Ward Kimball gave an indication of the war's impact on the Studio in a 1988 interview:

We took two million dollars out of Europe on *Snow White*, but after the war started we were only able to get $200 thousand out of *Pinocchio* and nothing out of *Fantasia*. We had a big market in Europe...we banked on that, that was our profit. The war cuts it off and what are you going to do?[7]

Everyday routine at the Studio changed dramatically the day following the Japanese attack on American naval facilities at Pearl Harbor. On December 8, 1941, Walt Disney received an urgent phone call at home—there had been an invasion of sorts at his studio. In an interview with his daughter Diane and author Pete Martin, Walt Disney recalled the fateful day when he received that call:

I was at home and we got word that they'd bombed Pearl Harbor... it was on the radio...shortly after that I got a call from the Studio Manager and he had been called, in turn, by the police. He said, "Walt, the Army is moving in on us...they came up and said they wanted to move in, and [he] said 'I'd have to call [Walt],' and [the Army] said, 'call him but we're moving in anyway.'" Five hundred troops moved into the Studio.

---

7 Strzyz, Klaus. *Walt's People: Volume 3* (edited by Didier Ghez). Xlibris Corporation, 2006. p.70.

I had a big closed sound stage. They said, "We want that, get this stuff out of here." We had to move all of our equipment. They moved into every area. We had some sheds...where we parked automobiles. They said, "What are these sheds?" I said, "Parking for the employees." They said, "Take 'em over." They moved in there and stored three-million rounds of ammunition. They posted guards at all of our gates.

They had 14 trucks on this sound stage because they could close the stage and work in a blackout. That's where they were repairing all of the optical systems for the anti-aircraft. These soldiers were part of the anti-aircraft force that was stationed all around. They had these guns all over the hills...because of the aircraft factories.

I had them there for eight months before they moved out...they were sleeping in every room. I had to double my artists up in rooms so that an officer could have a place to sleep. They had their sleeping bags down on the floor...they set-up their own mess kitchen.

It was kind of exciting. But it was kind of funny the way he said, "Well go ahead...call him up and ask him but we're moving in."[8]

In a television interview, artist Jack Hannah remembered arriving at the Studio the day after the attack on Pearl Harbor and finding "utter chaos and confusion". The fact there were military personnel stationed at the Studio was even reported in the press:

The studio swarms with soldiers making their headquarters on its stages: Disney offered them roofs over their heads when he learned they had been sleeping in nearby Griffith Park.[9]

Disney staff showed their support for the soldiers who were stationed at the Studio by holding a fund-raising raffle. An undated note sent to studio employees said in part:

Four paintings and one photograph remain unclaimed from the Soldier's Local Army Contingent Benefit Raffle held December 23. These remaining pieces of art will be raffled off again, the proceeds going as before to buy the soldiers quartered on the Disney lot cigarettes, candy, etc.[10]

On December 29, 1941, Bill Garity sent an inter-office communication to Dot Smith, a supervisor in the Ink and Paint Department, thanking her and the staff of Ink and Paint for their participation in a social event held for the soldiers:

---

8 Pete Martin interview, courtesy Diane Disney Miller.

9 *Coshocton Tribune*, January 25, 1942.

10 Author's collection.

> In case I forgot to do it on Wednesday, I wanted to express my appreciation to you and your gang for the swell results we had at the soldiers' party. All of the boys I have talked to said this was the best affair they ever attended and they all enjoyed themselves immensely.[11]

The troops stationed at the Studio heightened the level of anxiety felt by staff. Many employees wondered what would happen next. Americans living on the West Coast experienced uneasiness, fear, and worry. What exactly were the Japanese plans? Was an invasion imminent? Military units stationed along the coast were put in a state of readiness, emergency response plans were instituted, and black outs became standard fare. Apprehension and angst were the norm for many Americans from Anchorage, Alaska, to San Diego, California.

The feeling of apprehension was evident at the Studio as well. Just four days after the Japanese attack on Pearl Harbor, an inter-office communication was sent to all Disney staff from "The Nurse" (in all likelihood this was Studio nurse Hazel George):

> You probably know that the Studio has an active Disaster Committee preparing to meet "any eventuality". Every step relating to your protection in an emergency is being mapped and rehearsed.
>
> Since the black-outs, it becomes impractical to conduct any First Aid Class on the lot after dark. We can only suggest that you try if possible to take the course nearest your home; the Red Cross-sponsored course in home nursing is also very useful. When you receive either certificate, notify me.[12]

On December 15, an inter-office communication was sent to all staff from the Studio Publicity Department:

> It has been announced that there will not be any further "TEST" blackouts and with the change in the Studio working hours, it is unnecessary for any employee to be concerned as to the reaching of his home before a blackout. In this time of need for a united effort, a full day can be a means of doing your part.[13]

On December 18, just 11 days after the Japanese attack, Walt Disney addressed the topic of the Studio's emergency response plan in an inter-office communication that was distributed to all employees:

> In order to facilitate the movement of personnel to safe places during

---

11 Author's collection.

12 Author's collection.

13 Author's collection.

daytime emergency, squads of wardens have been appointed to cover every building on the lot.

> A check of the bulletin boards will show the wardens for your particular floor or building, and it is suggested that you become familiar with the emergency procedure in your working area in order that these precautions may function smoothly.
>
> Upon hearing the emergency signal, WALK—do not run—to the place designated for your safety, and co-operate in every way with the wardens for your particular area. Panic is dangerous. Please remain calm.
>
> These precautions have been taken for your protection and, while we hope that no such emergency will arise, we must be prepared at all times.[14]

Undated, but probably issued around this same time, was a memo sent to all staff from the Studio Publicity Department, asking for help with a civil defense matter:

> A request has come to the Studio for the donation of Army cots, preferably, although nor necessarily, of the folding type. These cots are to be placed in the St. Paul's Hospital Episcopal Cathedral, Figueroa and Seventh, which has been designated by defense authorities as an air-raid hospitalization point. If you have any cots which you can spare, please get in touch with Florence Gill [the voice of Clara Cluck], at OL.8193 and arrangements will be made to pick them up. For additional information, call publicity.[15]

When it became clear the Japanese had no intention of attacking the mainland and that Los Angeles area defense contractors were under no immediate threat, the anti-aircraft unit stationed at the Disney Studio left.

As Disney took on government work, the Studio was required to follow certain government security guidelines. The following interoffice communication was sent to all staff on March 3, 1942:

> U.S. Government regulations require all plants doing defense work to conform to a strict policy for personnel identification.
>
> In accordance with these regulations it shall be necessary for each employee to file his birth certificate with the Personnel Department not later than April 10, 1942. Such certificates will be held for the duration of the individual's employment and will be returned upon termination of service. Each employee will be given a receipt at the time he files his certificate.

---

14 Author's collection.

15 Author's collection.

At a time which will be announced later all employees are to be fingerprinted and new identification buttons will be distributed.[16]

In June 1942, Walt Disney's Studio was formally declared to be a war plant. In a letter to an unidentified contact in Washington, Walt Disney wrote, "[The] Army has now declared us a defense plant and they're setting up their regular identification and control system."[17]

In early June, employees were informed via an inter-office communication they were required to have their photo taken for security reasons. Artist Fred Kopietz received such a memo on June 8, 1942:

> It is necessary to photograph each employee in order to comply with government regulations for defense plants. Please cooperate by reporting promptly at 9:35 a.m., Monday, June 8th, in the Theater Lobby.[18]

The 1½ by 1¾ inch identification badges were constructed of clear Lucite plastic with a clip-type pin glued onto the reverse. The obverse of the badge featured a black-and-white, head-and-shoulder photograph of the employee, along with an identification number. The pin's reverse featured the signature of T.E. Harper who, according to the Walt Disney Archives, was head of the Studio's internal "police" force from 1940 until 1955.[19]

The reverse of the identification badge referenced California Penal Code law:

> "Section 529...prohibits use of badge by person other than one whose picture and name appears hereon. This badge must be worn by person identified hereon upon entering plant and at all times while on company property. Badge to be surrendered upon termination of employment.

Conviction under Section 529 carried a fine not to exceed ten thousand dollars or up to one year in jail, or both.[20]

Two Disney wartime identification badges have been offered for sale on eBay: one in 2005 and one in 2009. A third ID badge was sold in 2011 through auctioneer Howard Lowery's online site. A fourth ID badge is known to exist in private hands—in the spring of 2006, the

---

16 Author's collection.

17 Courtesy the Paul Anderson archives.

18 Author's collection.

19 Email from Disney Archivist Robert Tieman to the author, 2009.

20 Author's collection.

son of Lois G. Trimble provided the author with images of his mother's badge. Trimble worked in the Disney Ink and Paint Department from 1942 to 1944. This badge has been kept by Trimble's son and has not been offered for sale to the public. Walt Disney's own identification badge is currently on display at The Walt Disney Family Museum, located on the grounds of The Presidio in San Francisco.

A two-minute film clip recently surfaced that shows a Coast Guard Police officer checking Studio-issued identification badges, as staff and military personnel entered and exited the Studio grounds. While the clip was obviously shot for publicity purposes, the identification badges are clearly seen on the breast pockets of those coming and going. The clip features one nice close-up shot of a badge pinned to an employee's breast pocket.

In 1942, several magazines referenced the heightened level of security now in place at the Studio:

> Donald Duck and Dopey have enlisted. Goofy and Pluto are in for the duration. Mickey Mouse is now in khaki, doing his bit for Uncle Sam. Their home has become a fortress, its gates guarded constantly; troops are quartered in the buildings, which formerly housed artists and animators. An entire wing...has been taken over by the Navy Department and not even Walt Disney may enter its mysterious precincts without a pass.[21]

In November 1942, *Family Circle* reporter Harry Evans wrote about his visit to the Studio:

> Despite Walt's personal invitation to call, it took me 15 minutes to get into the place. There are soldiers at every entrance and in the office at the main gate. After several phone calls, a gent arrived, told the sergeant it was okay, they made a special pass and I was escorted to one of the main buildings.[22]

Bill Anderson, who started at the Studio in early 1943 and was assigned the title of Head of Production Control, remarked, "There was still security when I came, because certain projects were secretive. You had to be cleared to go into certain wings of the studio."[23]

The May 1943 issue of *Movieland* published a story that contained details about Disney's wartime security. The article stated in part:

---

21 *Coronet*, September 1942.

22 Dennis Books collection.

23 Thomas, Bob. *Building A Company*. NY: Hyperion, 1998. p.152.

"Halt!' The armed guard at the gate...was scanning my credentials more severely than the cops at the other studios—and Hollywood studio cops rank high among the nation's Tough Guys. He was wearing an arm-band: Coast Guard Police. The whole procedure was very strict. I was led into a waiting room while a few "we've-got-to-check-up-on-him" phone calls were made. A pretty girl was dispatched with a message obviously concerning my humble presence, and some more phone calls were made.

Finally, there were some more questions and signing one's name on a list, and I was given a visitor's badge, as in a Government office or defense plant. All day long, while I was out at Disney's, I was never left alone, not for a single moment. Which was all right—for the Disney studio is a defense plant, and one of our most important.

Employees working on classified projects received a multi-page list of laws and regulations that outlined their secrecy commitments, and the penalties they could face if they divulged information to unauthorized persons. The heading on the last page of the document read:

> Violations of any of the forgoing laws or proclamation, or suspicious circumstances relating thereto in the Walt Disney Studio, or pertaining to an employee, must be reported...

The document closed by listing F.B.I. and Naval Intelligence contacts that could be reached if any employee had concerns related to top-secret information.

As the war progressed, military and federal government officials became common sights around the Studio. In a letter dated September 17, 1942, Margaret Wheeler, Secretary to the Studio's Secretary-Treasurer George Morris, wrote to a friend stating, "The 'Mouse Factory' has almost as many Naval [sic] uniforms as the [Navy] Yard has. Most of our pictures are for the Navy now."[24]

Besides military personnel, the Lockheed Aircraft Corporation, a Burbank neighbor of Disney's, also occupied Studio space—Lockheed workers began assembling aircraft components on Disney property. Walt Disney's Studio soon became a beehive of war-related activity.

During World War I, several Disney employees served in the U.S. armed forces. Walt Disney had lied about his age in order to serve as an ambulance driver with the Red Cross in France. As World War I wound down, Disney tried to enlist in the military, but he was

---

24 Private collection.

rejected because he was too young. Disney found out the Red Cross Ambulance Corps was accepting applications, but he needed to be at least 17. When his father refused to sign the required paperwork, his mother acquiesced, saying she would rather sign the papers and know where her son was going than have him run away as his older brothers had done. Disney's mother penned the necessary signatures and Walt was accepted into the Red Cross.

Disney was sent to France just after the Armistice was signed. He spent most of his time there working as a driver and errand boy at a Red Cross canteen in Neufchateau. Disney returned home to America aboard USS *Canada* in October 1919.

Walt Disney's brother Roy enlisted in the Navy in April 1917, and was formally sworn in on June 22, 1917. After completing his "boot camp" training, he served as a Seaman aboard USS *Adonis* and later USS *Houston*. He was granted a discharge in February 1919 when the Navy began to downsize after the signing of the Armistice. Roy spent time convalescing at several different veterans' hospitals after being diagnosed with tuberculosis, which he contracted during his time in the military. Roy eventually made a full recovery.

Walt and Roy's brother Raymond (the second oldest child of Elias and Flora Disney), spent time in the military with a stint in the Army. Few details of his time in the service are currently known.

Story Director Perce Pearce joined the Navy. While in the service Pearce drew a cartoon strip featuring the antics of Seaman Si Dobbins, "The Funniest 'Gob' in the Navy". The strips were reprinted in booklet form with permission of the *Great Lakes Bulletin* in 1918, and featured 95 pages of newspaper strip cartoons.

Other Disney employees who served in the military during World War I included Producer Ben Sharpsteen (Marine Corps), Director Jack King (Army Signal Corps), and Dave Hand, who worked for a military contractor. Hand, who became the Supervising Director on *Snow White and the Seven Dwarfs*, "went to work as a timekeeper on horseback for a munitions factory".[25]

Disney staff members again answered the call of duty during World War II. Animator Frank Thomas was stationed with the First Motion Picture Unit with the Army Air Force at Culver City, director Wolfgang Reitherman was attached to the Aircraft Ferry Command at Long

---

25 *The Bulletin*, Disney employee newsletter. February 24, 1939.

Beach, and special effects animator Cy Young served in a Signal Corps unit.

A partial list of staff that either enlisted or were drafted into the military can be found on the reverse of a centerfold pin-up found in the employee newsletter, *Dispatch From Disney's*.

Besides the military, many employees served in war-related volunteer positions. Gagman Roy Williams became an air warden for both the Studio and the City of Burbank, while others assisted as firemen, first-aiders, and Red Cross workers.

During the war, service flags hung in the windows and on the walls of businesses all across America. This tradition originated during World War I, when families who had a son serving overseas hung a flag in their window that featured a blue star in the middle. Each star on the flag represented a loved one serving in the military.

In 1943, Mickey Mouse was quoted as saying, "We now have quite a service flag and all of us here are damned proud of it. We have it hanging in the 2nd floor window facing the theater and it's visible from the walk as you come in from the commissary. Nora and Esther made it at night after work and we think it's the best looking in the valley."[26]

By 1944, the Studio's service flag had 165 stars on it. The staff breakdown was 85 Army, 49 Navy, 21 Marines, seven Waves, two Merchant Marines, and one WASP.[27]

The Studio's service flag also displayed five Gold Stars, which represented a person killed in the line of duty. Disney employees killed in action included: Burdette Sykora, Assistant Direction; Gerald James from Animation; John Leighton Jr. from the New York office; Robert Squire from the Cutting Department; and Bernard Walmsley from Traffic.[28]

The December 20, 1940, issue of *The Bulletin* reported employee Gerald James had enlisted in the Army Air Force: "...six months ago he was flipping *Rite of Spring* in-betweens in room 16 of 1D...he was the first Disney man to lay down scripto for Vickers...*The Bulletin* has asked and received Jerry's story, which will appear as a series of several articles." While visiting with his mother in Canada, James

---

26 *Dispatch from Disney's*, 1943 Disney employee newsletter.
27 Disney Annual Report for Employees, 1944.
28 Disney Annual Report for Employees, 1944.

enlisted as a Sergeant in the Air Force. James went missing while on a mission over Northern Europe.

A story in *Dispatch From Disney's* indicated James had been reported missing from night operations. His mother said, "He had just been with us for such a happy week's leave; enjoying every moment of it, and had only returned on the Friday. So far we have no letter giving more information, but we believe they were out on Coastal Command, bombing enemy shipping or laying mines in enemy waters."[29] As the *Dispatch* went to press, Disney staff learned through the International Red Cross that James' body had washed-up on the shores of Holland—"a country he had sought to restore to freedom".[30]

Like many other Americans, Disney employees participated in several war-related home-front activities. At a time when the average salary per year was just $1,750, staff purchased bonds at the rate of $3,500 per week. "Since March 1942 when the payroll deduction bond purchase plan went into effect, total purchases have been $769,750.00 maturity value. The Treasury Minute Man (10%) flag was earned during 1944 when weekly payroll deductions reached 10% of the total Studio payroll with 91% participating."[31]

The Red Cross Mobile Blood Bank pumped 418 pints of blood from the arms of willing Disney employees over the course of three visits to the Studio. A publicity photo from the war years shows Walt Disney himself donating blood. Disney staff also donated over $7,300 to the Red Cross and over $5,600 to the War Chest.[32]

Before the outbreak of war, Disney artists created a short film for the Amarillo, Texas, Community Chest. An October 6, 1940, article in the *Amarillo News Globe* reported:

> A major contributor to the Amarillo Community Chest's current budget campaign is Walt Disney, famed originator of animated cartoons, who this year has produced in the Disney Studios a special film for use in the community chest campaign.
>
> The production, a brief scenario in full Technicolor, called *The Volunteer Worker*, shows Donald Duck, the hero, burning up the pavements—as

---

29 *Dispatch from Disney's*, 1943 Disney Employee newsletter.
30 *Dispatch from Disney's*, 1943 Disney Employee newsletter.
31 Disney Annual Report for Employees, 1944.
32 Disney Annual Report for Employees, 1944.

well as his feet—to solicit contributions, meeting the misadventures which dog his steps and, finally, his triumph.

In 1943 and 1944, Disney artists created comic-style booklets for the Los Angeles War Chest. The small booklets contained cartoon panels that told readers about the organization's war-related work. (These items are listed as HF035 and HF036 in the "Home Front Collectibles" section of Chapter 2.)

Chesty and His Helpers was published in March 1943. The booklet folds open to six double-sided pages, with cartoons on 10 of the 12 pages. Each page with cartoons contains six panels. The booklet tells the story of Chesty, his two helpers Polly and Paul, and their helicopter Coptie, who looks somewhat like the airplane Pedro, from Disney's 1943 South American film *Saludos Amigos*. The cartoon images show the group parachuting bundles of food, clothing, and shoes to Belgian children, Greeks, and Norwegian guerrilla fighters, as well as Russians and Chinese. While over China, Coptie is attacked by a group of Japanese Zero fighter planes. A squadron of P-40 Flying Tigers fighters (piloted by a group of American volunteer pilots who fought alongside Chinese Nationalist forces) saves the day by driving the attackers off. In real life, the insignia for the Flying Tigers was created by Disney artist Hank Porter. The group finishes their journey with a stop at a hospital and a boy's home where they deliver checks.

A second version of this booklet was published in 1944 under the title *Chesty and Coptie*. While this edition has a similar plot and layout to the one printed in 1943, it's different in that it makes reference to the Nazi's V-1 rocket-propelled "buzz bombs", which are referred to in the booklet as "robot bombs", and the D-Day invasion of France, which is referred to in the context "the second front is now a reality". The booklet has 27 cartoon panels.

An article in the November 2, 1943, *Los Angeles Times* promoted the first booklet, *Chesty and His Helpers*:

> Met with youthful enthusiasm by 300,000 children in local public schools, *Chesty and His Helpers*...bid fair to outdo the popularity of *Snow White and the Seven Dwarfs*. Chesty, who symbolizes the "spirit of giving", is a smiling little fellow...who wears the same tall, red and white and blue-striped headgear as does Uncle Sam in the cartoons. Every child of school age in the city may obtain his or her own copy of the travel story...published by the Los Angeles War Chest and distributed through the schools by courtesy of Vierling Kersey, Superintendent of Schools.

Disney artists contributed to the war effort in other ways as well. Artist Hal Adelquist reported:

> How can my training in art best serve in this war?
>
> The answer came from the U.S. Army Engineer Corps. There was an urgent need of preliminary camouflage planning for the protection of both industrial and military objectives. A unit was formed immediately on a volunteer basis. Scale models were made of larger installations. Photography showed both the "before" and "after" effects. Completed treatments were used by the Engineer Corps for training and for actual work in the field. On the strength of the initial work, more assignments were given.
>
> Soon the Marine Corps became interested, requesting contour maps of strategic objectives to aid in military operations. From the Army came a request for a slide film demonstrating the history and value of camouflage. The resulting production was distributed widely.
>
> Illustrations for Army and Marine Corps manuals, posters on camouflage, on discipline, and for the procurement of personnel were accomplished. Unassigned experimental work sought "new angles" on protective concealment. Much of the model work encompassed important industrial installations. In some cases, treatments were suggested for five square miles of surrounding terrain. Reports were compiled on systems for building models and making contour maps.[33]

According to retired Walt Disney Company Archivist Dave Smith, the volunteer unit Adelquist referred to consisted of 10 to 12 men who worked on their own time, usually in the evenings. The artists involved with the project manufactured a four-by-eight-foot model of the Lockheed plant, and then designed and crafted a camouflage net that was strung overtop a portion of it. The unit existed for approximately nine months and was disbanded in 1942 after most of the artists involved with the volunteer endeavor had been called to serve in the military.

Two books related to camouflage also had input from Disney artists. The first, *Camouflage Field Training Manual of the Second Marine Division*, carries an acknowledgement on page 26 that the models shown in the booklet were "prepared by the Walt Disney Studio for the 604th Engineer Battalion". The second publication, *War Department Field Manual 20-C Camouflage of Bivouacs*, was a 72-page booklet published in May 1944 that also contained Disney illustrations.

The maximum draft age in 1942 was 26 years for married and 35

---

33 *Dispatch from Disney's*, 1943 Disney Studio employee newsletter.

years for single men. Everyone over the age of 18 could be called upon to serve. The draft eventually took one-third of Disney's employees.[34]

The draft had an impact on one of the Studio's first war-related projects. In November 1941, Disney Production Manager Robert Carr wrote to the Commissioner of the National Film Board of Canada:

> Thank you very much for your telegram yesterday telling us that you liked *The Thrifty Pig* [a bond film being produced for the Canadian government]. Walt was glad that you are satisfied and sends his regards. Your French title sequences will not be ready at the same time as the English. Our special artist who was working on this and who had the whole thing at his fingertips has just been drafted. Ub is putting new people on it and doing everything possible to get the French title sequence to you as quickly as possible.[35]

When Disney complained that many of his best talent were being drafted, military officers working liaison positions at the Studio suggested he appear before draft boards to ask for deferments. Commenting on his situation Walt Disney said, "They seem to think we're still doing Mickey Mouse."[36] Disney instead invited draft boards to the Studio, where board members had to be cleared by military intelligence and the Federal Bureau of Investigation. Despite undergoing these two in-depth clearances, there were still areas of the Studio that were deemed off-limits because of the top-secret military projects artists were working on.

After their tour, board members allowed many of Disney's drafted employees to return to work. Those artists who could not be deferred often went to work as animators for the U.S. Army Signal Corps. The draft and the Studio's 1941 strike resulted in Disney's payroll falling from a high of just under 1,200 employees during the production of *Snow White*, to around 500 by the end of 1942.[37]

The June 18, 1942, edition of *Motion Picture Daily* showcased several lists of movie industry employees now serving with the military. The names were organized by studio, and the list for The Walt Disney Studios contained 56 staff including Xavier Atencio, Clair Weeks, and Wolfgang Reitherman.

---

34 Thomas, Bob. *Walt Disney. An American Original.* p.177.

35 National Film Board of Canada Archives.

36 Miller, Diane Disney (as told to Pete Martin). *The Story of Walt Disney.* Dell Publishing Co., NY, 1959. p.180.

37 *Fortune*, August 1944.

The drain on Disney's staff continued for the duration of the war. The effect of the draft on the Studio's ability to produce both commercial and government films was mentioned in the 1944 Annual Report:

> Costs of operation for the year reflected a substantial increase occasioned chiefly by heavy wartime labor turnover, the loss of certain skilled personnel to the armed forces and the necessity of maintaining flexible schedules to accommodate the demands of Governmental agencies for training films. This trend has characterized each of the three war years and in the face of postwar uncertainties seems likely to extend even past V-day.

Despite being upset he was losing so many staff to the draft, Disney fully supported employees who expressed a desire to enter the service. On September 22, 1942, Walt Disney wrote a letter of recommendation for a staffer applying for a commission in the Marine Corps. The letter read in part:

> Mr. [C.W.] Batchelder has been with our organization since June, 1934.
>
> In his capacity as head of our Camera Department he had, of course, a thorough knowledge of photography, both live action and animation. However, along with his technical knowledge, he proved to have unusual organizational and executive ability.
>
> The Camera Department is one of the most important links in the production of our pictures and in turning our great quantities of film on schedule, Mr. Batchelder showed by the handling of the men working under his supervision, outstanding qualities of leadership.
>
> In his personal qualifications we have found him dependable, likable, and intelligent. He leaves us with all the respect and good will we can extend to a thoroughly satisfactory employee."[38]

The Studio eventually fell under the jurisdiction of the Manning Table and Replacement Schedule. This piece of Federal legislation allowed companies to keep key employees who might otherwise be drafted by the Selective Service Act.

On March 21, 1944, artist Fred Kopietz received an inter-office communication regarding his draft status. The memo read, in part:

> You appear on our newly accepted Replacement Schedule for an "over six months" deferment. This is the maximum deferment allowed on any Replacement Schedule. A 42-A Form, which is a request for deferment and informs the Board of your status on our Replacement Schedule, will be mailed in by the company during the month of April. As a result

---

38 Private collection.

of this, and provided there are no drastic changes in Selective Service policies, you should receive another 2-A classification.[39]

The 2-A Classification was an occupational deferment available to those (other than students or agricultural workers) performing vital, war-related work.

As Disney staff members were artists, it's not surprising that about 70 formed their own theatrical group. The group performed at military camps and hospitals throughout southern California. In his book *Justice for Disney*, artist Bill Justice referred to the group as a "poor man's Bob Hope show". The group included dancers, singers, actors, and Ward Kimball's band, the "Hugajeedy 8". The 1944 Annual Report for Employees mentioned the performers:

> A camp show unit of employee entertainers gave many shows in nearby camps and hospitals, including several performances of the Drama Group production *Curse You Jack Dalton*.

Two "call sheets" from the spring of 1945 refer to the production as simply, "Disney Camp Show". On March 21, 1945, the group traveled to the U.S. Navy Hospital in Long Beach, while on May 2, 1945, the group drove north to the Biltmore Hotel in Santa Barbara, where they put on a show for the "Redistribution Station".[40] Each call sheet runs four pages in length, and documents who was involved in the show, what their responsibilities were, and what the program for each performance was going to be.

The May 2, 1945, call sheet listed the names of 47 staff members who had signed-up to participate in the program, as well as the following program information:

- 8:00 p.m.: Curtain opens
- Short cartoons: *Tiger Trouble* or *How to Play Football*
- Overture
- Can-can
- Quartette
- "Strolling Through the Park"
- Juggler
- Magician

---

39 Author's collection.

40 Author's collection.

- Entire olio company singing "By the Sea"
- Recitation
- *Curse You, Jack Dalton*
- Eadie Mae Moore sings, accompanied by Milt Banta
- Ward Kimball, Hugajeedy Eight play "Bugle Call Rag"
- Ward Kimball introduces Bill Justice
- Band plays "Jumpin' at the Woodside" as Justice draws Disney characters
- Georgia Skinner sings three songs
- Band plays "Heigh Ho"
- Entire company on stage singing "Heigh Ho"[41]

To keep in touch with employees serving in military units around the world, the Studio issued a newsletter in the spring of 1943. Ralph Parker edited *Dispatch from Disney's* and only one edition of the publication was produced. In a letter dated April 12, 1943, to artist George Goepper, Walt Disney made reference to the *Dispatch*:

> With so many of our gang scattered all over the world, we thought they might be interested in knowing what we are doing and what's going on while they are away. For this reason, we cooked up this little magazine and we hope it will do the job of letting everyone know what's happening back home. Rest assured we are all doing our best, working as hard as we can and we hope the day won't be too far away when this whole mess is straightened out and we can carry on again in what is known as the normal way of life."[42]

The *Dispatch* contained 38 pages of information and a gatefold featuring nude pin-up girls drawn by Freddie Moore, Bill Justice, and Milt Kahl. There were letters from Walt, Roy, and Mickey Mouse, artist profiles, project updates, and guest columns. The cover featured an adaptation of the *Der Fuehrer's Face* sheet music illustration with Donald Duck throwing an overripe tomato at Hitler's face, while the back cover pictured several Studio-designed military insignia (drawn by artist Hank Porter) in a V-shaped design.

In the newsletter's forward, Walt Disney wrote:

> People who write forewords are inclined to talk down to the audience.

---

41 Author's collection.

42 Author's collection.

Talking to you fellow employees in the services, I find myself looking up in a spirit of admiration.

Here is news of our effort to back you up, along with a glimpse of familiar faces and happenings. We hope this will make you feel like grabbing pencil, brush or camera and sending us news of yourself. Your contributions are welcome—the magazine will be the medium through which every employee can learn what you are doing and thinking.

Working, as we never worked before, on films for the Army and Navy, we are thinking of the time when you are coming back. Animation is proving that it can help with major problems. The lessons learned, you will apply constructively in solving the problems of peace.

Making training films about torpedo tactics, anti-tank guns, forming methods and others too hush-hush to mention, we are learning techniques for tackling our share of the reconstruction problems ahead. Films for the preservation of health and morale in war lead to comparable films for peace.

Making films for the development of better understanding between North and South America, we look forward to similar work on a worldwide scale. New and better types of educational motion pictures give cohesion to this torn earth. Light for China and India must reach their millions through the projection machine. Science, Economics, and Industry must be given a voice which all can understand. With these and a thousand other problems, the motion picture can be more helpful than any other force.

That is the work to which you will return with the ending of the war. It is an important part of the work to be done, a good thought to hold. Using the ways and means, which the art of animation is acquiring through films of war, you will make constructive educational films for peace.

Wherever you are, the good wishes of each of us are with you.[43]

In his letter, titled "Communique from the Film Front", Roy Disney wrote:

As I came into the Studio this morning and saw our service flag with 165 stars on it (two Gold), I was jolted into the realization that the war is rapidly making us an organization of veterans, and I do mean oldtimers [sic].

Many of us who are following through while you are scattered the globe over defending our freedom, thought we had settled that issue twenty-five years ago. Schicklgruber decided differently, however, and now we oldtimers [sic] find ourselves fighting with the one weapon we are most capable of handling—the motion picture.

---

43 *Dispatch from Disney's*, 1943 Disney Studio employee newsletter.

> You know better than we do at home what it means to see a good motion picture after a back-breaking day. Your morale, and that of every United Nations soldier, is very much our obligation. The training film, too, is most important, as our Army and Navy have found. So, too, are the pictures on health, and those which carry the message of America's might to all free countries.
>
> This work we are doing today under the heading of defense films has opened up a tremendous field for our medium. It's an education to us as well. When this mess is all over, and we are free men once more, I sincerely hope that you will be instrumental, with us, in bringing our medium to the heights which we now can see ahead for it."[44]

Ralph Parker's son Ron said the *Dispatch* was his father's personal project, and when his father left the Studio no further issues of *Dispatch* were produced:

> It was my father's thing, so [it] didn't continue. It was mainly to be an information update and morale booster for Disney employees who were serving in the WW II military. It was printed by the *Los Angeles Times* empire of the Chandler family, who at the time had the most advanced printing facility in North America, which explains the good quality of the printing job.[45]

As the war progressed, the Studio and its employees settled into their newfound role. Disney's artists soon began making significant contributions to the war effort. The same artists, who had entertained the public with the "feel good" fairy tales of *Snow White and the Seven Dwarfs* and *Pinocchio*, turned their talents to producing training films for all branches of the military and propaganda films to promote political messages, and designing insignia to bolster the morale of soldiers serving overseas.

---

44 *Dispatch from Disney's*, 1943 Disney Studio employee newsletter.

45 Quote courtesy Sam Grabarski, email interview with Ron Parker, June 2003.

Studio Collectibles

ST001a *Dispatch from Disney's.* 1943. 5½ x 8
This 38-page newsletter was sent to Disney staff serving in the military. Only one issue was published. The front cover was an adaptation of the *Der Fuehrer's Face* sheet music cover that featured Donald Duck throwing an over-ripe tomato at Hitler's face. The booklet-style newsletter contains letters written by Walt, Roy, and Mickey, guest columns, employee profiles, film and project updates, and a girlie gatefold. The front-cover illustration was created by Disney artist T. Hee, who had a reputation of being an excellent caricaturist. The art was based on the illustration found on the cover of the film's sheet music, which had been created by Disney artist Ward Kimball.

ST001b *Dispatch from Disney's.*
Detail found on the top of page one.

ST001c *Dispatch from Disney's.*
Detail from an inside page titled "If our World War I vets had looked then as they look now..." The illustrations were created by Disney animator and later storyboard artist Bill Peet.

ST001d *Dispatch from Disney's.*
The back cover features insignia designs created by Disney artist Hank Porter, whom Walt Disney once referred to as a "one man art department".

ST001e *Dispatch from Disney's.*
Detail from the mailing envelope used to post the newsletter to Disney employees serving in military units around the world.

ST002 Nude pinups for Servicemen. 1943. 10 x 16
This gatefold was included in copies of *Dispatch from Disney's*, an employee newsletter sent to staff serving in the military. Disney artists Freddie Moore, Bill Justice, and Milt Kahl drew the art found on the pinup. The reverse of the gatefold has an extensive list that showcases the names of Disney staffers and the units in which they were serving in.

ST003 *Dispatch from Disney's*, Walt Disney letter. April 12, 1943.
In April 1943, Walt Disney sent a copy of the Studio booklet-style newsletter *Dispatch from Disney's* to animator George Goepper. The newsletter's cover was signed by Walt Disney and several other prominent Studio employees. The letter read:

Dear George.

With so many of our gang scattered all over the world, we thought they might be interested in knowing what we are doing here and what's going on while they are away.

For this reason, we cooked up this little magazine and we hope it will do the job of letting everyone know what's happening back home.

Several of the gang have put their John Henry's on the cover of the magazine, which is just their way of saying "hello" and "good wishes".

Rest assured we are all doing our best, working as hard as we can and we hope the day won't be too far off when this whole mess is straightened out and we can carry on again in what is known as the normal way of life.

As ever,

Walt

P.S. If you like the magazine, please write us and if you have any material which would interest the rest of the gang, send it on as we would appreciate having it.

ST004 Walt Disney Studio corporate Christmas card. 1943.

Walt Disney began issuing corporate Christmas cards in 1930. The 1942 card has a war theme that pictures Santa Claus sitting atop a bomber with the caption, "The same old wish but never more sincerely, Merry Christmas and a Victory Through Air Power New Year." The card made reference to Disney's propaganda film, *Victory Through Air Power*. This is the only Studio Christmas card to make reference to World War II. Mickey, Minnie, Donald, and Pluto are pictured wearing military uniforms.

ST005 Inter-office memo. December 11, 1941.

This staff memo was circulated by the Studio's Nurse and announced that because of blackouts the First Aid class being held at the Studio was canceled.

ST006 Inter-office memo. December 18, 1941.

This memo was sent out by Walt Disney to all staff and addressed the issues of emergency planning, staff safety, and air raid wardens.

ST007 Inter-office memo. December 29, 1941.

In this staff memo from Bill Garity to Dot Smith, Garity thanked Smith and the staff of the Ink and Paint Department for participating in a social event held to benefit local soldiers.

ST008 Inter-office memo. June 8, 1942.

This staff memo directed artist Fred Kopietz to the Studio theater where he would have his photo taken for his employee ID pin.

ST009 Inter-office memo. March 21, 1944.

This staff memo to artist Fred Kopietz informed him the Studio had been notified he had been granted a six-month deferral from the draft.

ST010 Employee identification pin. Circa June 1942. 1½ x 1¾

In June 1942, staff had their photos taken in the Studio theatre as part of a federal identification program instituted for war plants. The pin consists of an orange-colored piece of paper bearing the staffer's black-and-white photo on the obverse, while the reverse bears the signature of the head of Studio security T.F. Harper and a quote from section 529 of the California penal code. The papers are encased in a Lucite-type plastic, to which is mounted a pin.

ST011 Walt Disney Studio bulletin board announcement. 1940. 9½ x 12½

This bulletin board announcement would have been tacked-up on boards around the Studio sometime in December 1940. The flyer invited staff to join Walt and Roy Disney at a local bar named Victor's for drinks. Negative headlines on the flyer appear in green over a white background. These headlines give an indication as to how badly the war in Europe was proceeding: the Nazis had occupied Paris, Denmark, and Holland. The headlines also indicate that *Fantasia*, the Studio's newest release, had a poor initial opening at the box office. A facsimile message printed on the flyer in orange crayon in what is supposed to be Walt Disney's handwriting states, "What the hell—come on over to Victor's and have a drink on us." Some researchers believe this item was an insert included with the 1943 Studio Christmas card (ST004).

CHAPTER 2
Home Front

"Now what are you going to do? Spend for the Axis, or save for taxes? Just remember, every dollar you spend for something you don't need is a dollar spent to help the Axis...and every dollar you sock away is another dollar to sock the Axis."[46]

During the war, Disney's stable of characters was used extensively to promote various home-front programs. Mickey, Minnie, and the rest of the gang happily performed their patriotic duties by promoting blood drives, victory gardens, and volunteer work.

Disney's characters were also pressed into service by numerous government agencies including the War Manpower Commission, Food Distribution Administration, Treasury Department, Department of Agriculture, War Production Board, and War Finance Committee. As government employees, Mickey and the gang promoted rationing, good nutrition, bond and savings drives, and the payment of income tax.

Walt Disney himself was called upon by government agencies to write patriotic and inspiring articles that appeared in magazines and newspapers, and scripts that were broadcast on radio throughout America and Europe.

One of the first home-front projects the Disney Studio worked on involved the Canadian government. One month after producing Lockheed's *Four Methods of Flush Riveting* (this film is discussed further in Chapter 5, Propaganda and Training Films), Disney met with John Grierson, the Commissioner of the National Film Board of Canada. At this meeting, Grierson secured the rights to the Lockheed training film, and he signed a contract with Disney for the production of four bond films and one military training film. As a member of the Commonwealth, Canada was already involved with the European conflict, having declared war on Germany on September 10, 1939.

---

46 Narrator, tax film.

A letter of agreement between Disney and the Canadian government was signed August 4, 1941. Later that month, a press release from the NFB outlined Disney's involvement in the Canadian war effort:

> The National Film Board has secured the cooperation of the Walt Disney Studios to make films for the Government of Canada. Walt Disney has offered his cooperation and that of his Studio staff as a personal measure of support. Two representatives of Mr. Disney's Studios, Mr. Robert Carr and Mr. Ub Iwerks, have arrived in Ottawa...to discuss two projects which the Disney Studios will begin working on immediately.
>
> The first is a series of films for the War Savings Committee. The pictures will be short animated cartoons, done in Technicolor in the inimitable Walt Disney style. Disney's characters will stage a war savings parade on Parliament Hill, Donald Duck will obey his better self...the Three Little Pigs will show how to beat the Big Bad Wolf and Snow White's famous Seven Dwarfs will hock their jewels to serve the national cause.
>
> The second project is a military training film ...to be made for the Minister of National Defense. Mr. Carr and Mr. Iwerks were sent to Ottawa by Mr. Disney to see Canada's war effort for themselves. They will remain for a week to consult with the NFB and other Government officials.[47]

Less than one month after the letter of agreement had been signed, Disney artists had assembled proposals for all five films:

> Ub Iwerks will be in the National Film Board offices on or about Thursday September 25, bringing with him sketches and complete continuities on these four War Savings films and also on the military training film. He hopes to obtain the necessary approval from all parties concerned in time to fly back Sunday September 28.[48]

In order to meet NFB deadlines and budgets, Disney artists re-used several animated sequences from previously released Disney films. The first Canadian bond film was titled *Thrifty Pig*. Animation from the Academy Award-winning film *Three Little Pigs* was used. The Big Bad Wolf was redrawn as a Nazi, while the pigs became loyal Canadian citizens.

Thrifty Pig opened with Fiddler and Fifer making fun of their brother Practical, who was fixing his chimney. In a letter to Grierson, the Chairman of the Canadian War Savings Committee wrote:

---

[47] National Film Board of Canada Archives.

[48] National Film Board of Canada Archives.

> One point we did not mention...was that a fairly liberal use of Union Jacks might be desirable. From our point of view it would make it distinctively a Canadian picture and would settle beyond doubt that the Disney organization did a picture for us, and that it is not an American film adapted to War Savings.[49]

The Union Jack was indeed featured prominently in the film. As the British ensign fluttered atop a flagpole in his front yard, Practical responded to his brother's taunts by singing, "You ought not to sing and dance, when there's danger all about. You should get your houses wolf-proof; bricks like these will keep him out." A camera close-up showed the bricks in question were Canadian War Savings Certificates.

Later in the film, the Big Bad Wolf, wearing a Nazi armband and cap, and carrying a bag emblazoned with a swastika, blew down Fiddler and Fifer's houses. When he tried to blow down Practical's house he was thwarted by the savings certificate bricks. Practical then chased the Wolf away by pelting him with bricks.

At the film's conclusion the Pigs sang, "Who's afraid of the Big Bad Wolf, the Union Jack's still waving. We'll be safe from the Big Bad Wolf, if you lend your savings." The film closed with a "buy 5 bonds for the price of 4" promotion showing a German fighter plane being shot down and savings certificates turning into bombers on an assembly line. The "5 for 4" slogan appeared at the end of each Canadian bond film and referred to the government's offer of a five-dollar certificate for the price of four dollars.

Thrifty Pig was ready for theatrical release in mid-December 1941. The film was released during a "War Savings as Christmas Gifts" promotion. A letter from Ross McLean, Assistant NFB Commissioner to a Columbia Pictures of Canada executive, asked for "...125 to 150 prints in order to secure rapid circulation."[50]

Thrifty Pig was so successful, the Australian government also requested prints of the film. The April 6, 1942, *Motion Picture Daily* reported:

> The Walt Disney subject *The Thrifty Pig*, made for the Canadian Government drive to encourage savings, has been requested by the Australian government, RKO announced. With the permission of Canada, RKO plans to provide 30 prints of the Technicolor subject for

---

49 National Film Board of Canada Archives.

50 National Film Board of Canada Archives.

Australian use, with special titles to meet requirements there. The deal was handled by RKO's Australasian managing director, Ralph Doyle, and Phil Reisman, vice-president in charge of RKO foreign sales.

By 1942, several other countries had requested use of Disney's Canadian bond films. "Sixty 16mm prints of three Walt Disney films made for the National Film Board of Canada are being distributed throughout the Dominion to promote the sale of war savings stamps and certificates."[51]

The second Canadian bond film was titled *Seven Wise Dwarfs*— this short re-used animation from the diamond mine sequence of *Snow White and the Seven Dwarfs*. The film opened with the Dwarfs leaving their mine to trade their jewels in for savings certificates. As the Dwarfs marched over a log bridge, the Canadian Parliament buildings were visible in the background.

The Dwarfs marched merrily on their way singing, *"Heigh-Ho, Heigh-Ho, we always help you know. We'll do our part with all our heart Heigh-Ho, Heigh-Ho, Heigh-Ho, Heigh-Ho, Heigh-Ho, we always help you know. We'll win the war with 5 for 4 Heigh-Ho, Heigh-Ho, Heigh-Ho, Heigh-Ho."*

As the Dwarfs marched into town, all but Dopey traded in their gems for savings certificates at the Post Office—Dopey traded in his gems at the bank. As Doc led the Dwarfs out of the Post Office, Dopey rejoined his friends for the march back home. The first print of *Seven Wise Dwarfs* was shipped to the NFB for approval December 20, 1941.

The third bond film was titled *Donald's Decision*. In this short, Donald engaged in a battle with the Devil and an Angel over how to spend his salary. The Devil wanted Donald to spend the money on himself, while the Angel wanted Donald to reinvest his savings in war bonds. This film re-used footage from the short *Donald's Better Self*.

The fourth bond film, *All Together,* featured 17 Disney characters marching past the Canadian Parliament buildings. Geppetto, Pinocchio, Figaro, Donald, Pluto, Mickey, Goofy, Huey, Dewey, Louie, Doc, Grumpy, Happy, Sleepy, Bashful, Dopey, and Sneezy carried placards, banners, and balloons which read, "All together for war savings. Get 5 F-O-R 4. All together for war savings."

While the bond films were produced specifically for the Canadian government, the NFB contacted Disney in July 1943 requesting that

---

51 *Motion Picture Daily*, July 22, 1942.

prints of *Thrifty Pig, Seven Wise Dwarfs,* and *Donald's Decision* be sent to England. The British National Savings Committee wanted to view the films to see if they could be used to entice the British public into investing in bonds. To date, no record has been found to indicate if the films were actually used in a British campaign.

Two of Disney's voice talents, Clarence Nash, the voice of Donald Duck, and Florence Gill, the voice of Clara Cluck, toured Canada promoting the sale of bonds. In a July 16, 1941, letter to Disney, Canada's Minister of Finance wrote:

> On behalf of the Government of Canada I wish to thank you most sincerely for the assistance you gave our Victory Loan Campaign by permitting Mr. Clarence Nash and Miss Florence Gill to make a trip to Toronto to participate in the excellent radio program broadcast on June 20.[52]

The trip to Toronto was the first of many bond promotion appearances Nash made during the war. The *Niagara Falls (NY) Gazette* reported:

> Indications are that there will be a large attendance at the Victory Loan dinner tonight at the General Brock hotel. The guest speakers will be Sir Clutha Mackenzie, son of the Prime Minister of New Zealand, and William McCraw, of the War Munitions board. The original voice of Donald Duck, Clarence Nash of Hollywood, will be a feature of the program.[53]

In addition to the savings and bond films, Disney artists designed a war savings certificate folder for the Canadian government. The cover pictured Donald stoking a fire while Mickey, standing atop a lion, stirred the contents of a "war savings" cauldron with a pole that had a British ensign attached to the end. The caption under the illustration read, "Keep the pot a-boilin'." The multi-page folder had room for saving stamps to be pasted inside, and once the required number of stamps had been accumulated, the folder and its contents could be redeemed for a bond.

On July 31 1941, Disney received a letter from W.H. Somerville, Joint National Chairman of the War Savings Committee, recognizing Disney's contribution to the production of the savings certificate folder.

---

52 National Film Board of Canada Archives.

53 *Niagara Falls Gazette,* February 16, 1942.

> The War Savings Committee has now completed production of a folder application stuffer which will be used as an insert mailing certificates to purchasers. We are enclosing a copy of the stuffer, which in our opinion, is considerably enhanced by the illustration of the cartoon whose reproduction you authorized so generously.
>
> On behalf of the War Savings Committee I would like to assure you of our deep appreciation of the many contributions you are making to the Canadian war effort. It is indeed gratifying to the Committee to have the donations of many talented American artists in various fields and your own efforts are amongst the most value of these expressions of goodwill.[54]

Walt Disney and his staff embraced dozens of American home-front programs, following the formal declaration of war by the U.S. government against the Imperial government of Japan, on December 8, 1941.

One of the Studio's biggest home-front endorsements involved the Treasury Department. In 1941, new revenue laws created seven million new American taxpayers.[55] Treasury Secretary Henry Morgenthau contacted Walt Disney on December 8, 1941. "Why don't we call Mr. Disney,' Mr. Morgenthau asked. 'That man can make even taxes fun.'"[56] Fearing a mass tax revolt, the Treasury Secretary wanted Disney's help in convincing new taxpayers it was their patriotic duty to pay.

Hollywood gossip columnist Louella Parsons wrote about Disney's upcoming meeting with Morgenthau in her January 5, 1942, column, which was syndicated in the *Los Angeles Examiner*:

> The classic walls of the Secretary of the Treasury's office will echo with a different kind of meeting…Walt Disney and his two writers, Joe Grant and Dick Huemer, authors of *Dumbo*, will meet Secretary of the Treasury Morgentheau [sic] at a "gag" meeting—the first of its kind ever to be held in a Government office. They will discuss an unrevealed plan to use all Disney characters in a wartime drive. I suppose Mickey Mouse, Donald Duck, Dumbo, Jimmy [sic] Cricket, and all the characters we love will do their part to help in propaganda—or shall we say morale—plan. The Disney contingent planed out for Washington last eve.

---

54 Courtesy the Paul Anderson archives.

55 Shale, Richard. *Donald Duck Joins Up*. Diss. U. of Michigan, 1982. Ann Arbor: UMI. p. 27.

56 *Movieland*, May 1943.

In his landmark interview with journalist Pete Martin in the summer of 1956, Walt Disney spoke about the Studio's involvement with the Treasury Department's income tax film:

> I got a call from the Treasury from John L. Sullivan...[H]e wanted me to come right back [to Washington, D.C.]. He said [the Secretary of the Treasury Henry] Morgenthau has some special project. He said, "Can you fly out tonight?" I said, "No, I can't." He said, "Can you get away tomorrow?" I said, "I'll try." He said, 'Well, this is very important and I want you to come back."
>
> My daughter's birthday is the 18th of December. I'd been away on a couple of her birthdays. I had promised to be here on her birthday.[57]

Disney immediately left for Washington, D.C. His first thoughts were that Treasury wanted some kind of bond promotion film.

> I felt, well, Treasury...war bonds. I was thinking of...things I could do to help them sell more war bonds.
>
> I met with Sullivan, [Treasury Secretary Henry] Morgenthau, and with [Guy] Helvering who was [Commissioner] of Internal Revenue. They said, "We have a problem and maybe you can help us on. We want to sell people on paying taxes."
>
> I said, "That's funny, you're the Treasury speaking. You're the United States government." I said, "Sell people on paying taxes? If they don't pay it you put them in jail." Helvering [said], "Well that's my trouble." He said, "We've got at least 15 million new taxpayers with this new tax bill. These people have never paid taxes before and I can't prosecute 15 million people. We've got to make them understand what taxes are and the part that taxes play in a war."
>
> I said, "Well, I came back all prepared to help you sell bonds." [Helvering] said, "That's the point. The people think they buy a bond that's going to help win the war but how are we going to pay off the bond? I don't want to have to prosecute these people. We want them to pay their taxes and be excited about paying their taxes as a patriotic thing." Morgenthau said, "You've got the idea now you can work it out."
>
> That evening I went out to Sullivan's house...in Virginia. [W]e had dinner...and over a couple of martinis, Sullivan, myself, and Helvering worked out this little thing. I got all the things they wanted to say. I thought up a little plan and I telephoned it right away to the Studio and I got some boys working on it. In the meantime, I had to call my daughter and wish her a happy birthday over the phone.
>
> They said [they needed] this in the theatres sometime in February. Now this was the 18th of December. I had to do this...complete cartoon,

---

57 Pete Martin interview, audio, courtesy Diane Disney Miller.

seven or eight minutes, and it had to not only be finished, it had to be processed through Technicolor, all the prints had to be run out and it had to run in the theatres so that it could get a complete penetration...before March 15.

Before I left Washington, Morgenthau wanted to know what it would cost. I said...I [didn't] know. I said my short subjects were running me about 43-thousand dollars but this [was] liable to cost more.

I got back [to the Studio and] got my group of boys in [and] I said "...this is important to the government." [T]he boys all went with me. We slept on the job. We got beds in...we stayed right there, we worked 18 hours a day [and we] got the film out.[58]

Disney returned to Washington in early January for a presentation to show what had been accomplished since his last visit.

I grabbed my storyboards and flew back to Washington...in case there were any last minute little chaps. I had to present it to Morgenthau. I came in the room all alone with Morgenthau, the secretary, and some other guy who was kind of an aide and the guys warned me, they said..."watch the secretary, she's influential."

I...went through this story [and] told Morgenthau what I was doing. I used Donald Duck. Donald Duck was this citizen, he'd do anything for the war effort and when he found out about taxes you know, why he...shrunk to the floor. But, when [it] was explained what taxes meant, he got patriotic. So, he's going to get his taxes in right away.

And I had to get him not only to sell taxes, but they wanted me to sell the simplified form [too]. [Donald] came in with headache pills...calculators, and all that stuff to make out his tax [form] and the guy said, "You don't need that, throw it away. You use the simple form and here's what you do." The duck made it out. He made this whole thing, Donald Duck. How much do you make? Put it there. He added up his taxes, you see. His dependents [were] Huey, Dewey, and Louie. That's his three little nephews. We filled the whole form out. "Now," [the narrator] said, "the most important thing," "Yes, yes," [Donald] said, "tell me, tell me," [and the narrator replied,] "Get it in the mail, get it in as early as you can. Don't wait 'til the last minute." The duck [replied] "Yes sir," and every time he'd salute he had red, white and flags in his eyes you know. He folded that all up and...he ran out to mail it, but he came to the mail box and we had the mail box open its mouth ready to receive it, but he ran right by it and I had him run all the way from California over to Washington to deliver his taxes.[59]

---

58 Pete Martin interview, audio, courtesy Diane Disney Miller.

59 Pete Martin interview, audio, courtesy Diane Disney Miller.

Morgenthau was initially cool to the idea of using Donald Duck. Instead, the Treasury Secretary advocated for the creation of a new character named Mr. Average Taxpayer. Disney insisted on using Donald Duck as he felt Donald had more of a connection to the American public. Disney stated that Donald's services were on par with any other "real life" Hollywood superstar. In the end, Walt Disney prevailed and Donald was used.

Morgenthau's meeting with Disney was reported in the January 6, 1942, issue of *The New York Times:*

> A meeting with Secretary Morgenthau today [January 5] which overflowed into his anteroom and delayed his press conference was revealed by the Secretary later as a discussion with Walt Disney and members of his staff of the details of a film being produced for the Treasury.
>
> It was inferred, although Mr. Morgenthau would not say so, that its object would be to encourage Americans to pay taxes early and to buy war bonds. Asked to lift the veil, which hides his tax plans, Mr. Morgenthau replied that in these matters he was like Mr. Disney's Dumbo, unable to speak.

The Treasury Department film was titled *The New Spirit* and was completed in less than four weeks.[60] This turnaround from conceptual idea to finished product was an extraordinary achievement, as most shorts took between six and eight months to produce. The film's slogan was "Taxes to beat the Axis".

Disney received a letter of appreciation from Sullivan dated January 26, 1942:

> I find it difficult to express to you my appreciation of what you have done to help us solve a difficult problem. I have never seen any type of picture that set out to do a particular job and which so completely accomplished its objective in an entirely effective way. How you were able to do this in such a short time is beyond my comprehension, but frankly I doubt if you could improve upon it if you had six months more time in which to do the job.[61]

Disney launched a massive publicity campaign for the film, treating the short as though it was a regular theatrical cartoon. Hollywood commentator Louella Parsons made mention of Disney's patriotic

---

60 Shale, Richard. *Donald Duck Joins Up.* Diss. U. of Michigan, 1982. Ann Arbor: UMI. p. 28.

61 Courtesy the Paul Anderson archives.

mission in her column, while promotional articles appeared in several magazines.

In a letter dated December 30, 1941, to George Buffington of the Treasury Department, Walt Disney detailed one publicity idea the Studio was working on:

> *Liberty* magazine appearing on stands March 11 will have a cover incorporating our characters making out their tax returns. Hope to place same idea with *Time, Life,* and other magazines…need Treasury Department okay to use income tax blanks as background for cover."[62]

The following day Disney received permission to use government tax forms as the background for the magazine illustrations. The March 1942 issue of *Liberty* featured a cover illustration with Mickey, Donald, Pluto, Dumbo, and Timothy Mouse completing a tax form. Disney was amused by the magazine artwork and in a letter to the Assistant Secretary of the Treasury Department he said:

> The Secretary also has a Kodachrome reproduction of the *Liberty* magazine cover. If you get a chance, take a look at it. You'll find it amusing—and please notice that Mickey and Donald have put me down as their dependent! Do you think your experts will allow this?[63]

The February 4, 1942, issue of *Motion Picture Daily* carried a full-page ad featuring Donald Duck saluting with the headline and caption, "Salute to Walt Disney for the New Spirit. The Donald Duck U.S. Treasury Department picture, which every exhibitor in America will be proud to play, and which will help gross billions of dollars for Uncle Sam."

The War Activities Committee of the Motion Picture Industry chose National Screen Service (NSS) to distribute the film.[64] NSS was formed in the 1920s to produce and deliver film trailers. In the 1940s, the company signed contracts with most of the major production companies to supply posters and other related advertising material. The January 27, 1942, edition of *Motion Picture Daily* reported "250 of the 1,000 Technicolor prints are being shipped to exchanges this week".

As publicity for the film mounted, a barrage of articles promoting the tax film began appearing in newspapers across the country. Under

---

62 Courtesy the Paul Anderson archives.

63 Courtesy the Paul Anderson archives.

64 *Motion Picture Daily*, January 27, 1942.

the headline, "Donald Duck to Clear Income Tax Mysteries", a story in the January 23, 1942, edition of *The New York Times* reported:

> The bad-tempered Donald Duck will show millions of American income taxpayers how to prepare their income tax returns in a new short color film being made by Walt Disney for the Treasury Department.
>
> It will be called *The New Spirit* and will be ready for showing within ten days in 12,000 theatres.
>
> Treasury tax experts decided that Donald Duck was "the head of a family" because he supports his three adopted nephews "for whose maintenance he has legal and moral obligation".

On January 12, 1942, the *Cedar Rapids Tribune* reported:

> Uh-oh! That Donald Duck Tax Film Got Made After All!
>
> The Treasury Department announces that it has available for labor unions or other groups a few 16mm films in Technicolor with sound track of the Disney movie *The New Spirit*, showing Donald Duck eagerly paying his income tax to help his country win the war, using the new simplified form to make out his tax return.
>
> The film shows the tax money transformed into war material and ends with the triumph of our military forces...requests should be sent to the Treasury Department, Washington, D.C. There is no charge except for transportation.

The January 23, 1942, edition of the *Modesto Bee* informed readers of the new tax film through the use of a bold headline, "Donald Duck is to Aid Payers of Income Tax". The accompanying story appeared in newspapers across the nation:

> If you are having trouble figuring out your income tax, just be patient and Donald Duck soon will explain the problem in Technicolor. The treasury has arranged with Walt Disney for production of a film, *The New Spirit*, in which Donald Duck figures out his income tax. The film is to be distributed free to theatres.

A facsimile letter addressed to exhibitors from Secretary Morgenthau, urging theater managers to showcase the Disney income tax film, appeared in several trade journals, including the January 29, 1942, issue of *Motion Picture Daily*. The letter read:

> Very soon you will be offered a new Donald Duck picture in [T]echnicolor entitled *The New Spirit* which is very entertaining. It was made especially for the United States Treasury by Walt Disney as a contribution to the nation's war effort. It carries a patriotic message to every American, showing through the medium of Donald Duck how each citizen can do his or her bit by paying his income tax promptly.

> This picture will have widespread publicity, and I believe your patrons will be looking for it eagerly. It will be offered to you free and I hope that you will elect to show it.
>
> Since its greatest effectiveness will be between now and March 16, I further hope that you will show it as soon as you can get it, and then send it along without delay so that the next exhibitor may show it promptly.

By March 5, 1942, the income tax film had "been given 7,764 bookings to date, exclusive of the as yet unreported Salt Lake City Territory". The bookings represented a domestic record for subjects approved for distribution by the War Activities Committee.[65] Within two weeks, the number of bookings had ballooned to 11,795. Morgenthau penned a letter of gratitude to NSS president Herman Robbins to express his gratitude. Morgenthau wrote, "With limited time to accomplish nationwide distribution, your cooperation has contributed largely to the success of the project."[66]

Walt Disney initially thought the film would garner positive attention. In a letter dated January 13, 1942, to John L. Sullivan, Disney wrote:

> From the looks of things at present, we are going to get a lot of swell publicity breaks on the Treasury Film. The response from the newspaper editors, columnists, etc. has been excellent.[67]

The Treasury Department had agreed to pay Disney $80,000 dollars to cover the cost of the film—half was to cover the actual cost of production, while the other $40,000 was to cover the cost of Technicolor prints. The Treasury Department included the monetary request in a deficiency appropriations bill. A Massachusetts Republican proposed an amendment to the bill to deny the funding stating that none of the money be used for motion pictures. Representative John Taber, a Republican from New York stated:

> I think the gentleman in the Treasury Department ought to know better than this. They have hired him [Walt Disney] to make a moving picture that is going to cost $80,000 to persuade the people to pay their income taxes ...can you think of anything that would come nearer to making people hate to pay their income tax than the

---

65 *Motion Picture Daily*, March 5, 1942.

66 *Motion Picture Daily*, March 20, 1942.

67 Courtesy the Paul Anderson archives.

knowledge that $80,000 that should go to a bomber, is to be spent for a moving picture to entertain people?[68]

Debate over the monetary bill was heated. The amendment passed on February 6 and Disney was denied the money owed to him. The Congressional debate was covered extensively in the press. The February 10, 1942, *New Castle News* reported how a local Congressman helped defeat the appropriations bill:

> Representative Louis E. Graham of Beaver this week helped defeat an $80,000 appropriation for a Walt Disney film depicting Donald Duck paying his income tax.
>
> The film has already been purchased by the Treasury Department as part of a propaganda drive to candy coat heavy tax payments. The House, however…declined to appropriate the money. Congressman Graham was among those who voted against the appropriation as an unnecessary and unjustifiable increase in the burden already confronting taxpayers of the nation.

Because of the adverse publicity, Walt Disney received several pieces of "hate" mail from Americans accusing him of being a war profiteer. Conversely, Disney also received several letters of encouragement that contained checks and cash from Americans wanting to help offset the unpaid for cost of the film.

A story published on the editorial page of the March 16, 1942 *Mansfield News-Journal* stated:

> The fact that Congress refused to pay Walt Disney $80,000 for the Treasury Department short *Donald Duck Pays His Income Tax*, is a bigger snicker than any in the amusing picture.
>
> If some are feeling sorry for Walt, they can save their sympathies. He will get paid all right—even if it has to come out of the president's private war chest, though it probably won't have to. The Treasury has other funds available that probably would apply.
>
> Proof that Disney isn't worrying is that he already is at work on another Treasury Department short—this time, I believe, with Donald going all out for the purchase of war savings, stamps, and bonds.

One letter of support appeared in the February 22, 1942, edition of *The New York Times*. The letter was written by Ned Kornblite Jr., manager of the Capitol Theatre in Waverly, New York:

> I am a theatre man and I would like to voice my opinion on the

---

68 U.S. Congress, House, John Taber, 77th Cong., 2nd Sess., February 6, 1942, *Congressional Record*.

subject of Congress's refusal to pay Walt Disney for his cartoon *The New Spirit*, which Disney made for the Treasury Department at the request of the Secretary of the Treasury.

I have seen this film, which is unquestionably one of Walt Disney's best cartoons, loaded with humor, beauty, and an important message. I had the pleasure of seeing an audience applaud and cheer this cartoon. It also was the first time that most of the people in the audience (whom I heard comment afterward) really knew how this new Federal income tax form for people who earn under $3,000 a year works.

It was shown in this cartoon in a simple but complete manner. It was impressive enough for me to go straight to my postoffice [sic] the next day and ask for this form so that I could help Uncle Sam by paying my taxes early, like Donald Duck did in the cartoon.

Since this cartoon is being distributed free to theatres from coast to coast, and since an effort is being made by all theatres to aid the Treasury Department by showing this cartoon prior to March 15 so that most of the 80,000,000 people who attend motion pictures in this country each week may learn in a painless manner how they can aid their country by paying their taxes early, I think that this reel is worth many times what Disney is rightfully owed by our government. It can't [but] help speeding up tax collections, which are so badly needed now. By what other means than the theatre screen could 80,000,000 people be reached so effectively?

As a theatre man, it will be my pleasure to have this reel on my screen, even though it does set back the regular schedule of Disney cartoons, which are the best added attractions, excepting news reels that we show. Disney has done his part. Our Congress, which has been passing appropriations for millions, should now do its part. They didn't take long to sneak through a bill for pensions for themselves. Now let them pay for a really wonderful manner in which to collect the money for all government purposes.

Besides the "bad publicity", another negative side effect generated by *The New Spirit*, and one that Roy Disney had foreseen, was the cancellation of Donald Duck cartoon shorts. The Treasury Department distributed over 1100 free copies of the film to theatres throughout the United States. Many theatre owners cancelled rentals of "regular" Donald Duck cartoons when they realized they would receive income from the tax film for no charge. Radio City Music Hall in New York City was one of just a few theatres that submitted a check to the Studio to cover the funds lost by Donald shorts displaced by *The New Spirit*.

Disney defended his production of the income tax short in a lengthy article that appeared in the February 10, 1942, edition of *Motion*

Picture Daily. In the article, Disney indicated the politicians who questioned the cost of the film "had overlooked the fact he had lost $6,000 to $7,000 in the production and stood to lose an additional $50,000 to $60,000 in bookings". Disney outlined the hidden costs that he and other companies absorbed over and above the production costs associated with the film:

> The $80,000 which he was to receive for the short, Disney explained, failed to pay for all overtime costs and other extra expenses by about $6,000. The cost of making 1,100 prints, also done on overtime, boosted costs, he pointed out. In addition to a loss on the production, Disney continued, he is losing playing time for his regular product. As an example, he mentioned the Radio City Music Hall where the booking on one of his regular short subjects has been reduced from two weeks to one to make room for the income tax short. The same thing is happening all over the country, Disney said, with the result that about $50,000 in bookings will be lost completely.
>
> Disney declared that he made no allocation in the costs for his own time, nor [sic] for the publicity staff which is exploiting the reel. He added that National Screen Service is distributing the reels free, the War Activities Committee of the industry is aiding in exploitation, and that Technicolor not only made the prints at a lower price than is usually charged, but also held up prints of other features in order to complete the Treasury prints.
>
> "If I had been asked to make this short in my regular schedule," Disney observed, "I would have done it for nothing. But I was asked to complete a subject in six weeks which would normally take my studio six months. I put everything else aside and 'beat the promise' by having it ready Feb. 1. I'm not running the war," he continued. "The Treasury asked me to do a job and I did it. The Government is paying nothing for mats, stills, and a publicity campaign. The motion picture industry has always done its part and it's time that somebody took a stand." The free playing time on 12,000 screens in the nation cannot be bought, Disney declared, but is given voluntarily to the Government.

Despite the Congressional veto on giving Disney the funds he was rightfully owed, Secretary Morgenthau told a Senate subcommittee on February 12 Disney would be compensated for his work. The February 13, 1942, edition of *Motion Picture Daily* reported:

> The subcommittee heard Secretary Morgenthau explain the purpose behind the behind the picture, but did not appear sympathetic. Assistant Secretary Sullivan said that if the Senate did not restore the item, which was kicked out by the House, payment could be made from funds previously appropriated for collecting taxes.

A story in the February 14, 1942, *El Paso Herald Post* also confirmed Disney would receive the funds due to him:

> Treasury says Walt Disney will get his $80,000 despite Congressional "veto" out of funds already on hand. D. Duck tax film, made by Disney at "cost", actually leaves him out of pocket. Reason: its use by theaters cuts into sale of regular Disney shorts.

Despite the negative publicity, Walt Disney must have felt vindicated when he received a letter from the War Activities Committee that estimated over 33.5 million people had seen *The New Spirit*, in the almost 11,800 theatres in which it had played. A Gallop poll estimated 37 percent of those who had seen the film said it had a positive effect on their willingness to pay.[2469]

On March 16, 1942, the Director of the Theatre Defense Bureau, B.V. Sturdivant, wrote to Walt Disney about the success of *The New Spirit*:

> After observing very closely theatre audience reaction to [*The New Spirit*] it undoubtedly is the most successful subject of its kind that has ever been exhibited. As a matter of fact, it is unfair to classify it with any other release since it is a pioneer in its own right. The demonstration of patriotic fervor which invariably followed these showings left no doubt in my opinion but that a great service was done in bringing about even greater unity among the American people in our all-out effort…there is no doubt whatever but that it encouraged the payment of income taxes.[70]

Because of the success of *The New Spirit*, work was underway six months later for a sequel. This time, production money was appropriated from Congress before work began on the film. In *The Spirit of '43*, Donald's Scottish alter ego battled with Donald over what he should do with his earnings. The Thrifty Scot wanted Donald to save his money so he could pay his taxes, while the zoot-suited Spendthrift wanted Donald to spend all of his earnings at the Idle Hour Club.

A tug of war between the two alter egos ended with the Thrifty Scot crashing into a brick wall that transformed into an American flag. The Spendthrift turned into a Hitler look-a-like after crashing through saloon doors that turned into swastikas.

---

69 Shale, Richard. *Donald Duck Joins Up*. Diss. U. of Michigan, 1982. Ann Arbor: UMI. p.32.

70 Courtesy the Paul Anderson archives.

National Screen Service also handled the distribution of Disney's second tax film. The War Activities Committee reported "677 Technicolor prints were made available at NSS exchanges".[71] And as he had done with the first Disney tax film, Secretary Morgenthau promoted *The Spirit of '43*. "Secretary...Morgenthau, in a telegram to the War Activities Committee addressed to film exhibitors, praised both independent and circuit houses for past assistance and urged early showing of *The Spirit of '43*, [a] Disney short aimed to stimulate income tax payments. National Screen Service reported yesterday that the Walt Disney short is scheduled to open...throughout the country Feb. 4, followed by thousands of bookings that will assure maximum playing time for the tax message."[72]

The Spirit of '43 ended with the narrator commenting: "Taxes to beat to earth the evil destroyer of freedom and peace. This is our fight. The fight for freedom. Freedom of speech, of worship. Freedom from want and fear. Taxes will keep democracy on the march." The four freedoms referred to by the narrator were the founding cornerstones of the Atlantic Charter, which later became the United Nations.

In January 1942, Disney received a letter from the Motion Production Code Administration. The letter stated Disney's tax films and any other Studio work produced for the government did not have to be reviewed by the Hays office or feature the Production Code Association seal.

Before the Motion Picture Code of 1930 was adopted, many Americans believed motion pictures were immoral, and Hollywood quickly became regarded as "Sin City". In a preemptive strike aimed at preventing the Federal government from intervening, the Motion Picture Producers and Distributors Association was created. Headed by William Hays, the Association sought to establish a set of moral guidelines that film studios would have to adhere to. Films meeting the Code's standards were given a "seal of approval".

As a tie-in with the income tax films, the Studio worked jointly with the Treasury Department to publish a children's book, *The Victory March*, published by Random House in 1942. The inside back cover of the book had a sleeve that held a war savings stamp album containing a 10-cent

---

71 *Motion Picture Daily*, January 15, 1943.

72 *Motion Picture Daily*, February 2, 1943.

savings stamp. The book's plot featured Donald Duck and his friends protecting Donald's savings stamps from the evil hands of the Big Bad Wolf, who once again was portrayed as a Nazi, and two of the Three Little Wolves who were dressed in Italian and Japanese fascist attire. The story took place in and around famous Washington, D.C. monuments.

Besides the American version, there were also British and Australian versions of this book. An advertisement in the April 25, 1942, issue of *The Publishers' Weekly,* the official journal of the American book trade, stated:

> Ready in May. First printing 50,000 copies! The great surprise book of the year for children with a 10[-cent] war savings stamp album. Walt Disney's THE VICTORY MARCH or the *Mystery of the Treasure Chest.* This will be one of the big juvenile bestsellers of the spring. Don't order by mail! Our salesmen will be in to see you with full details.
>
> Every boy and girl will want a copy of THE VICTORY MARCH. It's not only a game to play (with action gadgets on every page to make the Disney characters *run, fly, march,* and *swim*), but it's also a practical lesson in thrift and patriotism.

Five days after Pearl Harbor, Walt Disney wrote a letter to Jock Whitney of the Council of National Defense regarding a request for ideas dealing with a home-front campaign the Council was interested in mounting:

> The first set of sketches is intended for a series of posters entitled, "BE CAREFUL–YOU NEVER KNOW WHO'S LISTENING!" Then, continuing with the thought of warning people to be careful of what they say, several sketches are submitted for use as single ideas, rather than a series. Also included are miscellaneous sketches, which may be useful poster ideas.
>
> We would be happy to throw our entire resources behind any of these campaigns…we can throw our best talent in the studio to work finishing them up for the final reproduction stage.[73]

Disney added the Studio could turn the sketches into promotional films:

> The top production talent that you know is available can put any of these ideas into one minute trailers, or four or five minute subjects on any campaign that may be designed to reach the masses. I know we could put the bee on it and have it out in short order.[74]

---

73 Courtesy the Paul Anderson archives.

74 Courtesy the Paul Anderson archives.

The initial artwork featured caricatures of Japanese leader Tojo, but with the German and Italian Declarations of War, caricatures of Hitler and Mussolini were quickly added to the mix.

The Council of National Defense turned down the idea of using the art in any home-front campaign. Some of the material was sold by Kay Kamen and appeared in the March 1942 issue of *Good Housekeeping* magazine under the title, "Rough Sketches by Walt Disney". The accompanying text stated that the 15 comical sketches were "Submitted…at the request of the Office of the Co-coordinator of Inter-American Affairs".

In order to pay for the war and to keep a lid on inflation, President Roosevelt launched the War Bond Program. In 1941, the Treasury Department began issuing bonds in denominations ranging from $25 to $10,000. A total of eight bond drives were initiated during the war.

On June 6, 1944, the day Allied forces stormed the beaches of Normandy, the Fifth War Loan Drive was launched. This bond offer consisted of several series, the most popular being the "Series E publication participation" small denomination bonds.

To help promote the sale of series "E" bonds, Disney allowed a certificate to be printed using 22 of his most popular characters. The certificate featured the faces of Mickey, Donald, Pluto, Goofy, Huey, Dewey, and Louie, all of the Seven Dwarfs, Pinocchio, Figaro, Practical Pig, Bambi, Faline, Thumper, Baby Weems, and Jose Carioca.

The Disney certificate was used extensively as a promotional tool in the Treasury Department's "Bonds for Babies" campaign. An instructional kit distributed by the Women's Division, Oregon War Finance Committee, outlined the program's purpose:

> To give the babies and children of Oregon a nest-egg in the future—to give them security—to assure a better America in which children will have the right to laugh, play, speak or pray as they wish.
>
> You will find in your kits a Walt Disney certificate and a special application for it. The idea behind the Bonds for Babies program is outlined at the head of these application forms, which are given out only after a person has bought a bond for a child under twelve years of age. As this certificate cannot be issued unless the serial number is on the application, the bond must be purchased first.
>
> Through the Women's Division, a special Bonds for Babies certificate, issued by the United States Treasury, and featuring an original Walt Disney design in color will be given away to every baby and child who

becomes a War Bond owner. Certificates to treasure in your baby book, or frame, will be mailed after receipt of the filled-in form below.

Many states mounted special bond campaigns related to the Disney certificate. An article in the *Washington Evening Star* indicated that state's Bonds for Babies campaign would be launched on September 20, 1944. The article also reported, "[T]he drive will extend into day nurseries, kindergartens and hospitals."[75] The following month was declared "Buy a bond for baby month" by the Illinois War Finance Committee. The organization used the slogan "A bond grows with baby" to generate interest in bond sales.[3176]

First Lady Eleanor Roosevelt mentioned the Bonds for Babies campaign in her September 28, 1944, *My Day* syndicated newspaper column:

> The Washington, D.C. chairman of the "Bonds for Babies" drive is Mrs. Nathan Hurwitz. She has set herself the task of trying to inspire the purchase of a bond for every child in every home in the District; and she hopes that other cities and rural districts all over the country will follow suit. A very attractive certificate is sent to each child bondholder, decorated with all the favorite characters in the Walt Disney movies. As the babies grow, these bonds will grow in value. They are really a very good investment, and someday they may serve to remind some child, who has almost forgotten, that wars have been fought to give him a peaceful world and that these bonds were once part of the price gladly paid for the preservation of freedom."[77]

The Bonds for Babies certificate was marketed through various means. One multi-page booklet targeted new mothers:

> Walt Disney's war bond certificates for gifts to infants are on stock at local distributors of war bonds. Designed to stimulate purchase of bonds for small children and new born infants. Copies of the certificate are on display at both local hospitals so that parents of new born infants might be attracted to purchasing a bond for the child.[78]

A promotional pamphlet aimed at the juvenile market was also published. The circular's text read:

---

75 *Washington Evening Star*, September 3, 1944.

76 *The Daily Herald*, October 13, 1944.

77 Courtesy John Vargo.

78 Author's collection.

> Hey, dad—buy one for me! I want one of those dandy Walt Disney War Bond Certificates.
>
> Sure, you've signed up for extra bonds in the drive and you're buying bonds right along. So here's a special. Buy a bond for baby. In fact, buy a few for all the youngsters—for their education, their careers, their future. Any child will be proud to own one of these Walt Disney certificates.
>
> You can have a Disney certificate made out to any child through twelve years of age by buying a bond registered in the name of that child. All you have to do is buy a bond, have the issuing agent (or your employer) certify the card below, drop it in the mail, and you'll get the handsome, colored Disney certificate. That means a thrill for your youngster today. A bond for your youngster for tomorrow![79]

Even as the war was winding down, sales of bonds remained brisk:

> The children of…the State Teachers college at Fredonia have credit for $35,419 in stamps and the 7th War Loan bonds. One class has a total of $9,385, with two boys qualifying as junior lieutenants for selling ten or more bonds. Sixty-eight children, 10 years old or younger, have bonds in their own names. They received their Walt Disney bond certificate and their names are on the junior roll of honor displayed in the Nation Bank of Fredonia and in the Citizens Trust Company.[80]

The junior roll of honor mentioned in the newspaper story was a poster illustrated with Disney characters. The names of children who had purchased a bond were added to the poster, which was usually displayed in school lobbies.

In early 1944, the city of Buffalo decided to actively raise money, which would be used to buy fighter planes. An article in the January 30, 1944, issue of the *Buffalo Courier Express* reported:

> A bombshell was tossed into the Buffalo and Erie County Fourth War Loan campaign yesterday—and probably will mean plenty of bombshells in Nazi and Jap territories—when [the] chairman of the Retail Stores Division of the War Finance Committee announced that his organization will present Uncle Sam's War Department with a squadron of planes to be known as The Flying Bisons.
>
> To accomplish this, retail stores of the city and county will have to sell approximately $1,500,000 in War Bonds and Stamps in a campaign, which will get underway tomorrow.

---

79 Author's collection.

80 *The Evening Observer*, June 21, 1945.

> Many interesting angles have been developed to make this particular phase of Buffalo and Erie County's Fourth War Loan campaign of particular import to area residents. Foremost is the symbol that each plane will bear—a winged bison created by Walt Disney, creator of Mickey Mouse.
>
> In addition, adults purchasing War Bonds and children buying War Stamps will receive honorary membership cards in the Flying Bison squadron. The cards will bear the Disney emblem.
>
> Bond booths in all retail stores will be expanded for the remainder of the campaign and additional personnel will be enlisted to accommodate the expected rush. Appropriate window displays will be exhibited to spur the drive. Radio programs are being arranged and newspaper advertising will carry the messages of the retail stores.
>
> A spokesman last night asserted that "Buffalo will be expected to back its own Flying Bisons to the utmost, and we know that this expectation will be fulfilled."
>
> Tonight, the Town Barn…will stage Bond Night, according to [the] proprietors, with prizes being nylon stockings, toasters, and flatirons. Wini Shaw, who toured the African and Italian fighting fronts with Jack Benny's troupe, will give autographs.

It's not known if the city did in fact purchase any airplanes. The "Junior Honorary Member of the Flying Bison Squadron" membership card mentioned in the newspaper article is extremely rare. The front of the card gave "recognition of purchases of War Stamps or Bonds during the 4th War Loan Drive," while the reverse stated, "The Flying Bisons—A squadron of fighter planes sponsored by retail merchants of Buffalo and backed by the war bond purchases of patriotic citizens during February 1944."

Perhaps one of the most bizarre bond promotions the Studio was asked to participate in involved a real live duck that was christened "Donald Duck the Sixth". *The Ogden Standard Examiner* reported in part:

> How Donald Duck sold $15,000 worth of war bonds at a radio auction is one story of the sixth war loan local front, and an increasing number of firms already over the top of their war bond quotas is another story.
>
> The Ogden Exchange Club conducted a war bond auction over KLO Tuesday night at which merchandise was awarded to persons or firms making the highest bids to purchase war bonds. The auction produced the sale of $56,500 in war bonds.
>
> Donald Duck, a living breathing Donald Duck, fully certified by Donald's creator, Walter Disney, went to the Ogden Union Stockyards company, when the company purchased $15,000 in bonds.

With the duck and the war bonds went a telegraphic certification from Walt Disney saying: "Donald Duck and I are happy to christen the living breathing image of Donald's Donald Duck the Sixth. Donald sends this message to the Exchange Club: 'I trust you will exceed your quota far beyond your highest expectations.' The same goes for me. (Signed) Walt Disney."

The Elks Club was the chief competitor in the bidding, but the Elks dropped out after reaching $11,000. R.C. Albright, stockyards company manager, put Donald on display in the lobby of the yards office building today.

"We are happy to bid $15,000 in war bonds for the duck," Mr. Albright said. "We would have purchased the bonds without the duck because we believe in war bond purchases and like everybody else believe that heavy purchases will speed the war's end. But we are happy to get Donald with the bonds, because we can use him to good advantage to keep the idea of war bonds before the many persons who visit the stockyards."[81]

Besides having his artists create illustrations for use in the government's bond promotion campaign, Walt Disney took on a more personal role in the endorsement of government initiatives by writing a promotional newspaper article and by narrating a radio spot.

In a letter to Walt Disney, Vincent Callahan, Director of the U.S. Treasury's Press and Radio War Savings Effort Department, wrote that his department was:

> [P]reparing a newspaper feature for the promotion of war bonds in which we want to use a statement from a different outstanding American each day for a period of 2 or 3 months. We would be most appreciative if you would give us a…statement for use in this new feature which will go to all weekly and daily newspapers in the country.[82]

Walt Disney replied:

> Here is the statement you asked for in connection with the promotion of War Bonds. I am sorry that it has been held up for so long a time, but I've been kept pretty busy here in the plant for the past month or so and couldn't get around to it until now. I hope that it will meet all necessary requirements.[83]

Walt Disney titled his contribution "Don't Let Them Down", and he wrote:

---

81 *Ogden Standard Examiner*, November 22, 1944.

82 Courtesy the Paul Anderson archives.

83 Courtesy the Paul Anderson archives.

> As I write this…I am flushed with the news of our great sea victory… in the waters adjacent to the Philippines…this…Loan must have our full support…by purchasing bonds you help prevent ruinous inflation while at the same time putting away a little money for uncertain post-war days. But the war isn't going to end tomorrow. Our boys still need Superfortresses, Thunderbolts, amphibious tanks, aircraft carriers, bulldozers, and every other weapon of war. Don't let them down.[84]

Prior to the outbreak of war, Walt Disney took part in a radio show hosted by the newly-formed United Service Organization (USO). Created in February 1941, the non-profit group provided support services and entertainment to those serving in the military. The June 25, 1941, edition of *Motion Picture Daily* carried a full-page ad promoting what was being billed as "The Million Dollar Broadcast" in support of the USO. Besides Disney, the list of celebrities scheduled to appear on the radio program (broadcast June 29 on the Columbia Broadcasting System live from the Hollywood Bowl) included Fred Astaire, Gene Autry, Jack Benny, Eddie Cantor, Bob Hope, Carmen Miranda, Mary Pickford, and Buddy Rogers. All proceeds raised by the broadcast were donated to the USO. During the program, Edward G. Robinson pledged to contribute his entire $100,000 salary from his next picture to the USO.[85]

In September 1942, Walt Disney narrated a radio script written for the Treasury Department. The text promoted war bonds and savings stamps, and also featured the voice talent of Clarence Nash as Donald Duck:

> Donald Duck waddled into my office yesterday, his down standing on end and busting to get something off his chest.
>
> "You know Walt, in the last war people who avoided serving their country were called slackers and it was not a very nice thing to be branded one. Today we have hoarders who can be classified the same way. But I got an idea how everyone can hoard and still get a medal from the government for being patriotic. Yes sir, they can put every dime they can scrape up into war stamps and bonds and become the biggest of hoarders and their Uncle Samuel will give them a resounding slap on the back for it…everyone out of uniform should have a Treasury button on each lapel and be twenty percenters instead of ten percenters. I'll take four for three anytime, Walt."

---

84 Courtesy the Paul Anderson archives.

85 *Motion Picture Daily*, July 1, 1941.

Well, the Duck's got something there. If we must be hoarders, let's all hoard War Bonds and Stamps. Those who can't fight can at least furnish the weapons and at the same time, feather their nests against a possible rainy day after the war, with the soundest investment in the world today.[86]

Other Disney bond-related items include a poster that featured a sample Bonds for Babies certificate prepared by Adohr Milk Farms for the Southern California War Finance Committee; two different versions of a point of sale "Victory Bonds" poster featuring Donald Duck as the Thrifty Scot from *The New Spirit*; a 7th War Loan poster featuring Donald Duck and actress Aurora Miranda from *The Three Caballeros*; several different magazine ads that pictured the "Bonds for Babies" savings certificate; and a *Good Housekeeping* magazine page titled the *Victory March* that showed Donald's three nephews converting their hard earned "chore" money into savings stamps.

Three additional *Good Housekeeping* pages made reference to war savings and bonds—the three ads appeared in the October 1942 issue and pictured Donald Duck promoting bonds and savings stamps in Simplicity Pattern ads.

The Seven Dwarfs from *Snow White* were featured in a bond advertisement. The illustration pictured Dopey counting money, Grumpy writing down the names of those who have made a bond purchase, and the rest of the dwarfs pinning buttons onto their shirts that featured a slogan which read, "I gave".

Walt Disney allowed 7th War Loan stickers to be printed in his comic strips. In a letter dated May 15, 1945, Howard Smith, Feature Editor, War Finance Division, wrote:

> Dear Mr. Disney. The Treasury Department is most grateful to you for the use of the 7th War Loan stickers in your comic strips. That kind of cooperation is sure to result in the sale of a great many war bonds where your work is seen.[87]

Not only were children targeted in war savings and bond campaigns, but youngsters were also pressed into service as scroungers on scrap drives. The rallying cry of Boy Scout troops and groups of neighborhood kids was "salvage". Bands of children scoured alleyways,

---

86 Courtesy the Paul Anderson archives.

87 Courtesy the Paul Anderson archives.

backyards, vacant lots, and basements gathering all types of useable salvage including pots, pans, wire, and other assorted metal items, as well as newsprint, rags, silk, nylon, and rubber products.

Walt Disney himself became involved in a scrap drive. In August 1942, Walt Disney sent a telegram to Monroe Greenthall of the War Production Board (WPB) in which he wrote:

> It seems to me all of us ought to look around our backyards, attics and cellars in a concentrated effort to find the many useless articles lying around, which could be of such value today to Uncle Sam. As a matter of fact, I have in my front yard two iron deer which as you know we named Bambi several years ago…I would like Uncle Sam to have this metal if you would let me know where to send it.[88]

A return telegram from Greenthall three days later acknowledged Disney's contribution:

> Your [telegram] on iron deer received and we are working on same immediately. Will have one of the heads of WPB phone the salvage chief in Los Angeles area and arrange for handling of salvage as well as [the] story.[89]

On August 8, 1942, Disney received a letter from Lessing J. Rosenwald:

> We wish to acknowledge with thanks the receipt of your wire in which you so generously offer two iron deer from your front yard as a contribution to our national salvage drive. Our need for scrap metal is urgent. The War Production program is limited only by our supply of materials. The excellent example, which you have established in turning in this salvage material, we hope can be brought to the attention of the youth of America who have always been great admirers of Walt Disney. The executive secretary of the Los Angeles Salvage Committee…will contact you immediately and will arrange to have these iron deer start on their way toward being transformed into important elements of war.[90]

On August 11, 1942, *The New York Times* reported:

> Walt Disney's two iron deer are leaving his front lawn in Hollywood for the war front. The motion picture producer offered the two deer for scrap and…the War Production Board's Conservation Division accepted them. The deer, which weigh a ton, contain enough scrap for one 75mm field piece or 10 thousand incendiary bombs.

---

88 Courtesy the Paul Anderson archives.

89 Courtesy the Paul Anderson archives.

90 Courtesy the Paul Anderson archives.

Reference to Disney's salvage contribution also appeared in the September 7, 1942, issue of *Life*. The article, "Speaking of Pictures... This Is Scrap", contained a photograph of Walt Disney about to smash one of the deer with a sledgehammer.

Americans weren't the only ones involved with scrap drives. In England, the *Mickey Mouse Weekly* newspaper publication made several references to the "Salvage Waste Campaign". The November 1942 through January 1943 issues contained a salvage cartoon strip along the bottom edge of the center spread. The April 24, 1943, issue contained a plea from the publication's editor: "Save string, rag, bones, tins, bottles, paper, and old copies of *Mickey Mouse* for your local salvage man."

One of the most interesting and unique home-front items produced with the permission of the Disney Studio was a child's Mickey Mouse gas mask. Two versions of this mask exist: one manufactured in England, and the other in America.

The English produced four different gas mask styles during the war: masks for infants aged zero to two years; the so-called "Mickey Mouse" mask for two to five year olds; civilian respirators; and duty civilian respirators for nurses, law enforcement officials, air raid wardens, and others who performed work during enemy gas attacks.

The British child's gas mask was given the name "Mickey Mouse" in order to make the device more palatable to children. The donning of the mask was turned into a game to reduce a child's fear and anxiety, and while this mask bore the name of Disney's famous cartoon character, the actual device has no real physical semblance to the cartoon character.

An English firm did, however, produce a children's gas mask carrying tin that featured a fantastic wrap-around, full-color, tin lithograph illustration of Mickey Mouse wearing a gas mask. In 1942, the English Disney licensee Happynak produced a child's gas mask carrying tin that measures almost eight inches tall with a diameter of four inches. The canister featured a great color illustration of Mickey Mouse wearing a child's gas mask. As Mickey said, "Boo-oo", one child-sized mouse responded, "Oo-er," while a second said, "It's a bear," and a third stated, "S'only Unca' Mickey."

This tin is marked, "By permission of Walt Disney Mickey Mouse Ltd., Happynak Series No 50. Made in England", and was only produced for a short time. The metal used in the manufacture of the tin was eventually rationed and diverted to the production of war materiel. Less than 10 examples of this carrying tin are known to exist.

One month after the Japanese attack on Pearl Harbor, T.W. Smith Jr., the owner of the Sun Rubber Company, became concerned that Americans might be subjected to enemy poison gas attacks. Because Sun Rubber produced items made of rubber, Smith decided to pursue the possibility his firm could produce gas masks. T.W. Smith's son Richey Smith said:

> There was a fear of gas warfare…consideration [was] given to issuing gas masks to all civilians. My father thought they would scare children and went to [Walt Disney] with the idea to make a gas mask for children. Disney liked it. [The idea] was presented to the Chemical Warfare Department of the Army, which eventually approved the project.[91]

Correspondence between Sun Rubber and the Chemical Warfare Service began in late 1941. In January 1942, Walt Disney met with members of the Chemical Warfare Service to discuss the possibility of producing a gas mask for children molded in the shape of Mickey Mouse's face. The design for the mask was presented to Major General William Porter, Chief of the Chemical Warfare Service (CWS). Sun Rubber produced several prototypes and submitted them for review. Richey Smith said, "Bernard McDermott, a product-designer at Sun Rubber, made plaster impressions of children's faces. [The mask] was compression molded from rubber. Prototypes with canisters were produced."[92]

On January 13, 1942, the *Charleston Daily Mail* reported the news of Disney's latest venture when it ran a one-line story that stated simply: "Walt Disney has designed a Mickey Mouse gas mask for children."

As a result of the CWS meeting, and according to Major Robert D. Walk, a U.S. Army Reserve Command Weapons of Mass Destruction Instructor: "125 masks were ordered in February 1942. Production was canceled in April 1942 by the Chemical Warfare Service due to the divergence of all rubber to military purposes…protection of children was not an essential military purpose."[93]

---

91 Email interview with the author.

92 Email interview with the author.

93 Email interview with the author.

On April 19, 1942, Disney's licensing rep Kay Kamen sent a Mickey Mouse Hustlegram (memo) to Chester Feitel regarding the Mickey Mouse gas mask. Kamen wrote:

> At the present time no work on the production of Mickey Mouse masks has started due to the fact that this mask requires more rubber then the child's mask now being made. This does not mean that a Mickey Mouse mask will or may not be used ultimately. But at the present time it is not an actuality.[94]

Chester Feitel was hired as a Disney Sales Representative on September 21, 1942. Robert Tieman of the Disney Archives said: "1942 was too early for film sales/distribution being done in-house, but Dave [Smith, who was head of the Archives until his retirement in 2011] suggested perhaps [Feitel did have] something to do with merchandising. We surmise that Feitel possibly worked for [Disney merchandising rep Kay] Kamen. It looks like Walt was unsuccessful in obtaining a deferment [as] Feitel left the company on March 27, 1943. He was re-hired as a Sales Consultant on December 19, 1949, possibly to head the merchandising division after Kamen's own untimely death in a plane crash in October of that year. Feitel resigned on September 3, 1955."[95]

Very few of the American Mickey Mouse gas masks have endured the ravages of oxidation. The U.S. Army Chemical Corps Museum in Fort Leonard Wood, Missouri, owns a pre-mold prototype; the 45th Infantry Division Museum in Oklahoma City, Oklahoma, has a production specimen; the Walt Disney Archives has a face-piece without ears or lenses; and Richey Smith of Sun Rubber owns one in poor condition.

In 1942, Americans faced the inconvenience of rationing. Eventually, the price of almost every consumable was controlled by the Office of Price Administration. Sugar and coffee were the first items to be rationed, followed by processed foods, meat, and dairy products.

A ration stamp booklet was published with Disney artwork on the front cover (circa 1943). Mickey, Minnie, Donald, and Pluto were pictured carrying groceries. The back cover of the coupon holder was used as advertising space by local businesses.

---

94 Email interview with the author.

95 Email correspondence with author, August 2006.

During the war, the Koppitz-Melchers Brewery of Detroit, Michigan, employed a novel idea to cash-in on home front patriotism. Beginning in 1942, the company began distribution in Michigan of a so-called "Victory Beer". Approximately 100 different label variations were produced for this particular brand, and while most of the associated labels featured illustrations of American war-related materiel like tanks and airplanes, several labels featured images of Disney wartime insignia emblems. To date, three different Koppitz Victory Beer labels with Disney combat insignia have been discovered:

- A stubby bottle with a label featuring the design for the Mosquito Fleet of patrol torpedo boats. The label's caption read: "Mosquito Fleet emblem by Disney shows Uncle Sam has wartime sense of humor. Other emblems are brightly emblazoned on ships, tanks, trucks, and planes. Buy U.S. Defense Stamps and Bonds." The design pictures a mosquito atop a torpedo, which has just been fired from a PT boat.
- A label removed from a bottle with the designs for the 45th Air Base Squadron (baby Pegasus from *Fantasia*), 62nd Pursuit Squadron (boxing bulldog), and the Jacksonville Air Station (flying squirrel).
- A second label also removed from a bottle with the designs for the Alaska Defense Force (seal balancing letters on its nose), the 69th Quartermaster Battalion (figure made-up of tools), and the Bombardment Training Unit, Ellington Field (stork from *Dumbo*).

Food products were not the only items to be rationed. As the war progressed, fuel was added to the list of apportioned products, and the average American driver was limited to just three gallons of gas per week.[96] The Sunoco Petroleum Company used Mickey and Donald in an advertising campaign that featured the slogan "Reinforced for rationed driving". This slogan was used on promotional items including ink blotters and roadside billboards. In one ad Donald drove an army jeep, while in another Mickey fired an artillery gun shaped like a Sunoco oil bottle. Some of the advertising material made reference to the war savings campaign and some featured the silhouette of a Revolutionary War Minuteman.

---

96 By the Editors of Time-Life books. *Our American Century. Decade of Triumph. The 40s.* VA: Time-Life, 1999. p.85.

At least two gasoline rationing posters were created using Disney characters. In one, Mickey, Donald, and Goofy, dressed in work clothes, stand by the side of a road with their thumbs in the air hoping to hitch a ride with a passerby. The poster's tagline read: "Share your car for your country. Planes need gasoline." The second poster pictures Mickey, the Three Little Pigs, and Jose Carioca riding in a car, while Goofy and a rather upset looking Donald are pulled behind in a wood wagon.

One of the most successful civilian participation programs during the war was the Victory Garden, where Americans were encouraged to grow and preserve fruits and vegetables. The Secretary of Agriculture developed the idea shortly after the Japanese attack on Pearl Harbor. Factory workers tended crops for use in their cafeterias, while homeowners grew crops in their backyards, vacant lots, and boulevards. Gardens were even planted on zoo grounds and racetracks around the U.S. Participants in the program produced over one-million tons of produce worth an estimated $85 million dollars.[97]

When interest in the program began to wane, State War Councils sponsored fairs where gardeners could display their prize-winning produce. Disney artist Hank Porter designed the front-cover illustration for the National Victory Garden Institute's 1944 Victory Garden Green Thumb Contest Record Book. Two versions of the book were produced: one for adults and one for children. The illustration on both pictured Mickey dressed as a farmer, holding out his "green thumb" for all to see. The book created for youth gardeners used the same illustration with added text that read: "The Green Thumb 3-V's. Vegetables. Vitamins. Vitality." The youth book was promoted in the July 1, 1944, edition of the Illinois War Council's *Illinois Mobilizes* newsletter.

An article appearing in the May 22, 1944, edition of the *Dixon Evening Telegraph* promoted a local Victory Garden contest and mentioned the record book:

> "Any adult home gardener, city or farm, is eligible to enter the contest. A champion Victory Gardener in each classification...will be selected in this community to enter the county contest. The county winners will then enter the state competition. Each entrant will

---

[97] Lingeman, Richard. *Don't You Know There's A War On? The American Home Front.* NY: Capricorn, 1976. p.251.

receive a contest record book with a cover especially designed by Walt Disney to be used for keeping a record of planting and harvesting."

W.L. Stensgaard, a Disney licensee, produced a whimsical Victory Garden sign that featured Donald Duck chasing pests from his garden. The sign was available in two sizes and was sold through five-and-dimes, hardware, and grocery stores. One version of the sign was printed on a Masonite board attached to a 24-inch-long stake. This sign was produced in six colors, had a wholesale price of $10.80 per dozen, and a retail price of $1.69 each. The second version was printed in four colors on 100-point fiberboard, and was mounted on an 18-inch stake. The fiberboard signs wholesaled at $7.80 per dozen with a suggested retail of $1.00 each.

A promotional flyer sent to retailers read in part: "Everybody will want to identify their victory garden with this colorful durable outdoor marker. Creates a new spirit for gardens. Thousands will buy for own use, also gifts and prizes."

Stensgaard was also involved with the development of what appears to be a series of home-front campaign advertisements. The Disney Archives has no history on these items, but images exist for what appear to be four posters. The only known examples of this art appeared in an internet auction in 2003. The illustrations were printed in black-and-white on heavy-stock, glossy paper, and three of the four designs appeared to have been hand-colored. The number encoding found on all four illustrations indicates there may have actually been five designs in this series of images. The art featured Mickey, Donald, and Pluto, and all of them involved patriotic themes. These images appear to have been produced sometime in 1942 and were used to promote salvage and scrap drives, the payment of taxes, bond purchases, and worker productivity.

Disney artists designed numerous posters for use on the home front. In 1943, a series of three were produced for the Food Distribution Administration (FDA). These posters promoted balanced diets and nutrition, and pictured Donald Duck and Horace Horsecollar, Goofy by himself, and Max Hare and the Big Bad Wolf.

The posters were made available to factory managers, schools, and State Nutrition Committees. They could be imprinted with a name and logo for four cents each in lots over 500, or five cents each for lots under 500. Single copies without imprints were sold for four cents each. Most of the FDA posters currently found in today's secondary marketplace were produced for the California War Council. The Max Hare/Big Bad Wolf poster is the rarest of the three, while the Donald/Horace poster is the most common.

A related advertisement in the September 1943 issue of the *Journal of Living* included the tagline: "Movieland's famous creator of Mickey Mouse designed…posters for the Food Distribution Administration—for display in the nation's war plants. Better meals and snacks have cut accidents by 30 per cent [and] absenteeism by 19 per cent in some plants."

In 1944, Disney artists designed a "Job Hopper" poster for the War Manpower Commission. This government agency was responsible for the movement of workers from civilian to defense jobs. The poster featured a greedy, evil-looking grasshopper clutching a fistful of money with the slogan "Don't be a job hopper. Our soldiers are sticking to their guns. Stick to your job." The poster design also appeared as a magazine advertisement.

Disney artists created several other war-related posters: Daisy Duck promoted the United Service Organization (Donald Duck appeared as the mascot of the USO Theatrical Society on an emblem designed by Disney artists in 1941); Mickey and/or Donald appeared on a series of six posters promoting the Aircraft Warning Service; a poster on camouflage featuring Donald Duck was created for the 8th Air Force; and a set of five posters was designed in 1942 for soldiers in combat zones—these posters reminded service personnel about security measures and camouflage and featured images of Goofy, Pluto, and Donald Duck. A poster was also created with an illustration of a so-called Japanese "firebug". This poster warned those who enjoyed camping and hiking that careless forest fires were just as bad as enemy sabotage.

Disney artists designed a wide range of promotional material for numerous home-front causes including the Red Cross. In 1945, Perry Hamilton, Chairman of the War Production Board Blood Donor Program, sent a letter to Walt Disney in regards to a circular that was used by the board in a blood donor drive. Perry wrote, "The poster has created greater interest in the blood donor program and resulted in a very substantial increase in the number of donors."[98] The flyers were distributed to WPB employees in Washington D.C. and New York.

---

98 Courtesy the Paul Anderson archives.

At least four illustrations were created at the Studio for the Red Cross. One featured Donald's angel and devil alter egos (from the short cartoon *Donald's Better Self*) trying to respectively encourage or discourage the duck from giving blood.[99]

A second piece of art featured 19 different Disney characters encouraging the viewer to join the Red Cross—this image carried the tagline: "Always Room For One More!"[100] (The line was later resurrected and used in Disneyland's Haunted Mansion attraction.)

A third design, published in the July 10, 1940, *Brownsville Herald*, pictured Mickey, Donald, Minnie, and Pluto gathered around the Red Cross symbol, with the caption:

> "Look here," quacked Donald Duck. "What have you done to help those miserable millions of refugee children in Europe?" "Little children whom I used to make laugh are weeping bitter tears today," said Mickey Mouse. "Won't you give to help them?" barked Pluto. "I'd be a Red Cross nurse if they'd take a winsome mouse to help," promised Minnie.
>
> Disney's popular characters turn serious for a moment to urge all Americans to give generously to the American Red Cross War Relief Fund for rescue, feeding, shelter and medical care of millions of homeless and orphaned children in the European war zones.[101]

The fourth item was a small, eight-page brochure detailing the adventures of "Kit Bag". The booklet was distributed to Los Angeles-area school children in 1945, and detailed the adventures of Kit, a bag filled with useful, everyday items that was distributed to soldiers. The actual kit contained a needle and thread, playing cards, paper, pencil, envelopes, soap, razor blades, and a novel.

The brochure featured 12 panels of illustrations depicting Kit shaving, writing a letter, playing a card game, and sewing a tear on a jacket sleeve. The last panel carried the caption, "And so filled with gifts to take care of the fighting man's needs, 'Kit Bag' hurries off to war!" The back cover of the brochure stated:

> It costs $6 per second to provide: Blood donor service, U.S. Prisoners of War Aid, Aid to servicemen's families, Disaster Relief, Servicemen's Clubs Overseas, Nurse's Aides, Service in Military Hospitals…and

---

99 Courtesy the Porter family.

100 Courtesy the Porter family.

101 Author's collection.

61 other vital services and activities furnished by your Red Cross to the 11,000,000 men and women in our Armed Forces—their loved ones at home and our Allies all over the world. How many seconds will you buy?

The brochure's front cover indicated: "35,120 kit bags were made by Los Angeles chapter production workers in 1944."

Disney artists created the artwork found on an American Women's Voluntary Service's (AWVS) Christmas card. Alice T. McLean founded the AWVS in January 1940 to give women practical training in skill sets that were in demand during the war. By 1942, the organization had grown to 350,000 members.

AWVS staff worked alongside Red Cross volunteers helping with food production and conservation, health, nutrition, and scrap drives. The AWVS scheduled classes for women in auto mechanics, nursing, emergency aid, and civilian defense. AVWS staff also worked in draft board offices, and they drove ambulances and cars in the military motor pool.

An article in the November 29, 1942, *Los Angeles Times* reported:

YULE CARD AIDS SALE OF BONDS

Mrs. Pat O'Brien's Idea Executed by Walt Disney.

Fresh off the press is a new Christmas card! Appropriately introduced to Mr. and Mrs. Public during Women at War Week, it combines a festive holiday greeting with a definite patriotic gesture.

The idea was conceived first by Mrs. Pat O'Brien, who presented it to Walt Disney. Mr. Disney developed the card, giving to it the personality of an original Disney design.

Donald Duck is putting a small cellophane bag down the Christmas Chimney—a cellophane bag into which the sender inserts a War Stamp.

Next the Treasury Department was consulted and the project given their endorsement [and] Miss Harriett Elliott, head of the Women's Division of War Stamps and Bonds, also sanctions the cards.

The cards are on sale at American Women's Voluntary Services bond windows and at the A.W.V.S. headquarters for 25 cents each. All proceeds from Christmas card sales will be given to aid the A.W.V.S. activities.

The card features Donald as Santa about to go down a chimney. A "V" for Victory symbol made popular during World War I and revived during the World War II is visible in the left background. Donald flashes the "V" sign with his left hand and his sack is filled with toys in the form of the instruments of war.

In 1941, United China Relief, an organization formed to aid the people of China, set a goal to raise five million dollars in donations. The Sino-Japanese War, which had started in 1937, caused untold misery for hundreds of thousands of Chinese citizens who suffered under the yoke of Japanese occupation. The main purpose of United China Relief was to raise money to help ease the suffering of the displaced and sick, as well as aid wounded Chinese servicemen and guerilla forces fighting in the country's northwest region.

Walt Disney lent his support to the cause, and on May 17, 1941, Disney received a letter written on behalf of friend and fellow producer David O. Selznick:

> We want you to know how grateful we are to you for consenting to appear on the broadcast with which it is hoped to launch the West Coast drive for United China Relief.
>
> The airtime originally selected, May 27, has had to be changed since the same time has now been selected by the President of the United States for his fireside talk on the world situation. We still intend to make a brief fifteen-minute appeal immediately preceding the President's talk, but the broadcast proper has been transferred from 6:30 to 7:00, Pacific Time, on June 6. We trust that it will still be possible for you to appear for us at this time.
>
> Once again may we thank you on behalf of the Committee and all the members of the United China Relief drive.[102]

Almost one year later, on April 6, 1942, Walt Disney received a letter from United China Relief President W.R. Herod, who wrote:

> Your drawing of the universally appealing Donald Duck and Mickey Mouse showing "thumbs up" for China is one of our most captivating pieces of publicity. We are going to run this as an ad in the *New Yorker* magazine and are also planning to make a poster of it. We'll certainly send you copies, for your possible interest. My sincere thanks for your generous contribution to the 1942 promotion campaign of United China Relief.[103]

The image Herod referred to in his letter appeared in the September 26, 1942, issue of *The New Yorker* magazine and was also reprinted as a small poster.

To further aid United China Relief, Walt agreed to let the organization use Hop Low, the baby mushroom star of the "Nutcracker

---

102 Courtesy the Paul Anderson archives.

103 Courtesy the Paul Anderson archives.

Suite" sequence of *Fantasia*, in its fundraising efforts. The May 19, 1942, *Los Angeles Times* reported:

> Just how important Hop Low has become to millions of people even outside the entertainment world is shown by his adoption as the figurehead of the national United China Relief campaign. Disney has turned over his Hop Low royalty rights to the organization, with the result that funds coming from the sale of Hop Low match books, salt-and-pepper shakers, and pins all go to China's aid.

In 1942, the United China Relief fund drive resulted in donations totaling over seven million dollars. In 1946, the name of the organization was changed to United China Service, which remained in service until its dissolution in 1966.

In December 1941, artist Hank Porter designed an emblem for the Department of Agriculture. A January 28, 1942, press release issued by the Department of Agriculture read:

> The American eagle, poised on guard above a cargo ship is the design… which will be available to identify U.S. food products wherever they are sent throughout the world.
>
> The emblem was presented to Secretary Claude R. Wickard…in recognition of the vital part U.S. food is playing on both the home and foreign war fronts of the world. The new emblem, which will be available for voluntary use by packers, is expected to become a familiar part of the labels for food containers.
>
> "Farmers and all of us are proud of the contribution United States food is making, and will make increasingly, to the job of building and maintaining the fighting strength of the United Nations," said Secretary Wickard. "The new emblem is a symbol. It visualizes the determination to see that American food is used as a powerful weapon in winning the war—and building the right kind of world peace when peace comes."
>
> Copies of the design are being mailed today to several thousand food processors who are contracting with the Department to furnish food supplies needed for the Lend-Lease and territorial program shipment, for school lunch and domestic distribution to low income families, and to meet the other supply needs for the Food for Freedom program.
>
> The detail of the emblem…shows an American eagle poised protectively over a cargo boat, fending off a bombing plane. Stars representing the four freedoms are above the eagle…the four freedoms pledged in the Atlantic Charter and later by the United Nations are freedom of speech and expression, freedom of every person to worship God in his own way, freedom from want, and freedom from fear.[104]

---

104 Courtesy the Paul Anderson archives.

Roy Disney suggested the eagle be used on the emblem. In a letter to Walt, Roy wrote that the Studio artist responsible for creating the design should conduct research in the Studio's reference library on the use of the American eagle on symbolic patriotic devices, like the Presidential Seal.

The Disney-designed emblem was printed on canned lima bean and green pea labels in both black-and-white and color. These two labels also featured the Morse Code dot-dot-dash symbol for the letter "V", which carried the notion of "V" for Victory. The design also found its way onto an apple label, and was incorporated by three dairies onto two different-sized milk bottles.

The July 25, 1942, *Muscatine Journal and News-Tribune* reported the design was also being imprinted on packages of dehydrated eggs being sent to England:

> Walt Disney made a special trip to the capital to make the drawing for the box cover: a blue eagle, red stars, and U.S.A. in white—our national colors. At first London objected to any insignia revealing that the goods came from this country. But Food Minister Woolton was finally persuaded that he ought to approve the advertising for its propaganda value. He agreed with our contention that it would buck up Island morale by showing that Uncle Sam was saying it with poultry, fruit, [and] with bullets.

Besides military units and government agencies, Disney artists created mascots and emblems for contractors involved with war production and home-front activities. The "Beechcraft Busy Bee" was created for the Beech Aircraft Corporation in 1942. This mascot was used in the company's employee incentive program. The insignia featured a bee with four hands holding various tools, positioned on a field of blueprint paper shaped in the form of a beech leaf.

A short story in *Dispatch from Disney's* reported:

> The Beechcraft Busy Bee…is a decorative note of good cheer…serving a similar purpose is the Beechcraft song composed by Studio musicians. Prepared for use with training films, it has been declared the organization's official theme music and is used as marching song by Guards and Guardettes.

Jiminy Cricket was used to illustrate a fable that appeared in the October 20, 1944, issue of the Beech Aircraft's employee newsletter, *The Beech Log*. The one-page story was illustrated with several images of Pinocchio's conscientious companion. The story dealt with several issues that were prevalent during the war: job hopping, job security, and war savings.

The Beechcraft Busy Bee was also used on a certificate awarded to Beech employees. An article in the June 19, 1942, edition of *The Beech Log* described how the company's new logo was used on an employee Award of Merit:

> Many hundreds of "Award of Merit" certificates...are now being lettered with the names of Beechcrafters who have qualified as the first winners of the Beechcraft Busy Bee emblem. Judging has been practically completed in all departments for the initial awards, and the lists of super-active "Busy Bees", as determined by foremen and union committeemen, or department heads, have been turned in to the company's joint labor-management Production Drive Committee of the War Production Board. The method of distributing the Certificates and Busy Bee emblems was decided by the Committee yesterday, just a day too late to be described in this issue of the LOG. It seemed certain, however, that the awards should be ready for distribution on or before Friday, June 26.
>
> In making the first awards the Committee limited each department to a specific number...as a result, there were many borderline cases where men of equal value qualification with award-winners were eliminated by this restriction of numbers. These unlucky people were selected by lot for elimination and are in line for the next award.[105]

In November 1942, Disney artists created a grasshopper emblem for the Aeronca Aircraft Corporation. The design appeared in a 26-page booklet titled *Mr. Grasshopper Wins His Wings*. The booklet told the story of the Abel Grasshopper, a highly adaptable plane the firm produced. During the war, the Grasshopper was used for courier work, artillery observation, aerial photography, air patrol, and troop transportation, and the small plane could also be pressed into service as an air ambulance. The grasshopper emblem was also used in a series of magazine advertisements and was imprinted on matchbook covers.

In 1943, a license was granted to Press Alliance for the production of a newspaper comic-style publication that was to be marketed to war contractors as an in-house monthly. The periodical was tentatively titled *Walt Disney's Mickey Mouse on the Home Front*.

In a December 6, 1943, letter to Roy Disney, Disney merchandise licensing rep Kay Kamen wrote:

---

105 Private collection.

> After a very slow beginning and plenty of wrinkles to iron out, and many postponements and delays, etc., Paul Winkler finally got his House Organ under way and printed three issues. These were small "runs" and with very little, if any, profit. We agreed to have them print these three issues on a specialty royalty agreement instead of the regular royalty rates, and the other day I consented for them to do the next two issues on the same basis to give them that much longer to experiment. This special royalty basis for the first five issues is provided for in the contract.
>
> Personally, I have some doubt as to whether this publication will go over, and the fifth issue may be the last. I base my opinion on the reason that the war in Europe may end by that time, which might cause the cancellation of many war plant's contracts. On the other hand, if the war does end in Europe, it might still be used for those plants still producing for the Pacific War—or the title might be changed and it might be sold as a regular House Organ insert.
>
> There has been a lot of interest in this publication and I am sure that if properly merchandised, it can result in some interesting leads towards licensing or motion picture work.[106]

Roy Disney harbored misgivings about the publication from the outset. In his December 9, 1943, inter-office communication to Kamen, Roy Disney wrote:

> I was very disappointed and in fact, disgusted with it—so much so that I would like for us not to go ahead with this agreement. I feel they have done a very poor job. While the artwork in itself is often very poor and sloppy...their printing is bad, their jokes are so flat and corny...the paper is such that I think it is a disgrace to our names and characters.[107]

In the same letter, Roy expressed concern that King Features Syndicate, who handled the distribution of Disney's newspaper comic strips, would consider the publication an infringement on their license. Roy wrote: "King Features may even have reason to dislike this format. If it weren't connected to the war effort, I would worry about the King features angle."[108]

Kamen had addressed a similar concern as early as November 19, 1942. In a letter to the licensees for the house organ, Kamen wrote:

> The said publication shall be sold by you only to industrial concerns

---

106 Courtesy the Paul Anderson archives.

107 Courtesy the Paul Anderson archives.

108 Courtesy the Paul Anderson archives.

for the purpose of being given away to their respective employees; and the said publication, and the various issues thereof, shall not be sold at retail anywhere.[109]

Another concern was that if the publication was sold on newsstands, this would be a violation of the licensing agreement Disney had with Whitman, publishers of the *Walt Disney's Comics and Stories* comic book. In his December 6, 1943, letter, Kamen briefly discussed Whitman's existing licensing agreement:

> You have in your files a release from Wadewitz [who was in-charge of the comic book agreement at Whitman] to the effect that he does not consider this as competing in any way with the *Walt Disney Comics Magazine*. This is in the form of a Photostat…with Wadewitz's release written right on it.[110]

Roy was so unimpressed with the publication, he closed his December 9 letter to Kamen by saying: "I wish you would have them leave off their masthead the use of Walt Disney's name. Just let it go as *Mickey Mouse on the Home Front*, with the company copyright clearly visible."[111]

Spurred to action by Roy's letter, Kay Kamen wrote to the Home Front Publishing Company on December 14, 1943:

> Gentlemen. I have just seen a layout of your January issue and [have] made several corrections—also some of the reproductions of the characters were not very good. Your artist told me that he will make the corrections. One more thing—will you please omit "Walt Disney's" from the masthead. I think the title *Mickey Mouse on the Home Front* is sufficient. However, please be sure to have clearly visible the proper copyright notice.[112]

Tide Magazine carried a promotional reference to the new home-front publication in their July 15, 1943, issue:

> In a new house organ service called *Mickey Mouse on the Home Front*, Walt Disney is putting his inimitable gang to work combating absenteeism and other war plant headaches. Featuring four-color comic strips, the service offers four page and two page inserts tailored for standard house organs, as well as an eight page tabloid with articles, fiction, and space for company news."[113]

---

109 Courtesy the Paul Anderson archives.

110 Courtesy the Paul Anderson archives.

111 Courtesy the Paul Anderson archives.

112 Courtesy the Paul Anderson archives.

113 Author's collection.

Several war contractors purchased issues of *Mickey Mouse on the Home Front* for distribution amongst their employees, including Glenn L Martin, Delco-Remy, Aeronca, and Aero Parts. Companies often had their business name printed under the masthead to give the impression the newsletter was being printed specifically for them.

In the fall of 1943, artist Hank Porter created two mascots for the McClatchy newspaper and radio chain. The September 4, 1943, front-page headline in *The Sacramento Bee* declared: "Two Busy Bees, Straight from Pen of Walt Disney Make Appearance." The accompanying story stated:

> Born September 4, 1943—to the McClatchy newspapers and radio stations. TWINS.
>
> Figuratively, of course, the McClatchy newspapers and radio stations are passing out the cigars today in celebration of the double arrival of Scoopy and Gaby, the newspaper and radio bees.
>
> Here are the portraits of the little darlings. Not photographs mind you, but portraits by Disney—Walt Disney—world famous animator of Donald Duck, Mickey Mouse, and hundreds of other fascinating and enjoyable characters.
>
> Although they are not yet a day old, Scoopy and Gaby have their careers all mapped out for them. The three McClatchy newspapers… will feature Scoopy's sketch daily. The five McClatchy radio stations… will feature Gaby in their promotional materials. The animated bees are intended to lend personality and a familiar identity to all the products of both the newspapers and radio stations. That is their career.
>
> When Eleanor McClatchy, president of the McClatchy newspapers and radio stations, approached Walt Disney with the proposal that he create the twin bees, the animator was impressed with the fact that the organization had rendered service to the people of California for nearly a century.
>
> [Walt Disney] would like, he said, to add Scoopy and Gaby to his long list of characters, but, of course, he did not do that type of commercial work. Still…if the money for the job were to be donated into the Army Relief Fund instead of going into the Disney pocket, the matter could be arranged. It was agreed. Scoopy and Gaby came bounding out of the same inkwells, which gave Donald Duck and Mickey Mouse and Dumbo to the world. A check for $1,500 was sent to the Army Relief Fund.

The images of the two bees were used on several publicity and promotional items including a pinback button and decal. What is interesting about this project is that Disney refused payment for the work, and instead directed the McClatchy family to make an in-kind donation to a worthy cause instead. The July 9, 1944, *Fresno Bee* reported:

> Scoopy, the Walt Disney cartoon bee which appears daily at the top of the front page of *The Fresno Bee*, has gone to war.
>
> A reproduction of Scoopy and *The Fresno Bee*, which he holds aloft, has been painted on at least one American convoy truck now in Italy to help keep Fresno bright in the thoughts of erstwhile Fresnans overseas. Captain James H. Matthews…has sent home a photograph he made of the convoy truck. Scoopy and a Fresno serviceman he identifies only as Private Norman.
>
> The captain in a letter to his wife…said Norman insisted on naming his truck Scoopy and cajoled company artists into drawing a carton of *The Fresno Bee's* bee and putting the name Fresno on Scoopy's papers in extra-large letters.

Disney artists created a special war effort insignia for West Coast shipyard workers in 1945. The insignia used a beaver as the symbol of a worker set against a background of cranes. At the bottom of the insignia were the initials S.C.R.A.M., an acronym for Ship Construction Repair and Maintenance. The Navy's Industrial Incentive Division stated the insignia could be "…placed on helmets, lunch boxes and windshields, or worn as a cloth shoulder patch similar to the combat insignia worn by fighting men on the front".[114]

An article in the August 11, 1945, *Hayward Revue*, reported:

> The Navy announced today that a special Walt Disney insignia had been approved for shipyard workers on the West Coast. The announcement was made by Undersecretary of the Navy…who pointed out that the Disney Studios in Hollywood had been the originators of many combat insignias…and that Navy's approval of this special insignia for shipyard workers indicated their importance in the combined efforts of both home front and fighting front to hurry the day of victory. In San Francisco, Marinship Corporation will use the insignia on the bow of a new Navy tanker which will be launched August 10.

Several Disney short cartoons had home-front themes. An incentive film starring Minnie Mouse and Pluto was made in 1942 for the Conservation Division of the War Production Board. *Out of the Frying Pan and into the Fire* encouraged housewives to save cooking

---

114 *The New York Times*, August 10, 1945.

fat and grease, which were used in the manufacture of explosives. In the film, Minnie discovered that: "A skillet of bacon grease is a little munitions factory...one pound of grease can make five shells."[115]

Shortly after completing the first income tax film, Walt Disney was approached by the Secretary of Agriculture, Henry Wickard. In 1942 Wickard coined the phrase: "Food will win the war and write the peace." Bureaucrats in the Agriculture Department thought the slogan would make a good topic for a Disney film.

In an April 4, 1942, letter to Walt Disney, the Special Assistant to the Agriculture Administrator, Ben James, listed some reservations about the direction the film was heading after viewing the proposed script and storyboards:

> Nelson P. Poynter of the Office of the Coordinator of Information has reservations: 1) Net effect of film would indicate that the U.S. job of feeding the world is altogether too easy; 2) The United Nations and the Axis are skeptical—is the U.S. willing to sacrifice?; 3) Want to introduce the idea that blight of war and devastation could engulf the U.S, therefore: 4) Introduce that the U.S....is determined to share its larder... [and] is increasing its production of foodstuffs. From here on the sequences can be of the amazing productivity; 5) At the end of the film introduce more of the grim determination of the U.S. to fight to distribute these foodstuffs; 6) I have a definite reservation as to the wisdom of "And Write the Peace" from the standpoint of our foreign policy.
>
> The main objective of the picture as it now stands is to give assurances to the United Nations and the occupied nations that there is a gigantic food producing plant operating in this country; that we are geared to make the most of our food resources and determined to fight our way through to them and deliver the food they need; that it is a tough task for our farmers and an essential duty; that the job is being done and will continue to be done; we can produce the food and will fight to get it to them.[116]

The film's slogan was eventually shortened to just "Food will win the war", and this catchphrase became the actual title of the film. The production deadline was set as July 25, 1942, and the finished film was to run between 500 and 550 feet, and cost the government $20,000.

---

115 Shale, Richard. *Donald Duck Joins Up*. Diss. U. of Michigan, 1982. Ann Arbor: UMI. p. 34 & 33.

116 Courtesy the Paul Anderson archives.

Some of the catchphrases from *Food Will Win the War* included: "[O]ur tomatoes would tower over the Matterhorn...our potatoes would stack up twice as high as Gibraltar...if all the wheat in the U.S.A. were turned into flour it would be enough to snow under the Panzer army. If it were turned into spaghetti there would be enough to knit a sweater to encompass the earth."

The Studio contributed to the home-front campaigns of America's overseas Allies as well. An article in the November 15, 1940, issue of *The Bulletin* reported the ". . . opening gross (from *Fantasia*) is to be given to British War Relief funds".

Disney Artists helped the British government promote food products by designing a family of carrots for England's Food Minister. The January 11, 1942, issue of *The New York Times Magazine* announced: "England has a goodly store of carrots. But carrots are not the staple items of the average English diet. The problem...is to sell carrots to (the) country."

The Disney designed carrots included Carroty George, Dr. Carrot, Pop Carrot, and Clara Carrot. The vegetable characters were reproduced on a poster, recipe booklet, and the carrot images were used extensively in a newspaper ad campaign. A series of flyers was also distributed featuring the Carroty George character on one side, and recipes with carrots as the main ingredients on the reverse.

There is no doubt Mickey Mouse cheered the spirits of many an English child during the air war over Britain. The January 3, 1941 *Bulletin* reported: "...war to the contrary, the sales of the London published *Mickey Mouse Weekly* are still on the up and up according to a letter received this week from English staffer Silvey Clark." Miss Clark wrote that "...we're down to one Disney artist, the other having been called-up. And there seems to be no others in this country these days, though quite a number have had a shot at it." Commenting on the German air raids, Clark said: "... we've got so used to them now that unless we have a dogfight overhead, we don't even bother to stop work. Anyway, what's the use? If the beastly things have our number on them, then we should get them whatever we did."

The March 28, 1941, *Bulletin* contained another dispatch from Silvey Clark. The story, under the headline "Mickey Mouse Weekly Sales Up In London", stated there was an "increase in sales...despite the broken nights, daytime raids and an entailed staff. You will be pleased to know that on our 5th anniversary...our sales were up 10,000 on the year before."

Besides assisting the English, Walt Disney also gave moral support to the French, Turkish, and Chinese causes. Walt Disney voiced a broadcast aired by the Office of War Information on Christmas Eve 1943. An article in the December 25, 1943, *New York Times* reported:

> A series of messages promising that their hour of deliverance is fast approaching was broadcast last night to the people of Occupied France. The French nation was reminded of its noble history and urged to take courage so that its future will be equally bright. Those who took part in the program were Mrs. Franklin D. Roosevelt...and Walt Disney, movie cartoonist. Mr. Disney, whose Mickey Mouse and other film cartoons enjoyed great popularity in France before the war, said that Hitler was trembling before the mounting strength of the Allies. "Yes," he continued, paraphrasing the feature song of the *Three Little Pigs*, "Hitler, the Big Bad Wolf, is afraid."

In May 1944, Walt Disney voiced a recording that was to be broadcast in Turkey:

> It is a great privilege to speak as a representative of the motion picture industry to the people of Turkey. We like to think of motion pictures as a bond between other nations and ourselves. It is a bond of friendship—because entertainment brings friendship with it. The adventures and misadventures of Mickey Mouse and Donald Duck, for instance, are enjoyed by audiences in both our countries.
>
> It is very significant that American and Turkish people laugh and cry at the same things. They are moved to pity or stirred to anger by the same things.
>
> There was a time, before the war, when it was popular to talk about different national psychologies. But the longer this war lasts, the clearer it becomes that the people of democratic nations have much the same fundamental ways of thinking.
>
> That is a good omen and assurance that our legitimate hopes for the future have an excellent chance for success.[117]

Walt Disney also read a scripted message for an Office of War Information fifteen-minute short-wave radio program that played in China on November 10, 1944. The program featured music from several Disney films including *Saludos Amigos, The Three Caballeros, Pinocchio,* and *Snow White and the Seven Dwarfs*.[118]

As the war progressed, many Disney characters willingly enlisted in the

---

117 Courtesy the Paul Anderson archives.

118 Courtesy the Paul Anderson archives.

U.S. Armed Forces. Donald Duck starred as a member of the military in several short cartoons including *Donald Gets Drafted, The Vanishing Private, Sky Trooper, Fall In Fall Out, Commando Duck,* and *Home Defense.* Peg Leg Pete often co-starred as the stereotypical tough-as-nails Drill Sergeant. During his 50th birthday party in 1984, Donald was promoted to the rank of Sergeant and was given an honorable discharge.

Pluto starred in several shorts with a war theme. In *The Army Mascot,* Pluto replaced Gunther Goat as Camp Drafty's mascot. In *Private Pluto,* Mickey's pal was assigned to protect a pillbox, unsuccessfully matching his wits with two chipmunks that had been using the pillbox as a storage depot for their nut supply. (The pair of chipmunks went on to later fame as the duo Chip 'n' Dale.) In *Dog Watch,* Pluto watched over a ship while sailors enjoyed shore leave, and in *Canine Patrol,* Pluto was a member of the U.S. Coast Guard beach patrol.

Goofy starred in two military films. *Victory Vehicles* saw Goofy utilizing various forms of transportation that required no gasoline or rubber, both of which fell under strict rationing rules. *How To Be a Sailor* presented a historical and scientific approach to the art of sailing—in one scene, Goofy reported to his assigned battle station as an enemy warship approached, and, during the ensuing battle, Goofy launched himself instead of a torpedo at the enemy vessel.

While the production of Mickey Mouse cartoons stagnated during the war, Mickey starred in two comic-strip adventures with a war theme. The 1942 serialization of *Mickey Mouse and the Black Crow Mystery* had Mickey and Goofy uncovering a saboteur. In the 1944 strip *Mickey Mouse and the War Orphans,* Mickey befriended three children who turned out to be Royal refugees hunted by the Nazis.

While Walt Disney actively participated in various home-front campaigns, his wife Lillian took up the cause as well and partook in at least one event. On June 16, 1945, Walt Disney, his wife Lillian, their daughter Sharon, and actor Spencer Tracy's wife were on hand at the California Shipbuilding Corporation's shipyard at Terminal Island in Los Angeles, to participate in the launch of a victory ship.

Named in honor of the Rice Institute of Houston, Texas, SS *Rice Victory* was a 10,500-ton cargo ship, one of almost 500 built at the West Coast shipyard over the course of the war. The so-called "victory" ships moved supplies and materiel from ports on the American west and east coasts to overseas destinations in support of military campaigns taking place in Europe and Asia.

Publicity photos from the christening ceremony picture Lillian smashing the obligatory bottle of champagne on the ship's hull. Painted on the bow of the cargo ship is a now politically incorrect stereotype of a Japanese soldier (Tojo) with an "X" marked on his forehead—the "enemy" character's head was held in place by a smiling Donald Duck. While the image is inappropriate today, the caricature was not out of place during the war.

While Americans on the home front endured tough times, Disney's cast of cartoon characters was on hand to help ease the pain and share in some of the hardships. Disney's involvement in the war prompted one magazine writer to say: "[H]ow fortunate America is to have Walt on the job today. He's a propaganda genius for whom the Axis would gladly give a dozen crack divisions."[119]

Home Front Collectibles

Note: The collectibles referenced here can be viewed at: http://servicewithcharacter.com.

HF001 *Coronet* gatefold illustration. September 1942.
Several Disney characters support the war effort, led by Donald Duck as a member of the Marine Corps.

HF002 *The Victory March*. Random House. 1942.
This 12-page hardcover mechanical book was published in conjunction with the U.S. Treasury Department. The book depicts the Big Bad Wolf as a Nazi and two of the Little Wolves as Japanese and Italian fascists. In the book, the wolves steal Donald Duck's treasure chest, which contained a war savings stamp. The ensuing story has several Disney characters and the wolves chasing each other around various Washington, D.C. monuments. The book was written and illustrated by Disney artists on behalf of the Treasury Department, and contains a savings booklet and one free war savings stamp. Once the necessary number of stamps was collected, the savings booklet could be redeemed for one bond.

HF003a *The Victory March*. Ayers and James. 1943.
This 16-page soft-cover book is the New Zealand version of its American counterpart. There are no moving or mechanical parts in this adaptation of the book—all of the pictures are static. Differences between the New Zealand and American versions include:

---

119 *Times Weekly*, July 5, 1942.

- The New Zealand flag is featured on buildings. New Zealand monuments and buildings have replaced their American counterparts.
- The title page featured the American and British flags draped in a "V" for victory symbol.
- The inside front cover pictured Uncle Sam and his English counterpart, John Bull, rolling up their sleeves in preparation for a fight.
- The back cover pictured Donald Duck holding a New Zealand war savings stamp.
- The inside back cover pictured the "Flags of the 26 United Nations", along with a grid for pasting in war savings stamps.

HF003b *The Victory March.* Ayers and James. 1943.
Back cover illustration.

HF004 Donald Duck Army Paint Book. Whitman. 1942.
The cover pictures Donald Duck in uniform and Pluto standing at attention. The book bears the number "688" and features scenes from several of Disney's wartime cartoons including *The Vanishing Private, Sky Trooper,* and *The Army Mascot.*

HF005 Victory Garden sign. 1942. 12 x 18
This sign was manufactured by W.L. Stensgaard and Associates of Chicago, a Disney licensee in 1938 and from 1941 to 1962. Masonite-type board attached to a yellow colored ¾-inch diameter 24-inch long stake. The sign's multicolored scene pictures Donald Duck chasing a chicken, worm, and a caterpillar from his garden. This version of the sign was back coated, produced in six oil colors, and had a wholesale price of $10.80 per dozen. The suggested retail price was $1.69 each.

HF006 Victory Garden sign. 1942. 12 x 16
This second version of HF005 was constructed of 100-point heavy fiberboard, was produced in four oil colors, and was mounted on a ½-inch diameter, 18-inch long pole. The sign had a wholesale price of $7.80 per dozen. The suggested retail price was $1.00 each.

HF007 Victory Garden sign advertisement. 1942. 9 x 16½
Advertisement distributed to retailers by W.L. Stensgaard and Associates, with information about the Donald Duck Victory Garden sign. The ad stated that there were two versions of the sign: both had identical graphics but were different sizes and were constructed of different materials.

HF008 Green Thumb Contest Record Book. 1944.
This soft-cover book was used to record the types of crops grown, their

quantity, and weight. Contests were held across the United States at the local, state, and national levels. Community and company garden winners were awarded national green thumb blue ribbons, while each state's first prizewinner took home a special trophy. The prize for the national winner was a $1,000 war bond. The record book cover features Mickey Mouse dressed as a farmer holding out his green thumb for all to see. The cover art was created by Disney artist Henry "Hank" Porter, who also designed many of the insignia emblems created at the Studio during the war. Three different cover versions of the record book exist: one for adults, one for youth, and one dated 1944 for The Illinois Victory Garden Youth Program. The regular youth and the Illinois youth record books also feature the tagline: "The Green Thumb 3-V's. Vegetables. Vitamins. Vitality."

HF009 Green Thumb Contest Record Book. 1944.
Illinois Victory garden Youth soft-cover book.

HF010 Super Duper Market ration book. Circa 1942. 6½ x 5
This booklet was used to hold ration coupons. Mickey, Minnie, Donald, and Pluto are pictured on the front cover leaving a grocery store with their purchases. Space on the back cover was reserved for advertising. Most of the ration books found today have an ad for a grocery store that was located in Clovis, New Mexico.

HF011 War Finance Committee certificate. 1944. 10 x 8
This certificate was published by the U.S. Government Printing Office for the Treasury Department. The outside edge of the certificate is ringed with the images of 22 Disney characters including Mickey, Pinocchio, and Donald, one of the Three Pigs, Goofy, Bambi, Figaro, Baby Weems, Huey, Dewey, Louie, Thumper, Jose Carioca, Pluto, Faline, and all of the Seven Dwarfs. As each state had their own Finance Committee, several signature variations exist. An ad appearing in the September 3, 1944, *Washington Evening Star* stated the certificates were to be issued in connection with the War Bonds for Babies campaign, which was launched on September 30, 1944, by that district's War Finance Committee.

HF012 War Finance Committee bond certificate advertisement. 1944. 8 x 11½
This black-and-white magazine ad pictures a $100 bond, the Disney bond certificate, and an order coupon.

HF013 War Finance Committee certificate poster. 1944. 16 x 24
This poster was used in the Bondsfor Babies campaign. It pictures the image of a sleeping baby, below which has been affixed a Disney war savings certificate. The poster is marked: "Prepared for Southern California War Finance Committee by Adohr Milk Farms." The line above the image of the

baby reads "Buys Bonds for Babies", while the line below the image of the baby states: "They Shall Inherit The Earth—Nest Egg—Security—Emergency—Protection." The poster also lists the various bond denominations available for purchase: "$25—$50—$100—up to $5,000."

HF014 Treasury Department poster. 1944. 18 x 22
"Buy a Bond Junior Roll of Honor." Donald, Doc, Sneezy, Dopey, Pluto, Jose Carioca, Panchito, Pinocchio, and Bambi are pictured on this poster, which was used to promote the federal government's war savings program. The poster could be found in many school entrances or hallways and in factory lunchrooms during the war.

HF015 Flying Bison Bond Drive Membership Card. 1944. 3¾ x 2¼
The front of the card reads: "In recognition of purchases of War Stamps or Bonds during the 4th War Loan Drive. Albert C. Witzig is hereby made a Junior Member of the Flying Bison Squadron." Reverse reads: "The Flying Bisons. A squadron of fighter planes sponsored by the Retail Merchants of Buffalo and backed by war bond purchases of patriotic citizens during February 1944." The Disney-designed "Flying Bison" insignia is reproduced in the background on the front of the card.

HF016 *Playthings* magazine. May 1944.
Front-cover Kay Kamen ad features an illustration of the Disney "Bonds for Babies" certificate.

HF017 *Playthings* magazine bond advertisement. May 1944.
This one-page advertisement was placed by Disney's licensing representative, Kay Kamen. The illustration was taken from the "Bonds for Babies" certificate. The text reads: "Some Walt Disney characters are doing their bit on the far-flung battlefields—the others on the home front, but ALL OF THEM will be seeing you in the leading toy departments of the world soon after Victory. Buy still more war bonds."

HF018 *Playthings* magazine. May 1945.
Front-cover Kay Kamen ad pictures Mickey and Donald promoting the "Mighty 7th War Loan".

HF019 Bond advertisement. November 21, 1943.
"Give War Bonds For Christmas." This bond ad appeared in the Detroit versus Pittsburgh National Football League program. The ad pictured a scene from the "Ave Maria" segment of *Fantasia*.

HF020 Camp Allen newsletter. November 1944.
This mimeographed newsletter had an ad on the front cover featuring the illustration found on the "Bonds for Babies" bond certificate.

HF021 Walt Disney War Bond Certificate circular. Circa 1944.
This circular has an illustration of a young boy and one of the certificates. The boy is seen to be saying: "Hey, Dad—Buy One For Me!" The ad text goes on to state: "You can have a Disney certificate made out to any child through twelve years of age by buying a bond registered in the name of the child." The ad also had a cutout application form.

HF022 Bonds for Babies promotional booklet. Circa 1944. 6¼ x 4½
This softcover, eight-page booklet was printed for the Los Angeles County War Finance Committee Women's Division "through the courtesy of the Sears Roebuck Foundation". The booklet's front cover features an illustration of the Disney War Finance Committee bond certificate.

HF023 Donald Duck Victory Bonds poster. Circa 1944.
This poster features an illustration of Donald Duck as a Scotsman. Donald stands in front of a wicket and holds a change-purse in his left hand and paper money in his right. The poster reads, "Buy Victory Bonds Here!" A caption seen to the left of Donald reads: "Hoot Mon, 'Tis the right thing t'do!"

HF024 Shriners' Oasis Temple fundraiser premium. 1943. 8½ x 11
This illustration, titled "Courageous Hearts with Glorious Hopes", was printed on heavy stock cardboard/paper. The image pictures disabled children looking above themselves at other children who are positioned in a dream cloud. The children depicted in the cloud are engaged in various childhood activities that the children below cannot participate in due to their disabilities. These prints were used in a wartime Shriners subscription promotion. The money received from subscriptions was invested in war bonds, which were placed in an endowment fund. The interest earned from the endowment fund was used to maintain Shriner hospitals.

HF025 Donald Duck 7th War Loan poster. Circa 1945.
Donald Duck is smitten by Aurora Miranda. This illustration was from the South American feature *The Three Caballeros* and also appeared in a 1942 issue of *Coronet* magazine.

HF026 Savings bond promotional item. Oval shaped, 9½ x 5
In this illustration Grumpy signs a piece of paper, while beside him Dopey appears to be holding a large amount of cash. Dopey and the five other Dwarfs wear buttons that read "I gave".

HF027 Canadian War Savings Certificate Folder. July 1941. 3½ x 6¼
This savings folder, produced for the Canadian War Savings Committee, features a great illustration of Mickey standing atop a lion (that symbolized England). Mickey stirs a cauldron labeled "war savings" with a pole, to which is attached the British flag. Donald Duck stokes the fire with logs

that are labeled "loans". The illustration was also featured on the back cover of the September 1941 Canadian issue of *Reader's Digest*.

HF028 *Reader's Digest*. September 1941.
The back cover features an illustration also found on the front cover of the Canadian war savings certificate folder (see item HF027).

HF029 *Liberty* magazine. March 14, 1942.
The illustration, found on the magazine's front cover, was part of a joint venture between the Disney Studio and the Treasury Department that promoted the timely payment of income tax. In the illustration, Mickey Mouse indicates Walt Disney as a dependent. Disney artist Hank Porter created the cover art.

HF030 *Good Housekeeping*. October 1942.
This issue contained three advertisements for women's Simplicity clothing patterns. Each of the three ads featured a Donald Duck illustration promoting either the sale of savings stamps or bonds.

HF031 *Good Housekeeping*. October 1942.
Simplicity clothing pattern advertisement.

HF032 *Good Housekeeping*. October 1942.
Simplicity clothing pattern advertisement.

HF033 *Good Housekeeping*. August 1942.
This issue contained a picture promoting the sale of savings stamps. The title of the illustration was "The Victory March" and featured Donald Duck's three nephews. The nephews are paid for completing various chores at Uncle Donald's house, and, despite the temptations of a candy store, toy shop, and amusement park, the three boys give their money instead to Uncle Sam in exchange for war savings stamps.

HF034 Mickey Mouse wall plaque. 1942.
This kit contained a die-cut cardboard image of Mickey Mouse manufactured by the Youngston Pressed Steel Company. Pieces that came with the kit included a tank and a shell burst, which were to be colored and glued to a cardboard plaque. The finished product was supposed to be mounted on a child's bedroom wall. The Mickey Mouse plaque is the only war-related one in a series of six produced by the company. The image of Mickey measures 5½ x 10½. The envelope measures 11½ x 14½ and pictures what the finished picture would look like. The reverse pictures the other plaques in the series. This product was made by a company whose own product line was impacted by the war—so much so that they had to stop production of their pre-war merchandise due to metal rationing. The

HF035 *Chesty and His Helpers.* Walt Disney Productions. 1943. 5½ x 7¼
This small promotional booklet was published for the Los Angeles War Chest. The booklet opens to six double-sided pages. There are cartoons on 10 of the pages, and each page contains six panels. The booklet tells the story of Chesty, his two helpers Polly and Paul, and their helicopter friend, Coptie. The group travels the world dropping supplies gathered by the L.A. War Chest to children and guerrilla fighters in Belgium, Greece, Norway, Russia, and China. Over China the group is assisted by members of the Flying Tigers, whose unit insignia was coincidentally designed by Disney artists Hank Porter and Roy Williams. The story ends with the group returning to America where they deliver checks to a boy's home and to a hospital. Polly and Paul return to school where they encourage their friends and other children to help the War Chest with their charitable work.

HF036 *Chesty and Coptie.* Walt Disney Productions. 1944. 3¼ x 5¼
This small promotional booklet was the second created by Disney artists for the Los Angeles War Chest. It features the same two lead characters, Chesty and Coptie, as the first version. The booklet opens to two double-sided pages. There are 27 cartoon panels inside that tell the story of Chesty and Coptie traveling the world. This time the message has been updated to include current events: the German "buzz-bomb" attacks in England; the second front created by the D-Day landings on the Normandy coast in France; and B-29 bomber bases being built in China.

HF037 *It's Fun to Be Free.* December 10, 1941. 9¼ x 12
This 52-page spiral-bound program was published by the St. Louis chapter of the Fight For Freedom Committee to Defend America. The program was printed for the "Fun to be Free" stage performance held in the St. Louis Convention Hall Municipal Auditorium. The program included music by Irving Berlin and George Gershwin, narration by actors Burgess Meredith and Humphrey Bogart, a variety show performed by Phil Silvers, and a speech by Wendell Wilkie. The cover features a great Revolutionary War scene with Mickey Mouse carrying a flag with the "V" for victory symbol, Donald Duck playing the fife, and Goofy banging on a washtub drum with a pair of spoons. Disney artist Hank Porter created the cover illustration for this program.

HF038 It's Fun to Be Free. 1941. 5 x 7½
This 23-page soft cover booklet features the same Revolutionary War scene as the spiral-bound program. There is a one page forward, two pages of notes, a listing of the cast of characters, and 15 pages of text for the play. A note in the booklet states the play was first performed at Madison Square Garden in New York City. The original price of the booklet was 30 cents.

HF039 St. Louis Transit Passes. 1944–1947. 3¾ x 2¼

These multi-colored transit passes were issued by the St. Louis Public Service Company, and while many of them carry a post-war date, all of the insignia designs featured on the passes were designed by Disney artists during World War II. Disney insignia images appear to have been used exclusively on the student cards. The cards are either marked "U.S. Fighting Units Series" or "Insignia of U.S. Fighting Units".

HF039a St. Louis Transit Passes. 1944–1947. 3¾ x 2¼
USS *Piedmont*. Doc repairs a ship.

HF039b St. Louis Transit Passes. 1944–1947. 3¾ x 2¼
Second Photo Technical Squadron. Donald with magnifying glass.

HF039c St. Louis Transit Passes. 1944–1947. 3¾ x 2¼
31st Reconnaissance Squadron. Dumbo crow with telescope.

HF039d St. Louis Transit Passes. 1944–1947. 3¾ x 2¼
247th Anti-Aircraft Artillery Searchlight Battalion, Battery C. Bambi Owl with searchlight eyes.

HF039e St. Louis Transit Passes. 1944–1947. 3¾ x 2¼
556th Anti-Aircraft Artillery Battalion. Dumbo crow with fly swatter. Other passes include:
- September 24–30, 1944. Second Armored Corps.
- January 21–27, 1945. USS *Sea Dog*.
- February 10–16, 1946. Training Group 3, Army Air Base.
- March 31 to April 6, 1946. Phoebe the Seabee.
- June 2–8, 1946. Yuma Aerial Gunnery School.
- July 7–13, 1946. 82nd Airdrome Squadron.
- July 28 to August 3 1946. USS *Pogy*.
- August 25–31, 1946. Marine Scout Bomber Squadron.
- September 22–28, 1946. Big Bad Wolf.
- October 20–26, 1946. 21st Field Hospital.
- November 10–16, 1946. Calvary Troop.

HF040 Sun Oil Company blotters.

These blotters were produced between 1940 and 1945. Some of the images were also reproduced in roadside billboards. Several of the blotters and billboards carried a "Buy Defense Bonds" slogan and the silhouetted image of a Revolutionary War Minuteman.
Variations include:

- Donald Duck driving a jalopy touches the flexed muscle of a cartoon character glass container of Sunoco oil. The caption reads: "Plenty tough. Sunoco motor oil. Reinforced for rationed driving."
- Donald Duck wearing a suit of armor wields a sword in his right hand, while he steers a military jeep with the other. The slogan reads: "Reinforced for rationed driving. Sunoco oil. Resists motor clogging caused by less driving."

HF040a Sun Oil Company blotter.

Mickey Mouse in military uniform gives the "V" for victory sign with his right hand. Mickey stands beside a glass bottle of Sunoco oil, which is shaped to look like an artillery piece. The caption reads: "Defend your car's life. Sunoco oil. Reinforced to make motors run better, longer!"

HF041 National Amateur Athletic Union program. June 1942. 9 x 12

This program lists all of the track events for the Junior Amateur Athletic Union track and field championships, held at Randall's Island Stadium in New York. The cover pictures Mickey, Goofy, Pluto, Bambi, and Donald jumping hurdles. The hurdles are in the shape of the letter "V" for victory.

HF042 National Amateur Athletic Union program. June 1942. 9 x 12

This item is identical to HF041, except this program contains numerous war-related advertisements and several cartoon illustrations, featuring characters like Popeye extolling the virtues of war savings and service.

HF043 Lend Lease Isaac's Farm Brand Lima Bean label. Circa 1942. 11 x 4¼

This label features an image of the Agriculture Department's Disney-designed Lend Lease emblem. There is also a color version of this same label. Other labels featuring the Lend Lease insignia included one for green peas and one for Page Valley apples.

HF044 Lend-Lease Milk Bottle. 5¼ tall

This bottle features the Lend-Lease emblem Disney artists designed for the Department of Agriculture in 1942. The bottle's front features the same image as HF045. The image found on this milk bottle was reproduced by the following three dairies: Maple Grove of Shelby, Kentucky; Ringer and Son of Xenia, Ohio; and Live Oak Riviera of Santa Barbara, California. A larger bottle distributed by the Live Oak Dairy also exists.

HF045 *Liberty* magazine. October 19, 1940.

The cover of this issue pictured Donald Duck's car adorned with American patriotic symbols. The might of the American eagle was unleashed on her Japanese, German, and Italian adversaries less than 14 months after this issue appeared on news-stands. Disney artist Hank Porter created the cover art.

HF046 Scoopy and Gabby decal. Circa 1943. 4 x 4¾

The two bee characters were created by Disney artist Hank Porter. In return, the McClatchy's made a donation to the Army Relief fund. Scoopy represented the chain's newspaper holdings, while Gabby represented the chain's radio stations.

HF047 Scoopy pinback button. Circa 1943. 1¾ inch diameter

This colourful pin was distributed by the McClatchy newspaper chain in California.

HF048 Scoopy printing press block. Circa 1943.

This small newspaper printing block features an image of the McClatchy mascot Scoopy.

HF049 War Manpower Commission magazine ad. Circa 1943. 8½ x 11½

This black-and-white ad from an undated issue of *Women in Crime* magazine features the same graphics as HF050.

HF050 War Manpower Commission. Circa 1943. 14 x 20

"Don't be a job hopper. Our soldiers are sticking to their guns. Stick to your job!" This colorful poster features the image of an evil-looking grasshopper clutching a fistful of money. The poster was designed to try and convince employees to stay at the job they were trained to do. During the war, there was a critical shortage of skilled workers as men volunteered or were drafted into the military.

HF051 Australian war bond jigsaw puzzle. 1942. 8¼ x 10½

Produced by the John Sands Company of Australia, this puzzle is an adaptation of the cover illustration found on *The Victory March* book. Mickey, Minnie, Donald, Pluto, Goofy, Dumbo, Timothy Mouse, Jiminy Cricket, Practical Pig, and several of the crows from *Dumbo* promote war savings. The puzzle and the paper wrapper the puzzle pieces came in feature the same illustration.

HF052 Australian war bond jigsaw puzzle. Circa 1942. 8¼ x 10½

This John Sands Company puzzle features Mickey in uniform holding the Union Jack in his hand, and Donald wearing an Australian slouch hat and holding the American flag in his hand. The caption on the puzzle reads: "All Together. Keep the flags flying—buy war savings stamps."

HF053 Australian war bond jigsaw puzzle. Circa 1942. 8¼ x 10½

This John Sands Company puzzle features the Big Bad Wolf dressed as a Nazi with swastika emblems emblazoned on his hat, armband, and a suitcase in his right hand. The Wolf is walking towards the brick home of Thrifty Pig. Thrifty stands on the threshold to his home, while his two brothers play their musical instruments in his front yard.

HF054 Masquers Servicemen's Morale Corps program. 1943-1944. 5½ x 7

Two different illustrations were used for Masquers programs. One cover features Mickey, Minnie, and Donald saluting the American flag, while the other pictures Donald carrying a flag as Mickey and Minnie march beside him. The Masquers were a group of like-minded actors, actresses, comedians, and musicians who traveled throughout southern California entertaining troops at various military bases and hospitals.

HF055 Masquers Servicemen's Morale Corps program. 1943-1944 5½ x 7

The cover of the pictured program is signed in pencil by actor Spencer Tracy.

HF056 American Woman's Voluntary Services Christmas card. 1942. 6¼ x 9

Alice T. McLean founded the AWVS in January 1940. If you look closely at the card, you'll see a "V" for victory symbol in the background formed by stars. Donald flashes the "V" sign with his left hand. His toy sack is filled with the instruments of war, including a battleship, fighter plane, tank, and rifle with a bayonet

HF057 Mickey Mouse gas mask carrying tin. Circa 1941. 7¾ tall, 4 inch diameter

This extremely rare English children's gas mask carrying tin was manufactured by the English Disney licensee Happynak. The graphics on the tin were designed to help ease a child's fear of having to wear a gas mask.

HF058 Mickey Mouse prototype gas mask. Circa 1942.

Prototype American child's gas mask produced by Disney licensee Sun Rubber. There are no Mickey Mouse gas masks outside of the institutional collections referenced in this chapter.

HF059 Mickey Mouse gas mask promotional photo. Circa 1942.

In this U.S. Army Chemical Corps publicity photo, a little girl is seen wearing a prototype Mickey Mouse children's gas mask.

HF060 American Red Cross newspaper ad. July 6, 1940.

Mickey, Minnie, Pluto, and Donald are featured in this newspaper illustration, which implores readers to: "Give generously to the American Red Cross War Relief Fund for rescue, feeding, shelter, and medical care of millions of homeless and orphaned children in the European war zones."

HF061 American Red Cross Kit Bag brochure. 1945.

This eight-page brochure details the adventures of Kit Bag. The premise behind this promotion was for Los Angeles-area school children to solicit donations, which were then used to purchase items like playing cards, novels, paper, pencils, razor blades, and soap, which in turn were distributed to soldiers. The brochure's inside six pages contain 12 illustrations.

HF062 American Red Cross promotional item. 3½ x 3½

The illustration pictures Donald Duck walking down a country lane. Donald's alter-ego angel pulls him along the road towards a building that has a Red Cross flag mounted to it, while his alter-ego devil tries to pull him in the opposite direction. A signpost reads: "Give your blood regularly to the American Red Cross." Donald's alter ego angel says, "At'ta boy Donald! Now you're doing what every able-bodied American with a conscience should do!"

HF063 American Red Cross promotional item. 3½ x 3½

This hexagon-shaped item carries the caption: "Always Room For One More!!" An illustration contained inside the Red Cross symbol features 19 Disney characters. Dopey holds a sign that reads "Join Today", Donald Duck gives a Red Cross pin to Snow White, and Doc fills out an application form.

HF064 "Wipe That Smile Off His Face. Zip Your Lip." Poster. 1943. 11 x 15

This poster features a smirking caricature of Adolf Hitler, similar in design to an image of Hitler that appeared in the Disney propaganda film *Education for Death*. The poster is marked "Intelligence Poster No. 1" and "Walt Disney Prod."

HF065 1st Mapping Group newsletter. May 1943. 8 x 10½

The back cover of this unit's newsletter features an illustration of Donald Duck reminding personnel to be careful what they say in public.

HF066 *The Washington Post*. January 9, 1944.

The cover and two-page article promote the Goofy short *Victory Vehicles*. The article contains five illustrations that show alternate modes of transportation requiring no use of rationed items. All of the pictured vehicles were designed by Goofy.

HF067 *Good Housekeeping*. September 1943.

This page was titled "Walt Disney's Goofy in Victory Vehicles". In this short cartoon, Goofy demonstrates various modes of transportation that required neither gasoline nor rubber, both of which fell under strict rationing guidelines.

HF068 "Share Your Car—It's Patriotic." Poster. Circa 1943.

This poster represents but one of the multitude of posters designed by Disney artists for various home-front campaigns—in this instance, gasoline rationing. The illustration features Mickey Mouse sharing a car ride with the Three Little Pigs and Jose Carioca. Donald Duck and Goofy are pulled behind the car in a trailer. Artist Hank Porter created this poster illustration.

HF069 " Share Your Car—For Your Country." Poster. Circa 1943.

This poster represents another home-front gasoline rationing promotional item. The image shows Donald Duck, Mickey Mouse, and Goofy with their thumbs out looking for a ride, while several airplanes fly overhead. Two of the hitchhikers have lunchboxes, and Mickey holds a wrench in his left hand. A caption at the top of the poster reads "Planes Need Gasoline". Illustration by Hank Porter.

HF070 *Good Housekeeping*, March 1942.

"Rough Sketches by Walt Disney." The accompanying text for this one-page article explained that the 15 sketches shown in the article were "[S]ubmitted...at the request of the Office of the Coordinator of Inter-American Affairs [COIAA]. Poster designs of this type probably will be seen in the near future." Many of the designs depicted Japanese racial stereotypes and all dealt with home-front issues, including the importance of not speaking about military-related matters in public where enemy spies could hear the information being discussed. When the COIAA declined the use of the material, Disney's licensing rep Kay Kamen sold the illustrations to *Good Housekeeping* magazine.

HF071 "Appreciate America." U.S. Department of Education poster. August 1941.

This poster features a head-and-shoulders illustration of Donald Duck saluting with the caption: "I get exasperated at people who squawk." This was Donald's way of asking people to support rationing. The tagline at the bottom of the poster reads: "Red for Courage. White for honor. Blue for justice."

HF072 "Appreciate America." U.S. Department of Education poster. August 1941.

This poster features a head-and shoulders illustration of Mickey Mouse waving an American flag with the caption: "Come on gang—all out for Uncle Sam." The tagline at the bottom of the poster reads: "Buy United States Defense Bonds and Savings Stamps." This image was reissued recently by the Walt Disney Company on a pin issued to employees attending a company picnic.

HF073 "Appreciate America." Envelope.
This mailing envelope is imprinted with the same Mickey Mouse image as HF072.

HF074 Aircraft Warning Service poster #1.
Mickey Mouse as a member of the Aircraft Warning Service peers through a telescope held in his left hand, while his right hand rests on a telephone. The caption reads: "Thousands of Eyes in the Dark. Keep Your Eyes Open!" The poster also has the "Remember Pearl Harbor" logo featuring a hand with a string tied in a knot on one finger.

HF075 Aircraft Warning Service poster #2.
This poster has head-and shoulder illustrations of Mickey Mouse and Donald Duck. The caption reads: "Look. Listen. Speak. Only to Your Post Commander." Donald's eyes peer through the two-letter "oo" in the word "look", while Mickey holds a phone in his right hand and cups his ear with his left hand. The word "only" is spelled out using the telephone cord. This poster also features the "Remember Pearl Harbor" logo.

HF076 Aircraft Warning Service poster #3.
Mickey Mouse as a member of the Aircraft Warning Service stands proudly at attention, saluting with his right hand. A large reproduction of the AWS insignia is in the background, while the "Remember Pearl Harbor" logo is pictured in the lower left corner.

HF077 Aircraft Warning Service poster #4.
Mickey Mouse as a member of the Aircraft Warning Service sternly looks out towards the viewer and points to the poster's caption which reads: "It's Time You Keep Awake! 24 Hours A Day, 7 Days A Week." Mickey also wears an AWS armband on his right arm. A telephone and the "Remember Pearl Harbor" logo are also pictured.

HF078 Aircraft Warning Service poster #5.
Mickey Mouse as a member of the Aircraft Warning Service is taken aback by a shot that rises up through the poster from the "Remember Pearl Harbor" logo to strike the letter "t" out of the word "can't" in the caption, which reads: "It Can('t) Happen Here! Keep Awake. Remember Pearl Harbor!"

HF079 Aircraft Warning Service poster #6.
Mickey Mouse as a member of the Aircraft Warning Service points to the background, in which a menacing stereotype caricature of a Japanese soldier drools from the mouth and advances with two knives drawn. The poster's caption reads: "A Reminder—Mr. Ground Observer—Keep Awake!" Mickey points to the soldier with his left hand and to the words "Keep

Awake" with his right hand. The poster also features a very large illustration of the "Remember Pearl Harbor" logo.

HF080 Forest Service poster. Unknown date and dimensions.
This poster was created for the United States Forest Service. The illustration depicts a stereotyped Japanese character with wings on his back riding atop a cartoon-type vehicle. The character is flicking a lit cigarette into the brush at the side of the road and there is a blazing forest fire in the background. The poster's caption reads: "Don't be a firebug! A careless fire is sabotage."

HF081a Food Distribution Administration posters. 1943. 13 x 19
Disney artists designed a series of three posters for the Food Distribution Administration, which were used to promote good nutritional habits. The posters were made available to factory workers, managers, schools, and state nutrition committees, and they could be imprinted with a name and logo for four cents each in lots over 500, or five cents each for lots under 500. Single copies of the posters were sold without imprints for four cents each. Most of the FDA posters found in the marketplace today were produced for the California War Council. The Donald Duck/Horace Horsecollar poster is the most common. Caption: "You can't breakfast like a bird and work like a horse."

HF081b Food Distribution Administration poster. 1943. 13 x 19
The Goofy poster is uncommon. Caption: "A Goofy lunch packs your punch!"

HF081c Food Distribution Administration poster. 1943. 13 x 19
"There's fightamins in fruit and vegetables!" This Max Hare/Big Bad Wolf poster is the rarest of the three posters in the series.

HF082 Carroty George flyer. January 1942. 5½ x 8½
The caption on the front of this double-sided flyer, printed in red and white tones, reads: "Carroty George says 'I'll tell you what to do with me.'" The flyer is "No. 2" in what is presumed to have been a series of flyers. The front of the flyer features a large illustration of the Disney-designed carrot character, while the reverse gives recipes for six different carrot recipes, including carrot-and-fish pie; carrot and cheese cream; carrot-and-bacon casserole; carrot spice pie; steamy carrot pudding; and chocolate pudding with carrots and grated potato. The reverse has illustrations of Pop Carrot and Clara Carrot.

HF083 *New York Times*, January 11, 1942.
Short article details the history behind the creation of the Carrot family by the Disney Studio.

HF084 Carroty George recipe book. 1942.

This booklet features Carroty George, Dr. Carrot, and Clara Carrot. Disney was asked to design the characters at the request of England's Food Minister. England had large stockpiles of carrots, and this was an attempt by the government to get their citizens to eat more of them.

HF085 Dr. Carrot Ministry of Food poster. 1942.

The caption on this poster reads: "Dr. Carrot—the children's best friend." The poster features a drawing of a carrot on the left side with the slogan on the right side. The carrot has a top hat in his left hand and a briefcase with the caption "VIT-A" (vitamin A) in his right hand. The carrot also wears glasses and spats.

HF086 Pop Carrot flyer. Circa late 1941. 5½ x 8½

The caption on the front of this double-sided flyer, printed in black-and-white tones, reads: "Pop Carrot says, 'Try me—I'm nice *all* ways.'" The flyer is "No. 1" in a series of flyers. The front features a large illustration of the Disney-designed Carrot character, while the reverse gives recipes. This flyer is similar in design and layout as HF082, and is therefore presumed to be from the same series.

HF087 Stensgaard Home Front posters. Circa 1942.

Stensgaard was involved with the development of a series of income tax and salvage campaign advertisements. The Walt Disney Company Archives has no history on these items. The only known examples appeared in an internet auction in 2003. The illustrations were printed in black-and-white on heavy-stock, glossy paper.

"Taxes will bury the Axis. Pay your taxes gladly." This design featured an angry looking Donald Duck wearing a star-spangled top hat and swatting caricatures of Hitler, Mussolini, and Tojo with a fly swatter. Stars in the illustration contain the phrases: "Taxes to buy guns." "Taxes to buy planes." "Taxes to buy ships." This image is the only one of the four to be printed in color. The words "Walt Disney" appear under Donald's backside, and the notation "CM 1146-1" is printed in the lower right corner.

"Get in the scrap! Save scrap metal. Save rubber. Save paper. Save rags. Save fats and greases. SAVE!" This illustration shows Mickey Mouse and Pluto involved in the collection of scrap material. Mickey is seen placing a metal pipe into a bucket strapped to Pluto's back. The words "Walt Disney" appear to the right of Mickey's left foot, with the notations "Produced by Stensgaard & Associates Inc." and "CM 1146-2" in the lower right corner.

"Invest in Freedom! Buy United States Defense Savings Bonds and Stamps. On Our Way to VICTORY every dollar means a step ahead." In this illustration, Donald Duck charges to the right. The barrels of the shotgun he carries are fashioned from two rolled war bonds. Caricatures of Hitler,

Mussolini, and Tojo are present on the right side, while a Revolutionary War Minuteman appears on the left. The words "Walt Disney" are in the lower left corner, with the notations "Produced and Distributed by W.L. Stensgaard & Associates Inc." and "CM 1146-4" in the lower right corner.

"Yankee Doodle Do. There's work to do in '42." This illustration pictures Donald Duck wearing patriotic-themed clothing. Donald is portrayed as a factory worker with a hammer in his right hand and a piece of steel in his left. A steam whistle wearing a star-spangled top is pictured on the right side of the illustration. The words "Walt Disney" appear in the lower left hand corner, with the notations "Produced and Distributed by W.L. Stensgaard & Associates Inc." and "CM 1146-5" in the lower right corner.

HF088 *Walt Disney Paint Book.* Whitman. 1942, 1943.

This 128-page paint book has a generic cover picturing Mickey Mouse, Donald Duck, and Pluto. Almost all of the interior pages to be colored have a military theme and feature scenes from several of Disney's wartime cartoons, including *The Vanishing Private, Sky Trooper,* and, *The Army Mascot.*

HF089 *Mickey Mouse Annual.* Dean and Sons. 1944

This 189-page annual was published in Great Britain. The cover illustration pictures Mickey, Minnie, and Pluto marching down the street dressed in various English military uniforms.

Home Front Collectibles: Contractors

HFC001 Aeronca Aircraft, *Mr. Grasshopper Wins His Wings* booklet. 1943. 5¼ x 7

This 26-page booklet was published by the Aeronca Aircraft Corporation and told the story of the Aeronca Grasshopper, a multi-purpose airplane manufactured by this defense contractor. The plane was used for artillery spotting, scouting, and air ambulance duties. Disney artists drew all of the illustrations. The cover also features the company's Disney-designed insignia. Members of the general public could receive the booklet by sending 10 cents in stamps to Aeronca's Publicity Department. The booklet was dedicated to "All American Aviators—Past, Present, Future."

HFC002 Aeronca Aircraft ad. Circa 1943. 10¼ x 14

This ad has a rhyming verse about the company, its employees, and the plane the company manufactured that was affectionately called the Grasshopper. The ad also pictures a very large reproduction of the company's Disney-designed insignia.

HFC003 Aeronca Aircraft ad. Circa 1943. 10¼ x 14

This ad shows a Grasshopper light plane at work dropping a packet of supplies to a stranded tank crew. The Aeronca logo is in the bottom left corner, and an ad for the *Mr. Grasshopper Wins His Wings* booklet is in the bottom right corner. There is also an illustration of a cartoon grasshopper scurrying across the top-right hand margin of the page.

HFC004 Aeronca Aircraft ad. Circa 1943. 10¼ x 14

This ad pictures three Grasshopper planes flying over a group of officers. The caption at the bottom of the page reads: "They're Grasshoppers B'Gawd". The ad also pictures the Aeronca logo in the bottom left corner and an ad for the *Mr. Grasshopper Wins His Wings* booklet in the bottom right corner. A cartoon grasshopper stands at attention in the top right corner.

HFC005 Aeronca Aircraft ad. Circa 1943. 8 x 11½

This ad pictures the PT-23 training aircraft. The Aeronca logo is pictured in the bottom left corner, with the *Mr. Grasshopper Wins His Wings* booklet pictured in the bottom right corner.

HFC006 Aeronca matchbook. Circa 1943.

The front of this matchbook has an advertisement for "Buck's Flight School, Lovell Field, Chattanooga, Tennessee", and a color reproduction of Aeronca's Disney-designed Grasshopper insignia. The matchbook's back cover pictures a generic Aeronca ad.

HFC007 ELCO employee pin.

The Electric Launch Company (ELCO) manufactured patrol torpedo boats for the Navy during World War II. By war's end, ELCO had built over 300 of the 80-foot craft. This cloisonné pin uses the Disney-designed "Mosquito Fleet" insignia as part of its design.

HFC008 Adel flyer. 1943. 7½ x 12

The front of this flyer features Mickey Mouse as the Sorcerer's Apprentice with the caption: "Oh boy, your future looks bright!" Mickey holds a crystal ball in his right hand that contains the word "Adel". When opened, the flyer measures 15 x 24. An interior illustration shows Mickey balancing an Adel symbol (industrial clamp) in his hand. In the background and off to the sides are various line drawings that show homemakers, filmmakers, and engineers using Adel products during peacetime. One inside page pictures three artist's renderings of Adel production facilities, while another inside page features a *Victory Through Air Power* ad, which was used in Adel's national advertising campaign: the invention of the synchronized machine-gun, used on World War I fighter planes, taken from the film's "History of Aviation" sequence.

HFC009 Adel flyer. 1943. 12 x 7½

The front of this flyer features Mickey Mouse and the caption: "This marks the end of the world." The flyer opens to 12 x 15 and the tagline continues: "[A]nd the beginning of a new one, the likes of which you've never seen!" An inside page lists 76 different companies which used Adel products. Another inside page features a *Victory Through Air Power* ad, which was used in Adel's national advertising campaign: the Wright Brothers airplane atop the wing of a B-19 bomber, taken from the film's "History of Aviation" sequence.

HFC010 Adel flyer. 1943. 12 x 7½

The front of this flyer features Donald Duck and the caption: "This will put you in your place." The flyer opens to 12 x 15 and the tagline continues: "[I]t will be a place of profit and prosperity for you." An inside page lists 76 different companies which used Adel products. Another inside page features a *Victory Through Air Power* ad, which was used in Adel's national advertising campaign: the first American transcontinental flight, taken from the film's "History of Aviation" sequence.

HFC011 Adel *SAE Journal* advertisement. September 1943. 8 x 11½

Over the course of September, October, and November 1943, Adel Precision Products ran advertisements for their line of synthetic rubber products. All of the ads featured the antics of a Disney-designed character named Sporty. The anthropomorphic fellow was "composed of standard Adel line supports and Adelite synthetic rubber material — all except the droopy drawers".

HFC012 Adel *SAE Journal* advertisement. October 1943. 8 x 11½

HFC013 Adel *SAE Journal* advertisement. November 1943. 8 x 11½

HFC014 North American Aviation Engineering Flight Test decal. 4¼ x 4½

This decal features an illustration of Donald Duck riding a stylized bird, which was the corporate symbol of North American Aviation. The illustration of Donald and the bird is superimposed over a triangle with the letters "NAA" enclosed inside.

HFC015 North American Aviation sign. 31 x 33

This aluminum sign features Donald Duck riding a flying bird. The "NAA" logo is in the background. This item was offered for sale in an eBay auction in March 2002. A letter from the author stated the seller had purchased the item from the son of a retired NAA worker who had taken the sign from an Ohio N.A.A. plant when he retired from the company. The item had a $4,500 opening bid and went unsold.

HFC016 Beechcraft Busy Bee ad. 1943. 8¼ x 11¾

This ad has an illustration of the company's Disney-designed insignia: a bee with various tools in his hands printed atop a blueprint background in the shape of a beech leaf. The ad's text explains how a "badge of merit" featuring the design was awarded to outstanding employees.

HFC017 Beech Aircraft employee handbook. Circa 1942.

This multi-page employee handbook is illustrated with images of the company's Beechcraft Busy Bee logo.

HFC018 Beechcraft Busy Bee Honorary Award of Merit. 1943. 13 x 10

This colorful certificate features the company's Disney-designed insignia and was awarded to both employees and contractors who met or exceeded productivity levels, and who contributed ideas to help the company operate more efficiently.

HFC019 Beechcraft Busy Bee calendar. 1943.

This company calendar was distributed to employees and features illustrations of the company's Disney-designed insignia on the cover, transparent title page, and on page number one.

HFC020 Beechcraft Busy Bee man's sterling pin. 1943. Large size.

This sterling silver and cloisonné pin was produced in the shape of the company's Disney-designed insignia. The large pin was given to male employees.

HFC021 Beechcraft Busy Bee woman's sterling pin. 1943. Small size.

This sterling silver and cloisonné pin was produced in the shape of the company's Disney-designed insignia. The small pin was given to female employees.

HFC022 Beechcraft Busy Bee insignia patch. 1943. 3½ x 5½

This colorful felt patch was worn by company employees and is in the shape of the company's Disney-designed insignia.

HFC023 Beechcraft Busy Bee employee club patch. 1943. 3" diameter

The design for this patch was created by Disney artists and was used for the Beech Aircraft "Ski-B's" ski club. The patch may have been created post-war.

HFC024 *Mickey Mouse on the Home Front* newspaper. 1943–1944. 11½ x15

This comic-style newspaper was distributed by defense contractors to their employees. The monthly publication ran from September 1943 to at least April 1944. The paper contained stories with titles like *Factory Follies, Wise Quacks, Donald's Loaf Life,* and *Patter Up.* Companies would have their name printed under the masthead to give the impression the newsletter was published specifically for them. Roy Disney expressed concern to licensing rep Kay Kamen over both the quality of the gags and drawings and the fear the newspaper may have been infringing on an existing license with another Disney merchandiser. Glenn L. Martin, Delco-Remy, Aeronca, and Aero Parts are some of the companies that distributed issues of this newspaper to their employees.

CHAPTER 3
Gremlins and Friends

> *"Everybody has heard about the Gremlins. The fantastic little people whose antics have become one of the great legends of the R.A.F. The Gremlins, it seems, started bothering pilots when they were driven from their homes in the trees as men began building airplanes and airplane factories."*[120]

In July 1942, Walt Disney received a letter from Sidney Bernstein of the British Information Services. Bernstein wrote to alert Disney to a story authored by Royal Air Force Flight Lieutenant Roald Dahl about "a new dream community in the Air Force". Bernstein thought the story had great film potential and said if Walt was interested he could reach Dahl through the British Embassy in Washington, D.C., where Dahl was stationed as an Assistant Air Attaché.

Thinking Dahl's manuscript contained enough material for a feature-length film, Disney sent Bernstein a thank-you telegram on July 13. That same day, Walt contacted Dahl and shortly thereafter the Studio acquired the rights to the story.

The history of the word "gremlins" has been traced back to the old English word "greme", which meant "to hex". The gremlin association with the R.A.F. dates back to tales told by British pilots stationed in India in the 1920s.

In Dahl's story, the neo-mythical creatures tampered with R.A.F. airplanes during dogfights with the Germans because the British destroyed the Gremlins habitat when they built an airfield on their land. By the end of the story, however, both the Gremlins and the British pilots reconciled their differences and joined together to fight the Nazis.

In mid-September 1942, another R.A.F. pilot came forward claiming the idea behind the Gremlins was his. On September 18, 1942,

---

[120] *The Gremlins*, Random House, 1943. The description is from the book's dust jacket.

Douglas Bisgood wrote to Dahl outlining his concerns. Bisgood had just ferried a bomber across the Atlantic from the U.S.A. to England, and after arriving back home had read a newspaper account of Disney's plans to produce a Gremlins film. Bisgood's letter read in part:

> I read in the *Times* that [Walt Disney] is making a film of the little fellas. What careless talk have you been up to...who originated the chaps? The names of Fifinella, Widget, and Flippertygibbet are my own private property. I shall take an extremely dim view of it if my name doesn't figure somewhere.

Two days later Bisgood sent Disney a letter outlining his concerns:

> I learn with keen interest that you are making a film on "Gremlins". I view with dismay the fact...you are using family names which I claim as being my originals and which I am in fact...using in a book I am writing.
>
> It may be that Flight Lieut. R. Dahl has mentioned these titles to you as I discussed them with him when I was on my way to Canada this year. I am not so much perturbed at the monetary consideration as I am at my titles being used without any reference to myself. I hope that your new film will be as successful...but I do feel that I have a very definite claim on the family titles you propose using.

Hoping to stave off any legal dispute with Bisgood, Walt wrote back to the pilot, indicating any royalties from the use of the characters would be donated to the R.A.F. Benevolent Fund. Disney also mentioned the project had "the full cooperation of the British Air Ministry, and Commander Thornton of the British Embassy in Washington". Disney closed his letter by writing: "It is our hope that this film will help to bring about a better understanding between the British and American people."

On October 1, 1942, Disney wrote to Dahl regarding the potential problem with Bisgood:

> If you have any feeling that this fellow may be inclined to cause trouble, I believe it would be wise to straighten it out now. [W]hen we undertake the production of a film, the cost of which runs into many thousands of dollars, we must surround ourselves with every precautionary measure. I would appreciate having your reactions to this particular situation.

On October 7, 1942, Dahl wrote to Disney regarding Bisgood. Dahl admitted he had spoken to Bisgood about the Gremlins, but added he didn't think Bisgood would cause any problems:

> I am quite sure that he will not cause any trouble. More particularly when he finds out how we are treating the matter and what we are doing with the proceeds.

By late October 1942, Disney had registered a number of Gremlins-related film titles with the Hays office. Suggested film names included *Gay Gremlins, Gremlin Lore, Gremlin Gambols, Gremlins in the Sky, We've Got Gremlins, Gremlin Trouble, Widgets Next in Wings, The Helpful Gremlins, The Gremlin Legend, We Fly with Gremlins, Hi-Flying Gremlins,* and *Look! Gremlins!*

Because the subject matter was not original, Disney needed to establish copyright. In November 1942, Disney penned an article about the Gremlins that was published in an R.A.F. journal that same month. (The story was also reprinted in the 1946 edition of *Slipstream, A Royal Air Force Anthology*. This hardcover book featured a collection of R.A.F. short stories.) On December 2, 1942, Dahl sent Disney a note of thanks on behalf of the Air Ministry for sending along the story for the journal:

> I have just received a telegram from Air Ministry asking me to convey to you their thanks for sending along the article on Gremlins for the R.A.F. Journal, which they happily received on time. They said it was just what they wanted and seemed very pleased about it all.
>
> I, myself, want also to thank you and all those in the Studio for the extremely pleasant time which you gave me during my short visit. I must say that never in my life have I seen so many "good types", as we call them, gathered together under one roof. I haven't enjoyed myself so much for ages.

After shopping the story idea to *Colliers* and *American, Cosmopolitan* magazine agreed to publish the story—the December 1942 issue featured Dahl's Gremlin story illustrated by Disney artists. Shortly thereafter, Dahl received numerous requests to turn his manuscript into a book. Disney liked the book idea, and in 1943 Random House published *The Gremlins*. Disney artists Al Dempster and Bill Justice provided the illustrations—Dempster was responsible for the 13 full-page color paintings, while Justice drew the black-and-white illustrations.

According to an article in the May 1, 1943, Rome, New York, *Daily Sentinel*, "The original manuscript for the book...[was] presented to the New York State Historical Association by the Artists' and Writers' Guild." The article went on to say the manuscript was signed by Dahl and was to be displayed for several weeks in the "Gremlin Center" in Cooperstown (the museum of the New York State Historical Association), before being permanently placed in the association's library.

After seeing the Gremlin characters created by Studio artists, Dahl wrote to Disney to express his concern with the preliminary character designs. Dahl believed the Gremlin characters should be drawn with derby hats. The issue quickly turned contentious. Dahl had a very specific design in mind, and it was one that Disney apparently failed to capture:

> I am very glad to see that you had not very definite views about Gremlins not wearing bowler hats (which I think are called derbys in this country); but their omission in your drawings did cause a little trouble, because *Cosmopolitan* wanted to cut out my description of Gremlins because it did not tie up with your drawings. I am afraid that I took a very strong line with them and told them, just because you happened to have drawn a Gremlin slightly differently to what he really looks like, this does not mean that all the Gremlins in the world will suddenly change to conform with your drawings.
>
> I...told them that they had to leave my original description in, whether it tallied with your drawings or not. I hope you don't disapprove of this.

None of the approximate three-dozen Gremlins pictured in the *Cosmopolitan* story wear derby hats. All of the headwear worn by Gremlins in the article has the appearance of being pull-down winter toques with horns protruding from either side.

The editors at *Cosmopolitan* contacted Dahl in January 1943 wanting permission to publish the story in the British edition of the magazine. Dahl wrote Disney again reiterating he did not like the original illustrations, which had been published in the American edition of the magazine:

> Another point is that it would, of course, entail a completely new set of drawings from you, because the ones you originally gave *Cosmopolitan* would not be suitable.

On March 19, 1943, Walt Disney wrote to Dahl indicating plans to produce a combination cartoon/live-action Gremlins film had been shelved. Disney indicated his staff was now working on ideas and plans to produce the subject as an animated feature-length film instead—the focus of the film would be from the Gremlins' perspective. Walt wrote that his artists seemed to be having a problem formulizing the idea or plot behind the film: "[W]e do get stuck on a lot of the GREMLIN business."

Included in the March 19 letter was Walt's appeal to have Dahl travel to California to help work out the details of the film:

> [A]t this point there are several very important things upon which

you could assist us, and we don't want to go too far with our present treatment and then find it was not in good taste.

Gremlins lore soon dominated the American psyche, and Walt was afraid public interest in Gremlins would begin to wane before he could get a film produced and distributed. As evidence of the Gremlins fad, the January 9, 1943, *New York Evening Post* reported: "The R.A.F.'s Gremlins will become swing fodder in Count Basie's new song, 'Dance of the Gremlins', sub-captioned 'There's a Gremlin in the Groove'."

On March 25, 1943, Roy Disney sent his brother an inter-office communication regarding gremlin films being produced by other studios. Roy indicated Walter Lantz said he would abandon the idea and withdraw his suggested movie titles; Dave Fleisher said he would do everything in his power to not use the name or topic in any films, although he added he didn't have final authority in such decisions; Fred Quimby said he'd drop titles and indicated the subject matter would be avoided; and Leon Schlesinger indicated he had two pictures in production with scheduled release dates of July and later that fall.

Fully aware Gremlins lore may have outrun its popularity before the Disney version could be completed, on April 16, 1943, Roy Disney wrote to Columbia Pictures President Harry Cohn asking him to shelve any Gremlin-related projects. Roy indicated the Studio had spent roughly $50,000 on developing the picture to date, and added he didn't want to spend another $600,000 to $800,000 and a year's worth of time if their picture was going to be "undermined and hurt by a lot of single reels that may saturate the public's desire to see a 'Gremlin' feature and really do us considerable harm in the marketing of it". Roy received an answer to his request on May 25 indicating Columbia had no plans for making any Gremlin-related films.

As the Gremlins idea wound its way through the development process, seamstress Charlotte Clark, (who designed and produced the popular Mickey Mouse doll in 1932), created several dolls based on the Studio's character designs. The dolls included a Gremlin, a Fifinella, and a Widget. In May 1943, Roald Dahl requested 12 Widget dolls, and seven months later, on December 18, 1943, Dahl sent a telegram to Disney's secretary Dolores Voght Scott requesting several more character dolls:

> A very special request for a Fifinella Doll, and two Widgets, but especially Fifinella. [A]re there any chance any around [?] [I]f so most grateful. [S]end [by] airmail. Very Merry Christmas you, [and] Walt.

Two days later, Walt Disney responded to Dahl's request by return telegram:

> Terribly sorry, but there isn't a Fifinella in the place. Widgets, yes. In fact, they have sold so very well that Mrs. Clark (the lady who personally makes all of our dolls) has been devoting all of her time to Widgets for the past several weeks. At no time have we ever had more than just a few Fifinellas. They didn't sell well so we discontinued making them. However, three Widgets were air-expressed to you today. Best Christmas Greetings. Sincerely, Walt.

On May 22, 1943, Dahl sent a letter to Walt Disney addressing the problem of another member of the R.A.F. who was making claims against the subject matter. Dahl told Walt the Air Ministry had intervened, and with the help of several civilian lawyers the complainant relinquished any claim to the Gremlins product.

As Disney's artists struggled to turn Dahl's story into a film, Gremlin sightings around the Studio increased. Artist Jim Bodrero wrote:

> Ever since work started on Flight Lieutenant "Stalky" Dahl's Gremlin story, complaints are heard that Gremlins have moved into Disney's—reports of Movieola Gremlins, sound Gremlins, splice-cutting Gremlins, and Monday morning Gremlins have filtered down the corridors.
>
> To put an end to these rumors, Studio Gremlinologists want to remind all parties that there is only one way to see, feel, or be infested with Gremlins—that is to be shot at while piloting or serving in the crew of a military or naval aircraft on operational duty.
>
> Flying schools have no Gremlins, nor do they appear on training planes or airliners. As for the Monday morning stomach things—everyone knows those aren't Gremlins, they're butterflies.[121]

Hollywood gossip writer Louella Parson wrote lightheartedly about Gremlins in her April 10, 1943, syndicated newspaper column, reiterating what Bodrero had told Studio staff:

> They don't tear stockings, wreck automobiles, and they aren't responsible for any accidents outside of the air. The only place Gremlins appear is in a plane and can only be seen by airmen.

On May 19, 1943, Disney received a rather terse letter from Dahl in which the airman reprimanded Disney for allowing Gremlins images to be used in a Lifesavers magazine advertisement. Dahl felt the use of the characters in this manner was demeaning:

---

121 *Dispatch from Disney's*, 1943 Disney employee newsletter.

> I nearly fell off my chair when I opened *Look* magazine...and saw the Life Saver [sic] advertisement with our Gremlins in it. [We] have spent many hours wondering how we can make sure of preserving in the eyes of the public...basic principles of Gremlinology, and of convincing them once and for all that Gremlins and their kin do not associate themselves with things other than aircraft and pilots.
>
> Imagine then my horror at finding a group of the little men, not to mention the Widgets and the Fifinellas, busily engaged in playing around with a lot of over-sized...life savers!
>
> I was horrified not only because the Gremlins were being completely misrepresented, but also because I could see you destroying in the eyes of the public the legend.
>
> [S]urely you realize that if the public are going to see Gremlins playing with peppermints...then...I am convinced, that the legend will be ruined. [P]eople are beginning to regard you as an authority on these things...therefore, anything you say about Gremlins from now on, goes.
>
> I suggest...that the use of Gremlins in advertising should, where possible, be confined solely to aircraft manufactures or to makes of aircraft parts, and that the things you make them do in your pictures should be the things which they normally do anyway. This will reserve the whole idea. If financial considerations make it impossible for you to narrow down the sales of advertising rights to this extent, then the makers of peppermint tablets, gum, and tooth paste will have to have an airplane, a real, well-drawn airplane, embodied in their advertisements if they wish to utilize Gremlins. And on this airplane the Gremlins can be shown going about their business. I can see that there might well be difficulties over this, but surely it is the only way of dealing with the matter and of preserving the true character of the story.

Walt addressed Dahl's concerns in a return letter on May 26, 1943, and he also requested Dahl come to the Studio to help work on the film's script:

> Your letter of May 19 received and contents noted. You may rest assured that any suggestions you have will always be given careful consideration.
>
> I would like to correct an impression which was indicated in your letter. It is not the financial returns, with which we are concerned, but through this medium we are able to establish our rights to characters through various forms of publication, and unless these rights are established we may not have any control over the Gremlins when they do come out. Our entire idea is one to establish our copyrights with no thought whatever of financial gain.

> We have reached a point in the story where…it would be very helpful if you could make arrangements to come out for a period of at least two months so that, together, we can whip the story into its final shape. If you are not able to do this, I do not feel that I can be held responsible to the Royal Air Force for the finished treatment of this material. Therefore, I wish you would please do what you can to come to the studio for at least the time necessary to put the script into shape for production.

Two months later, on July 2, 1943, Walt sent a letter to Dahl informing him he was not going to make the Gremlins into a feature. Walt was now considering putting the film out as a short instead. One of the main reasons, at least the one stated to Dahl, was the fact the R.A.F. retained control over the final product through a clause in the contract:

> The complications that arise with the R.A.F. are other reasons why we do not want to consider the feature angle. Every time I refer to Clause 12, I become a little apprehensive of what I may be facing. With the amount of money that is required to spend on a feature of this type we cannot be subjected to the whims of certain people, including yourself. I do not mean this unkindly or in any sense as criticism, but we feel it simply is not good business to undertake the production of the Gremlins as a feature at this time with so much risk involved.

On October 13, 1943, Dahl sent Walt a letter:

> The purpose of this letter is to enquire whether you have yet come to any definite decision in regard to the Gremlin film, because I have now to reply to a question which has been put to me by Air Ministry on this subject.

On December 18, 1943 Walt replied:

> I was in Washington a couple of weeks ago and fully intended to see you while there, but was bedded with the grippe which shot my plans all to pieces.
>
> Gremlins will not be made as a feature because of the feeling on the distributor's part that the public has become tired of so many war films. We have given considerable thought to the possibility of making the Gremlins into a short and I have personally endeavored to generate some interest among the various crews, but haven't met with any degree of success. However, if we ever hit upon an angle that seems right for production, we'll get in touch with you.

Studio artists had struggled for months to complete a full-length feature Gremlin film (initially as a blend of live-action and animation), and when artists working on the project couldn't develop a workable script, a decision was made to produce the story as a short cartoon instead. Unfortunately, Disney and his artists were vexed by the imps of the air, and despite the massive investment in time, labor, and money, the project was scrapped altogether in mid-December 1943.

As far as the species was concerned, Gremlins were adult males, Fifinellas were adult females, and Widgets were their offspring. Spandules were the winter relatives of Gremlins who lived in altitudes over 30,000 feet. Spandules hampered the maneuverability of fighters by causing ice to form on the aircraft's key components.

In 1943, Spandules were the subject of a 26-page booklet Studio artists illustrated for the Army Air Forces Safety Education Division, Flight Control Command. The booklet was titled *Winter Draws On—Meet the Spandules*, and was used to teach pilots how to fly, maneuver, and land in winter conditions. The booklet was filled with illustrations of Spandules wreaking havoc with aircraft. Part of the booklet's introduction read:

> Whenever an airplane enters their domain, they pounce aboard. They like to test a guy out. If he is on his toes they probably won't bother him much, but if he looks sound asleep or a little thick between the ears they are almost sure to plaster his wings with ice, load down his propeller, and do all sorts of tricks that can be real serious. If you know where to look for Spandules and if you keep a close watch on their handiwork, you can usually avoid a run in with them.

The patron saint of the Women's Airforce Service Pilots (WASP) was Fifinella. The design for the WASP insignia was based on illustrations found in *The Gremlins* book.

WASP were responsible for piloting military aircraft from defense plants to overseas debarkation points. The unit was formed at Houston Texas in November 1942, and fell under the jurisdiction of the Army Air Forces Training Command. Women trainees were between 18 and 34 years of age, possessed U.S. citizenship, had completed high school, and were required to have at least 35 hours of flying experience.

The first unit of WASP was designated the 319th Army Air Force Flying Training Detachment. The class underwent an intensive 27-week training period at Houston Municipal Airport. Upon graduation the pilots received about $250 per month in pay.

Byrd Howell Granger graduated with the first class. She was editor-in-chief of the WASP newsletter, affectionately titled *The Fifinella*

Gazette. Granger wrote to the Disney Studios in late November 1942 requesting an insignia. When the Studio agreed to provide the WASP with a mascot, Granger published the exciting news in the unit's newsletter:

> In answer to a telegram forwarded to Walt Disney asking for permission to use Fifinella...the following message was received. Permission granted for two years from date hereof...to use without charge, the name and design of Fifinella. The cheers which greeted the above when it was announced at mess are an indication of the group's thanks to Mr. Disney and his staff.

The Fifinella insignia was awarded to the WASP in January 1943. The insignia was forwarded to Houston in time to be incorporated into the March 1, 1943, issue of *The Fifinella Gazette*. Granger wrote:

> The original drawing of Fifi arrived in time to become part of the masthead...the final issue also contained a surprise for the girls, for as a slip-in, we had inserted color repro's of our emblem. What a kick that was!

During the war, patches, stationary, and decals were produced using Fifinella's likeness. In 1995, WASP Shutsy-Reynolds wrote:

> Fifinella was worn while in training...on the A-2 jackets and on the white blouse. The patch was not part of our uniform—in fact it wasn't even official. The patch was not available commercially. They were handmade by both trainees and instructors. To get a patch made at Sweetwater we made our own. I remember buying a large side of leather and with lacquer from the field paint shop made up about 50 which I sold. Money was always in short supply and the venture made for a fine weekend.[122]

The first class of WASP graduated April 23, 1943. Because the Houston Airport could not adequately accommodate the WASP training program, the detachment was relocated to Avenger Field in Sweetwater, Texas. The unit was renamed the 318th AAFFTD. Members of the 319th agreed to pass the Fifinella insignia on to the 318th.

The *Fifinella Gazette* reported:

> Within a matter of weeks the 319th will be no more. Its present members, such as have not graduated, will join the thriving 318th at Sweetwater. The matter of the Fifinella emblem of the 319th was taken up with a number of them Gremlins on Fifinella Field and after due consultation it was decided that the emblem would remain with the 319th until

---

122 Correspondence with the author.

its demise, after which...the emblem would transfer to the 318th."[123]

It seems that the impish Fifinella harassed women pilots just as their male counterparts were harassed by Gremlins. The following excerpt was printed in an undated WASP newsletter:

> There is a recent fallacy going the rounds that the Fifinellas have taken to riding the air waves recently. I knew their mother well...I first met up with that irascible and dangerous female Gremlin over the Rocky Mountains...she pulled my compass off by some 45 degrees and held it there until I was about to crash land. In the London to Australia race...she changed the signs on my fuel controls from off to on, locked my cockpit hood so I couldn't get it open and froze the flaps so as to give me a hair-raising landing. I called her lady Borzia and I suspected on that day she had obtained help, although I never saw a Gremlin until sometime later, and then only sketchily.

WASP were classified as Civil Service employees during the war. When a WASP died, she was not accorded the same benefits as a male pilot in the armed forces. The bereaved family was not allowed to display a gold star, nor were they allowed to place an American flag over the coffin. A total of 38 WASP were killed in the line of duty.

During the program's operation more than 25,000 women applied to become part of the WASP unit. Only 1,830 were admitted and of that number only 1,074 earned their wings. WASP logged sixty-million air miles during the war, and flew all manner of aircraft including drone targets, the B-17 and B-29 bombers, C-47 Transport, P-38, P-39, P-40, P-47, and P-51 fighters, and the YP-59A experimental jet.

Besides the Random House book, Disney's licensing representative Kay Kamen signed contracts with several manufacturers for the production of merchandise including hand puppets, a puzzle, and luminous pictures.

Disney licensee W.L. Stensgaard created several Gremlins figurines constructed of papier-mâché. One set was used by the Dayton Company, a fur storage company in Minneapolis, Minnesota. One display featured a group of four, full-relief, papier-mâché Gremlins and was titled "The Gremlin Fur Destruction Committee". The display measured four feet in height and was 42-inches in diameter. On May 26, 1943, Stensgaard representative Bennet Cert wrote to Random House Publishing:

---

123 *The Fifinella Gazette*, undated WASP newsletter.

This display was sold or rented to certain stores in connection with their fur storage and repair promotion plans ...the Dayton Company... purchased one of these and is using it very effectively. They have also used certain of the characters in their advertising promotion on the same subject. Of course the stores can use this Gremlin series in many situations aside from Fur Storage.

While Disney artists were unable to tackle the lighthearted Gremlin feature, they were able to produce more serious propaganda films. The Studio produced a total of six propaganda films during the war, several of which contained stark and terrifying images of fascist oppression and destruction. The U.S. government underwrote five of these films, while Walt Disney financed one. These films would be a far cry from the cuddly Gremlins characters Disney artists had worked so long to develop.

(The source material used in writing this chapter is courtesy the Paul Anderson archives.)

Gremlins Collectibles

GR001 *The Gremlins*. Random House. 1943.
This 48-page book tells the story of Gremlins, mythical creatures who played havoc with Royal Air Force planes as revenge for an R.A.F. base being built atop their natural habitat. The book contains 12 full-page color illustrations in addition to one two-page spread. The book also contains numerous black-and-white illustrations. Disney artist Al Dempster created the color plates, and Bill Justice produced the black-and-white illustrations. The book was published with a dust jacket.

GR002 The Gremlins. 1943.
The Australian edition was published by Ayers.

GR003 The Gremlins. 1944.
The British edition was published by Collins one year after the American and Australian editions.

GR004 *Cosmopolitan*. December 1942.
The issue contains a Gremlins story illustrated by Disney artists.

GR005 *Look*. June 1, 1943.
Full-page Gremlins Lifesaver candy ad.

GR006 *War Heroes.* April-June 1943.
This Dell comic book features a six-page color cartoon story on the legend of the Gremlins.

GR007 Gremlins Jaymar puzzle. Circa 1943. Box 10 x 7 x 2 deep. Puzzle 22 x 14
The very colorful 300-piece puzzle pictures 11 Gremlins, one Widget, and one Fifinella attacking an Allied fighter plane. The left and right vertical margins feature characters from the unproduced film. The puzzle is marked "Louis Marx and Co."

GR008 *Playthings* magazine. May 1943.
Front cover features a Kay Kamen ad for the cartoon, *Walt Disney's Gremlins of the R.A.F.* The illustration features a Gremlin drilling holes in the wing of a British fighter plane as a Widget and a Fifinella look on.

GR009 Royal Air Force Journal. January 1943.
This issue contains a Gremlin's story written by Roald Dahl with two illustrations by Disney artists.

GR010 Gremlins print. Circa 1944.
This item was marketed by Henry A. Citroen and was advertised as a luminous picture. This line of pictures was sold from 1944 to 1946, and the pictures are marked "© Walt Disney Productions".

GR011 Gremlins photograph. 8 x 12
This black-and-white photograph pictures the Gremlin insignia for the 12th Combat Camera Unit.

GR012 Gremlins animation script. May 18, 1943. 154 pages
This item was offered for sale through an internet auction site in the 1990s with a $1,200 reserve. The script originally belonged to Disney artist Herb Ryman.

GR013 *Flying.* Unknown month from 1943.
Magazine contains a four-page article and three photographs featuring the WASP.

GR014 *Flying.* Unknown month from 1944.
Magazine contains a four-page article and four photographs featuring the WASP.

GR015 *Winter Draws On—Meet the Spandules.* 1943. 6 x 4½
This 28-page booklet was published by the Safety Education Division, Flight Control Command, United States Army Air Force. The booklet contains 20

pages of Disney illustrations and tips on how to avoid cold-weather-related airplane problems. The booklet's introduction reads:

> In this book for the first time is pictured a close relative of the Gremlin, the Spandule. These little fellows inhabit the space above 30,000 feet except in the winter time, when they have come down to lower altitudes and have been known to play around on the ground. Although not mean at heart, these little guys are forced by their very nature to do a lot of things to get a pilot in trouble. Whenever an airplane enters their domain they pounce aboard...they like to test a guy out... they are almost sure to plaster his wings with ice...and do all sorts of tricks that can be real serious...if you keep a close watch for first evidence of their handiwork, you can usually avoid a run in with them.

GR016 Widget hand puppet. 1943. 7 x 9

The Character Novelty Company, a Disney licensee from 1940 to 1947, manufactured this puppet which was originally sold in a generic box for $1.50. The paper tag reads: "This is an exclusive Walt Disney design of one of the famous Gremlin characters discovered by the RAF."

GR017 Widget doll. 1943. 4½ x 9

Cloth doll. The tag reads "Copyright Walt Disney Productions".

GR018 Wasp stationary. 1943. 8 x 10

Script along the top edge of the paper reads "Avenger Field, Sweetwater Texas". A multi-colored Fifinella insignia is also pictured in the upper right corner with the caption "318th AAFFTD".

GR019 Wasp sticker. 1943. 3¾ x 3¾

This multi-colored sticker pictures Fifinella, the patron saint of the WASP. The sticker is marked "318th AAFFTD, Aviation Enterprises Ltd., Avenger Field, Sweetwater Texas".

GR020 Wasp decal. Post 1944. 2¼ inch diameter.

This decal features Fifinella, the Disney-designed mascot of the Women Airforce Service Pilots. This decal makes reference to the Order of the Fifinella. Appendix III contains a letter regarding the post inactivation organization of the WASP, which was tentatively given the name "Order of the Fifinella". As the WASP unit was decommissioned in December 1944, one could assume this decal was created in early 1945, or perhaps even later.

GR021 318th WASP Army Air Force Flying Training Detachment. 1944. 72 pages.

Embossed leather yearbook-type publication for WASP training class 44 W-6 – W-7. Cover features a fantastic reproduction of the unit's Disney-designed "Fifinella" mascot.

GR022 Fifinella matchbook.

The front of the matchbook features the Disney-designed "Fifinella" mascot of the WASP. The back cover reads "Avenger Field, Aviation Enterprises, Contractors to the Army Air Force".

CHAPTER 4
Insignia

"Every year we receive hundreds of requests for designs of various comic sketches. Naturally, that would be too great an undertaking. But in the case of the boys who are doing their share in the nation's defense program, we are only too happy to try to please them."[124] —Walt Disney

Over the course of the war, Disney artists designed military emblems for all branches of the United States armed forces, as well as emblems for military units serving with Allied countries including Canada, Britain, France, Poland, New Zealand, South Africa, and China. Between 1939 and 1945, Disney artists created an estimated 1,200 combat insignia.

The use of military insignia dates back to the Crusades, when Western European Christians battled Middle Eastern Muslims for control of Palestine. Knights displayed their heraldic crests on shields and flags so their followers could identify them in the heat of pitched battle.

During World War I, combat air units used identifying markings to help establish friend from foe. Some pilots spelled out their name across their plane's wing tops, while others, like German Ace Manfred von Richtofen, painted his Albatross fighter blood red, earning him the nickname "The Red Baron". Richtofen's idea proved so menacing that by the end of the war his entire pursuit squadron had painted their planes red.

During World War II, many units used a Disney character in their insignia design without obtaining proper authorization from the Studio—enterprising and artistic servicemen drew whatever design a senior officer or fellow serviceman wanted for their unit's insignia.

This was the case in the fall of 1931, when someone at Naval Reserve Aviation Base Floyd Bennett Field in New York created an

---

[124] Walt Disney, *Freeport Standard Journal*, March 4, 1941.

insignia design featuring Mickey Mouse. The emblem pictured Mickey sitting atop a goose that had a bomb and trident under its wings, with the Statute of Liberty visible in the background. This particular emblem represents the first documented used of a Disney character on a combat insignia.

Floyd Bennett Field was dedicated by Rear Admiral Richard E. Byrd in June 1930 as New York's first municipal airport. The field was named after Navy Warrant Officer Floyd Bennett, a New York native who had accompanied Admiral Byrd on the MacMillan Expedition to Greenland in 1925. Bennett was also Byrd's pilot on their attempted first flight over the North Pole in 1926.

Floyd Bennett Field was built on Barren Island at the southern tip of Manhattan. From 1931-1941, the field was one of eight Naval Reserve Aviation Bases that focused on providing primary flight training for Navy pilots. The base received a compliment of Curtiss O2C-1 Helldiver planes from the active fleet in 1931. The Helldiver was a multipurpose plane used as a dive-bomber and observer aircraft.

According to Lawrence Suid's book, *Guts and Glory: The Making of the American Military Image in Films*, an RKO Studio location manager contacted the Navy in December 1932 asking for the use of four Navy Helldivers for one day's flying time of two-and-a-half hours. RKO wanted to use the planes in the film *King Kong*. In late December, the Navy denied RKO's request.[125]

When RKO camera crews traveled to the East Coast to film location shots for *King Kong*, a company representative contacted the commanding officer of NRAB Floyd Bennett Field with an offer: RKO would donate $100 to the Officer's Mess Fund and pay the pilots $10 each to fly around the Empire State Building. The commanding officer, not knowing his superiors had previously denied RKO's request, accepted the offer.[126]

Four Helldivers took part in the filming. The fuselage of each sported the squadron's unofficial Mickey Mouse emblem. According to Suid's book, then-Lieutenant John Winston recalled he and three other pilots were given orders to "go and jazz the Empire State

---

125 Suid, Lawrence. *Guts and Glory: The Making of the American Military Image in Film*. University Press of Kentucky, 2002. p.52.

126 Suid, Lawrence. *Guts and Glory: The Making of the American Military Image in Film*. University Press of Kentucky, 2002. p.52.

Building".⁴¹²⁷ It took the pilots less than 15 minutes to accomplish their mission. Winston recalled: "We didn't know what it was all about. They just said there was some kind of movie being made."[128]

RKO cameramen captured footage of the planes flying in formation, peeling off, diving at an imaginary target, then looping and attacking from the opposite direction. RKO "intercut twenty-eight scenes of the Navy aircraft with process shots and miniatures to create the fatal assault on Kong atop the Empire State Building".[129]

The Mickey Mouse emblem is visible on the fuselages of the Helldivers in several of the film's scenes. The design can be seen in two live-action sequences: when the four Helldivers depart Floyd Bennett Field, and when the planes attack the giant ape as he stands atop the Empire State Building. The emblem is also partially visible on the plane's fuselages in close-up shots filmed inside an RKO sound stage.

The first "official" request for a Studio-designed insignia came in June 1939, when Naval Reserve Aviation Cadet Burt Stanley wrote to Walt Disney requesting an insignia for the "Fighting Seven" Naval Air Squadron, based aboard the aircraft carrier USS *Wasp* (CV-7).

Staney wrote: "During the last world war various aviation squadrons had their own insignia, such as the "Hat in the Ring" design used by Captain Eddie Richenbacker. Today, we don't have clever ones, the kind needed to kick up our morale and give us a feeling of personal pride in our outfit. Why don't you design us a suitable insignia?" Walt responded enthusiastically: "You bet I can."[130] The job was assigned to Studio artist Van Kaufman who fulfilled the request by designing an insignia featuring an angry wasp with boxing gloves.

Ten different American naval vessels have been christened USS *Wasp*. Cadet Stanley's carrier, CV-7, was sunk on September 16, 1942, while escorting troop transports carrying elements of the 7th Marine Regiment to Guadalcanal. During the mission, *Wasp* was crippled by

---

127 Suid, Lawrence. *Guts and Glory: The Making of the American Military Image in Film*. University Press of Kentucky, 2002. p.52.

128 Suid, Lawrence. *Guts and Glory: The Making of the American Military Image in Film*. University Press of Kentucky, 2002. p.52.

129 Suid, Lawrence. *Guts and Glory: The Making of the American Military Image in Film*. University Press of Kentucky, 2002. p.52.

130 *Flying*, April 1942.

two torpedoes fired from the Japanese submarine *I-19*. The carrier was abandoned and later sunk by USS *Lansdowne*.

Later in the war, when CV-18 (the second aircraft carrier to bear the name *Wasp*) was commissioned, Disney artist Hank Porter designed an insignia for the namesake based loosely on the illustration created for the original *Wasp*. Porter incorporated seven waves into the design, honoring the predecessor's designation as CV-7. The new image featured an updated wasp in a fighting stance with boxing gloves at the ready, standing astride an aircraft carrier.

CV-18 arrived in the South Pacific in March 1944. Planes aboard the *Wasp* participated in the Marianas Campaign, including the Battle of the Philippine Sea, as well as the fight for Okinawa and the invasion of Iwo Jima, and they launched raids against the Japanese Home Islands. The carrier finished the war by transporting servicemen back to the United States as part of *Operation Magic Carpet*. The *Wasp* met an inglorious end when she was sold for scrap in the spring of 1973.

Walt Disney received the next insignia request in March 1940. Lieutenant E.S. Caldwell, a Naval Operations officer in Washington, D.C., asked for a design representing the American torpedo boat squadron which was known as the "Mosquito Fleet". The ensuing design featured an angry-looking mosquito with a Navy tar hat on his head, skimming over the water with a torpedo clutched between his legs.

The March 4, 1941, *Van Wert Times* referenced the mosquito emblem:

> A dispatch from Hollywood states that Walt Disney's already busy studio is turning out insignia for the nation's armed forces. The local significance is that the first request for a "saucy" insignia came from Lieutenant Commander E.S. Caldwell, son-in-law of Lee R. Bonmmewitz, who stated that a humorous character was desired to be placed on a new fleet of high-speed mosquito (torpedo) boats to be commissioned shortly. Lieut. Com. Caldwell is in command of the "mosquito" boat squadron.
>
> When word got around to other units, in came more requests, and Disney assigned two of his best artists to fill them. Disney is donating the time and labor incurred in designing the humorous sketches.

The crew of the Mosquito Fleet torpedo boats gained a reputation of daring attack-and-rescue while plying the waters around the Philippines. In a letter of appreciation to Walt Disney, Lieutenant John Bulkeley, Commander of Motor Torpedo Boat Squadron Three, wrote:

> This squadron carried an insignia designed and painted by you of a mosquito riding a torpedo symbolizing the Mosquito Fleet. The

officers and men of the squadron all feel that your insignia contributed materially to the spirit and morale of the Squadron. I feel that you have had a definite part in the successful operations of the Squadron…and General MacArthur's successful withdrawal from Bataan. Well done![131]

Bulkeley's squadron was responsible for sinking three enemy ships and two landing barges, damaging two other ships and downing four enemy aircraft while on duty in the South Pacific. The unit's most famous accomplishment was the evacuation of Philippine President Quezon and General MacArthur from Corregidor.

Several months before America entered the war, Walt Disney was speaking of his desire to help design insignia for those serving in the military:

> Disney has consented to donating the time and labor incurred in designing the humorous sketches. Some of them bear striking resemblance of Donald Duck and too many of the queer looking sprites, which recently made their screen debut in *Fantasia*.
>
> "Every year," says Disney, "we receive hundreds of requests for designs of various comic sketches. Naturally, that would be too great an undertaking. But in the case of the boys who are doing their share in the nation's defense program, we are only too happy to try to please them."[132]

By the spring of 1941, the Studio began receiving letters from servicemen in all branches of the Armed Forces asking for an insignia design. With the U.S. Declaration of War in December 1941, there was a marked increase in requests. "The armed forces were growing so rapidly that new units…were being organized almost daily. Every self-respecting outfit had to have an insignia…every military organization wanted our designs," wrote Bill Justice in his 1992 autobiography, *Justice for Disney*.

The daily arrival of requests prompted Walt Disney to summon Henry "Hank" Porter to his office in early 1942. "Mister, you have yourself a job," Disney explained. "Just settle down to it. Make as many insignia as you can. If you get overloaded with work, let me know."[133]

---

131 *Dispatch from Disney's*, 1943 Disney employee newsletter.

132 *Freeport Journal-Standard*, March 4, 1941.

133 *Flying*, April 1942.

Porter began his career at the Studio in June 1936 as an animator on *Snow White and the Seven Dwarfs*. Prior to coming to Disney's, Porter had worked as a political cartoonist with the *Knickerbocker News* in Albany, New York, and later operated his own commercial art studio in Buffalo.

Porter had previously suffered through a one-month bout of temporary blindness, while working as a political cartoonist. Fearing a relapse when the light from his animator's board strained his eyes, Porter requested a transfer and was subsequently moved to the Studio's Publicity Art Department. Porter thrived in his new role, where he created a wide range of art including the *Snow White and Pinocchio* newspaper strips; feature-length and short cartoon publicity art; presentation art given to dignitaries, business leaders and celebrities; magazine covers and illustrations; and even the Studio's yearly corporate Christmas card. Porter also had authority to sign Walt Disney's scriptive signature. Disney was so impressed with Porter's creativity and output he once referred to Porter as a "one man art department".[134]

One facet of Porter's work that he truly relished was the creation of combat insignia. An article in the Studio's 1943 employee newsletter *Dispatch from Disney's* reported: "Henry Porter's favorite assignment is assisting in the creating of insignia for the armed services—insignia which are a gift from Disney's to our armed forces." Seven examples of Porter's insignia work were reprinted in color on the newsletter's back cover.

The majority of insignia requests arrived at the Studio via mail. Occasionally, a request would be placed over the phone or in-person, but these instances were rare. When servicemen arrived at the Studio in-person, Porter was more than happy to entertain the men for as long as his production schedule allowed.

Porter's daughter Maxine, who worked alongside her father at the Studio in the summer of 1944, recalled:

> Once in a while [military personnel] would show up in person, two or three of them would come, marines, sailors. They'd come in to a main office. [The receptionist] called and said, "We're sending these guys up", or somebody would escort them up. [My father] opened up the door and [would] say, "Hello." They just were admiring all his stuff. They'd stay as long as they could without keeping him away from his

---

134 *Dispatch from Disney's*, 1943 Disney employee newsletter.

work. He was excited when people came in person. He was happy to have these personal calls.[135]

The volume of requests quickly outpaced Porter's ability to keep up with the demand. The April 4, 1941, *Charleston Daily Mail* reported:

> Walt Disney's Burbank Calif. Studio has lately been flooded with requests for insignia designs from newly formed units of the United States army, navy and air corps. To fill these requests, Disney has put one of his artists on the job, full time.

By 1942, Porter was swamped. *Flying* (formerly *Popular Aviation*) magazine reported: "Porter's six-foot, six-inch frame was entirely snowed under and he let out a muffled cry for help from the bottom of the pile. He got it."[136]

Porter assembled a team of fellow artists he would call on for assistance. The group consisted of Van Kaufman, George Goepper, Ed Parks, and Roy Williams. Porter was the most prolific of the group, and created upwards of 80 percent or more of the estimated 1,200 insignia designs that eventually came out of the Studio.

An article in the April 1942 issue of *Flying* highlighted the members of Porter's unofficial insignia team:

> Van Kaufman, a very talented young man from Georgia who went to art school in Los Angeles and who has been working at the big Disney plant for two and a half years; George Goepper, skilled drawer of Pluto the pooch; and Ed Parks, a Connecticut boy who has been with Disney for four years. Of the lot, Parks is the only one who flies, having taken instruction in Connecticut.

Before being drafted, Kaufman was featured in a photo that appeared in the April 2, 1942, edition of the *Los Angeles Evening Herald and Express*. The headline above the photo was "Junior Army Sees Demonstration on Defense Cartoons", and the caption read:

> Junior Army members, who were guests of Walt Disney at his studio, are shown as they applauded Van Kaufman, studio artist, after he showed them how he drew insignia for Army and Navy planes using characters made famous in *Fantasia* as themes.

During the war, Kaufman attained the rank of Tech Sergeant. He spent the duration as a member of the First Motion Picture Unit (FMPU), a branch of the Army Air Force whose men were stationed on

---

135 Phone interview with author.

136 *Flying*, April 1942.

the grounds of the old Hal Roach studio in Culver City. (Kaufman also designed the unit's cartoon insignia, which was used on a matchbook cover. The design features a man with a camera flying in a plane that is being shot at.) Many Hollywood artists, writers, photographers, and animators served with the FMPU, including Disney animator Frank Thomas.

The FMPU was the brainchild of General Hap Arnold, head of the Army Air Forces. As Warner Bros. had produced films for the military months before the outbreak of war, Jack Warner was commissioned Lieutenant Colonel in the Army Air Forces and was given command of the unit. One of the first films produced by the unit was *Winning Your Wings,* a film designed to inspire young men to voluntarily enlist in the Air Force.

Kaufman returned to Disney's after the war, but left in 1949 at the invitation of famed automobile artist Art Fitzpatrick. The two produced dozens of magazine car ads with Fitzpatrick illustrating the cars and Kaufman drawing the backgrounds and people. The pair eventually produced 285 illustrations for Buick's *Wide Track* campaign.

Based on photographic research, and information from Kaufman's family, it appears Kaufman created many of the designs found in the Hearst newspaper insignia stamp albums. In all, Kaufman created the art for approximately 85 designs.

George Goepper began his career at the Disney Studio on June 1, 1933, as an in-betweener. He was quickly promoted to assistant animator on Norm Ferguson's team, where he worked on several short cartoons. In the mid-1930s, Goepper began training junior staff in preparation for work on Disney's first feature-length film, *Snow White and the Seven Dwarfs.* His film credits include *Fantasia, Bambi,* and *The Reluctant Dragon.* Goepper helped Porter design combat insignia for several months before being drafted in 1942. During the war, he attained the rank of Specialist First Class and was stationed in Washington, D.C.

Ed Parks started at the Studio as special effects animator on March 7, 1938, and by 1941 had transferred into the Publicity Art Department. Studio employment records indicate Parks left on September 3, 1942, for military service, and upon his return on October 30, 1945, he was assigned to work in the Animation Department. Parks left the Studio in 1961. His only on-screen credit was as an effects animator on *101 Dalmatians.*

Roy Williams started at the Disney Studio after watching the *Silly Symphony* short "Flowers and Trees" at a local Los Angeles theater. After declining a sport's scholarship at the University of Southern California, Williams applied for work at the Disney Studio on Hyperion Avenue, and after speaking with someone he thought was an office boy, but who was in fact Walt Disney, Williams was hired on the spot. Williams spent most of his career at Disney's as a member of the Story Department. The Walt Disney Company credited Williams with the creation of about 100 insignia designs during the war.[137] In the mid-1950s, Williams became a part of television lore as the "Big Mooseketeer" on the *Mickey Mouse Club* TV series. He later traveled the country as a Disney goodwill ambassador, worked on Disney comic strips, and created sketches for guests at Disneyland.

Animator Bill Justice also created insignia designs. Justice spoke of his insignia work in his autobiography, *Justice For Disney*: "Hank Porter did hundreds of beautiful insignias in full color…but…occasionally he was swamped. Since by then I could draw almost every character, I was asked to help. I did about twenty or thirty designs."

It didn't take long for requests to overwhelm Disney's insignia artists. By the spring of 1942, Porter's group had fallen more than 200 requests behind. "But we'll catch up," Porter enthusiastically declared to a magazine reporter.[138] This figure grew as the war progressed. In a March 17, 1944, interview Porter gave to *Yank: The Army Weekly*, he claimed he was "always three hundred designs behind".

As fellow co-workers were drafted or assigned to important film projects, Porter singlehandedly fulfilled all of the requests that came in from late 1942 onwards—after careful study, it appears fully 100 percent of the insignia created in 1943, 1944, and 1945 were designed by Porter.

The creation of an insignia was a fairly straightforward affair. After a recognizable Disney character was selected, or a fanciful non-Disney character or entity was created from scratch, the various design elements were established. Rough sketches of the design were developed on either Hammermill Bond animation paper or a thin tissue-type paper.

---

137 Walt Disney Company Disney legends page: disney.go.com/disneyinsider/history/legends/Roy-Williams

138 *Flying*, April 1942.

Most of the preliminary work was completed in black lead pencil, although Porter occasionally used colored pencils during the creation of the initial design. In several extremely rare instances, Porter actually painted the initial conceptual sketch using watercolor paints. Occasionally, Porter made notations on the preliminary drawings (like a color model sheet) to indicate the colors he wanted used in the final design.

Most if not all of the finished art was painted on heavy stock artist's board. Black-line outlining was done first and then the artwork was painted with vibrant watercolor paint. Maxine painted several of the combat designs created by her father:

> I painted probably a couple dozen. It took about five minutes. To me it was just like a coloring book. My dad did the inking. [My father] just told me what I couldn't do. I chose the colors on the insignia I painted, unless it was a given color such as Donald Duck who always wore a blue coat, you know, that kind of stuff. I could do anything I wanted as long as it came out looking good in black-and-white.[139]

The media used to create the final art was a water-based paint called Dr. Martin's, and in several publicity photos small bottles of this paint can be seen lined up on the side of Porter's desk. Maxine said:

> They came in...bottles like the little bottles of food dye, probably an ounce-and-a-half maybe. They were variegated. They had every color in the rainbow and they were graded up and down like a color chart. All you had to do was pick some, put it down on a palette, put a little water on your brush, and have at it. They actually were dyes and they were beautiful, bright, vivid colors. All of his paints were labeled... all the way through every color of the rainbow.[140]

Despite having beautiful, vibrant paints to work with, Porter was never able to see any of his finished work in the brilliant colors used to paint them. During her interview, Maxine revealed a little-known fact about her father:

> My father's big secret was, he was colorblind! I don't think a lot of people knew it. He never divulged his secret to many. He could see tones real good. He could tell by the tones what color of paint was being used.
>
> When he [drew] a picture it went somewhere else [at the Studio] to be photographed in black and white—glossies they called them. He

---

139 Interview with the author.

140 Interview with the author.

could tell when…[the insignia] were photographed in black and white what they were going to look like. He seemed to know. Red would photograph black. Blues…and greens photograph the same. Light yellow fell to white. That's how I learned about tones.[141]

Subtle clues visible in two Studio black-and-white publicity photographs give an indication Porter was colorblind. In one photo, a chart showing paint swatches labeled with the names of the color written beside the sample can be seen pinned to the wall beside his desk. As this photo is black-and-white, one can clearly see the differentiation in tones that Maxine referred to. One could imagine this is, in fact, how Porter could tell if the colors he was using at that particular moment looked correct in his mind. In a second photograph, the paint Porter had placed onto a palette has the name of the paint color written beside it.

The creation of so many different insignia was a taxing job complicated by War Department restrictions. The restrictions were imposed on service personnel to ensure no tactical information be disclosed about the designation or nationality of any unit. An article in the February 21, 1941, issue of the Studio's employee newsletter, *The Bulletin,* outlined some of these restrictions:

> All insignia ideas must observe the following: no numbers may be used according to a War Department ruling…insignia should be simple and designed for insertion within a circle. They may convey the purpose of the service for which they are intended. Example: an eagle wearing boxing gloves and doing a power dive submitted to a dive bomber squadron.

One example of a designation used and then deleted was in the design for the 108th Reconnaissance Group, an observation squadron serving with the Illinois National Guard. The original design, created in February 1944, featured an eagle standing on the number "108" while peering through a telescope. In a later modification, the number has been deleted and the eagle is standing on a cross symbol. In the final design. the eagle is standing atop a mountain peak.

To circumvent the "number" restriction, Porter often incorporated stars, thunderbolts, waves, or other elements into his designs to indicate a combat unit's designation. For example, the insignia for the 4th Field Artillery Battalion was a donkey pulling one cannon.

---

141 Interview with the author.

Atop the donkey's back were four pack bundles containing one star each. The insignia for the 75th Squadron of the 42nd Bombardment Group featured an eagle peering through a telescope while riding atop a bomb. The seven stars above and the five stars below the eagle represented the squadron's designation.

Other examples included the Third Weather Squadron, the 56th Pursuit Squadron, the 32nd Pursuit Squadron, and the U.S. Naval Reserve Ninth Naval District—all of these units had stars in their designs—while the 22nd Pursuit Squadron used thunderbolts in its design to indicate the unit's designation.

Another restriction that confronted Disney artists was their ability to use Disney characters in their insignia creations. "We have been informed that up to now no commercial characters could be used in the designs," explained Porter in April 1942. "That is why, to date, no Mickey Mouse, Minnie, Donald Duck and a few others in the Disney family haven't appeared. Naturally, it might look as if the various branches of Government were advertising the Disney product."[142]

Porter's statement was somewhat misleading. Despite the fact their use does appear to be limited, several Disney characters did appear on insignia prior to Porter's 1942 interview. Between 1939 and the end of April 1942, the images of 17 recognizable Disney characters were used on insignia designs a total of 38 different times.[143] The characters included Donald Duck, Pluto, Thumper, Max Hare, and several characters from *Fantasia*, including a Cupid, a baby Pegasus, a Centaurette, Hyacinth Hippo, and Ben Ali Gator. By the summer of 1942, the restriction had evaporated and Disney's characters began to be incorporated into designs on a more frequent basis.

Donald Duck was the most requested character. Many units related to his abrasive, no-nonsense, combative attitude. Donald became so popular, Navy officials began asking personnel not to request the character in their designs. Under the headline "Eschew the Duck", *Naval Aviation News* ran the following story in September 1943:

> Naval Aviation is receiving too many designs for squadron insignia that are doing that patient old prototype—Duck—to death. Progeny of the grand-daddy are becoming too numerous, with the result that

---

142 *Flying*, April 1942.

143 From a database maintained by the author that contains detailed information on over 1,000 Disney-designed combat insignia.

insignia lack distinction...not to mention the great many demands being made on the Hollywood designer [Disney]. Squadrons forming, therefore, should hire a new model. (Also lay off the eagle.)

Porter's insignia creations were so popular Admiral Willet E. Spencer sent a letter to Disney executives on November 31, 1943, informing them of Navy Directive #428:

> Feeling that there has been an overabundance of insignia designed by the Walt Disney organization and especially by one individual in said organization, we hereby notify all Navy personnel not to request or accept any insignia designed by Henry L. Porter of the Walt Disney organization.
>
> We feel that Mr. Porter has done more than his part in this work, which has been deeply appreciated by the Navy, yet we feel that any more insignia bearing the unmistakable characteristics of his draftsmanship would be a burden.[144]

The fact Hank Porter is mentioned by name in Admiral Spencer's directive gives an indication as to the popularity of his designs amongst Navy personnel.

Besides the ever-popular Donald Duck, other Disney character choices included Pluto, Dumbo, Goofy, Jiminy Cricket, Pinocchio, the Reluctant Dragon, Flower, Daisy Duck, Huey, Dewey & Louie, Little Hiawatha, all of the Seven Dwarfs, Ferdinand the Bull, Snow White, and Peg Leg Pete. Mickey Mouse was used to a much lesser extent, probably due, in part, to his wholesome image.

The bulk of combat designs created at the Studio didn't feature Disney characters. Hundreds of emblems were created using fanciful images of mammals, birds, insects, fish, and caricatured inanimate objects. "How do I get my ideas?" Porter asked rhetorically in 1942. "Well, you tell me. They just come to me, I guess. I study the request then I write for additional information about the duties of the organization if I need to know. Then I go to work."[145]

Porter further explained that he gave each request a "logical treatment"—fighting squadrons would get a combative animal as their mascot, a newly organized squadron might get a fledgling bird, while submarine designs almost always featured an image of the fish the submarine was named after.

---

144 Courtesy Tom Horvitz.

145 *Flying*, April 1942.

In October 1941, one of the most famous military insignia of all-time had its birth at the Disney Studio. Hank Porter and story man Roy Williams created the insignia for the legendary American Volunteer Group, Chinese Air Force—more commonly known as the "Flying Tigers".

"General Chennault gave me credit for the Flying Tiger insignia in his book *The Way of a Fighter*," noted Williams, "but I must give credit where credit is due. I did the original idea and rough design, but Hank Porter drew it."[146] The Flying Tiger emblem featured a winged tiger springing upward against a background letter "V".

On April 6, 1942, General Chennault wrote to Harry B. Price of China Defense Supplies Inc., the official representative of China in all Lend-Lease matters. The organization maintained an office in the Chinese Embassy in Washington, D.C.:

> I have delayed acknowledging receipt of your letter, the group banners, and the flying tiger insignia, because of the urgent press of other matters. The banners and the insignia were warmly received by all members of the group and the insignia are being worn by all who were able to get one or more. The second shipment has not arrived yet and we are looking forward impatiently to its arrival.
>
> The group to the last man seem to be quite satisfied with the designation of the "flying tigers" and we believe that the Japanese understand the reasons for that designation very thoroughly. Because of the peculiar nature of the war at present, our pilots literally "spring out and over the jungles" to get at the Japs, so that the "flying tiger" is quite appropriate.
>
> Please convey our individual and collective thanks...to all who contributed toward designing the insignia.[147]

Porter received a gold and cloisonné clasp pin in the shape of the insignia from Price. On June 2, 1942, Porter sent Price a letter in which he expressed his gratitude:

> Thank you very much for sending the copy of General Chennault's letter to me and the insignia pin as well. To know that the insignia is being worn so valiantly is a real thrill. It's the next best thing to being in the middle of the scrap myself. Again, thanks for your thoughtfulness; it certainly is appreciated.[148]

---

146 *American History Illustrated*, April 1979, "When Tigers Flew in China", by Wanda Cornelius and Thayne R. Short.

147 Courtesy Sam Grabarski.

148 Courtesy Sam Grabarski.

Porter's daughter Maxine remembered the pin:
> Yes, I remember that. He brought it home. Everybody saw it. He was thrilled to death with that. That pleased him because somebody gave him credit for something he did.[149]

Porter's Flying Tiger pin was sold to a collector in the summer of 2007. According to Brad Smith, whose father Robert T. Smith was a pilot in the AVG's 3rd Squadron, each member of the unit received a cloisonné Flying Tiger pin.

The AVG were disbanded on July 4, 1942. In October 1942, a second Flying Tiger design was created, this time for the 23rd Fighter Group, and in the fall of 1943 a studio-designed flying tiger emblem became the official insignia of the 14th Air Force.

War-era photos show several AVG P-40 fighters with an image of the Disney design on the plane's fuselage. Brad Smith said:
> There were two versions [of the fuselage decal], one for the right and one for the left side of the aircraft. A thin paper sheet protected the top and bottom of each decal. A sticky sheet from the bottom of the decal was first peeled off and the decal applied to the fuselage with… lacquer, smoothed down, and the top sheet was removed with water dissolving the paper. After the decal dried, another layer of lacquer was applied over the top.[150]

Disney artists designed an insignia for another famous unit, or rather vessel. In 1941, British Prime Minister Winston Churchill gave Lord Louis Mountbatten, great-grandson of Queen Victoria, command of the British aircraft carrier HMS *Illustrious*. While it underwent repairs at drydock in Virginia, Mountbatten embarked on a goodwill tour of the U.S.

En route to Pearl Harbor, Mountbatten had a stopover in California. During his brief layover, Mountbatten visited the Disney Studio. The October 9, 1941, *Fresno Bee* reported:
> Although the visit in Hollywood of Lord and Lady Mountbatten was very brief…they did visit the studios. Lord Mountbatten particularly was interested in the Walt Disney pictures, which are extremely popular in London. He visited the Disney studios with Lady Mountbatten, their daughter Patricia, Mr. and Mrs. Douglas Fairbanks Jr., and Charles Chaplin, and was shown part of *Dumbo*. He was so enthusiastic he asked if he might see it all that evening at dinner.

---

149 Interview with author.

150 Email correspondence with author.

While touring the Studio, Mountbatten witnessed Hank Porter designing insignia. "Say," he exclaimed, "I like that! How about one for the *Illustrious*?"[151] The resulting insignia featured Donald Duck in admiral's uniform astride a toy model of the distinguished carrier.

Disney artists created several different insignia designs for units that were either stationed at, or received training at, Naval Air Station Jacksonville (NAS JAX). The first insignia created for the base was not designed specifically for NAS JAX but for a class of aviation cadets training at the base.

On March 7, 1941, Aviation Cadet Clifford Hemphill Jr. wrote to Disney with his request:

> This squadron is a training group, with that as its sole activity, and with other things such as pursuit, observation, completely non-existent. It would, therefore, be fitting to have some animal which cannot fly or which has the rudiments of that art as our official insignia. My sole idea…is to have a flying squirrel, of a type and identity of those contained in many of your *Silly Symphonies*, soaring toward the viewer with some expression of semi-astounded surprise and happiness on its face.
>
> It would embody, it seems to me, the elements of a novice at flying, an easily animated mascot, and an appropriate symbol of we embryo aviators.[152]

The art and a letter from Vernon Caldwell of Walt Disney Productions was put in the mail on March 21, 1941. Caldwell wrote:

> Mr. Walt Disney has referred your letter…to the writer for attention. In executing this design we followed the suggestions contained in your letter. We hope the insignia meets your approval. Mr. Disney has asked the writer to inform you that he is glad to be of assistance to your squadron.[153]

The illustration featured an image of a flying squirrel and was one of several designs featured in the May 26, 1941, issue of *Life* magazine.

The station's second design was created in May 1941 by Class 2A-41-J Aviation Cadet Edward Skully, who was also the photographic editor of the Jacksonville NAS section of the 1941 *Flight Jacket* yearbook. The cadets in this class were part of VN-11 at JAX. Skully created a design that featured Donald Duck sitting inside a split eggshell, representing a fledgling cadet/airman about to learn to fly.

---

151 *Flying*, April 1942.

152 Correspondence with JAX base historian Ron Williamson.

153 Correspondence with JAX base historian Ron Williamson.

Cadets in the class wanted to use Skully's creation as their squadron's insignia. The squadron's commanding officer, Captain C.P. Mason, forwarded the request to Walt Disney in a letter dated May 8, 1941:

> I know you have been plagued recently by requests from aircraft squadrons desiring insignia. Primary Training Squadron Eleven-A has been casting about for some time for an appropriate insignia, and has decided on the enclosure. Permission is requested to use this replica of Donald Duck's nephew as the official insignia of Training Squadron Eleven-A.[154]

This group of new aviators began their training in February 1941 and received their wings in September 1941. Walt Disney gave his permission and sent the men a cleaned-up version of Skully's work in May 1941.

While the original request for the NAS was the squirrel design, according to base historian Ron Williamson:

> The squirrel never really caught on. When the letter of approval [for VN-11's duck in the eggshell design] came back to the station, it somehow got adopted in place of the squirrel logo for the [entire] station. [In addition to becoming the station's logo,] VN-11 also used it. That logo ended when the station transferred our flight training from JAX to Corpus Christi.[155]

In 2002, the duck in the eggshell logo was re-adopted as the station's unofficial insignia. Today, the design can be seen on a flag that flies in front of the station's administration building as well as on the side of one of the station's large fuel tanks. The design was also reproduced on a challenge coin issued in 2000 celebrating the station's 60th anniversary.

In the summer of 1943, the Jacksonville Naval Air Station's Donald in the eggshell design was updated when the station transitioned to a training facility for so-called "top gun" pilots.

A fourth design was created for Operations Delts., N.A.A.S. Municipal #1, Jacksonville, Florida, in April 1945. N.A.A.S. No. 1 began life as Jacksonville's municipal airport. The facility became part of NAS Jacksonville on April 12, 1944. The planes stationed there were the PB4Y Liberator and the PB4Y Privateer patrol-bomber. The Navy returned the airport to the city of Jacksonville after the war.

---

154 Correspondence with JAX base historian Ron Williamson.

155 Correspondence with JAX base historian Ron Williamson.

In March 1944, a fifth design was created for a unit stationed at JAX. A Disney artist created an insignia for an as yet unidentified fighting squadron that featured what appears to be a fighting rooster with razor-type fighting instruments on the bird's legs. An anchor is also seen in the background.

Porter created a relatively unknown design for the OSS, a top-secret government unit, in the fall of 1943. The Office of Strategic Services was established by Presidential Order on June 13, 1942, to collect and analyze foreign intelligence, and to conduct special operations. A precursor to the CIA, the OSS employed operatives worldwide and assisted those whom the federal government considered their friends with the means to conduct guerrilla warfare against America's enemies.

On August 9, 1943, Walt Disney received a letter from Joseph E. Alderdice, a Captain in the newly formed Office of Strategic Services:

> Dear Mr. Disney.
>
> Knowing and appreciating the great work that you are engaged upon in the furtherance of our war effort, I feel it quite an imposition to add to your labors.
>
> We have seen numerous examples of the symbols and insignia that you have made for various branches of the services and we would like to have you create something special for us.
>
> We are the Operational Groups of the Strategic Services, and our role in the nations [sic] war program is, of necessity, extremely secret, therefore we cannot flaunt the usual banners & insignia as do the rest of the Armed Forces. The design would be placed in the lecture room at one of our instructional centers to symbolize the supreme achievement of our groups.
>
> The attached chit rather crudely expresses something of the sort that we should like to have as the fundamental design; and as previously stated, would have to be treated as a military secret until the powers that be should rule otherwise.[156]

There is no record as to what type of design Alderdice submitted in his letter to Disney. The illustration, however, must have been unworkable, as on October 4, 1943, Vernon Caldwell of the Disney Public Relations Department wrote to Alderdice:

> We have been endeavoring to create an insignia along the lines suggested in your letter of August 2nd but find that these ideas do not work out as a design.

---

156 Courtesy Les Hughes.

The insignia that we have been doing for the army and navy have been symbolical using Disney characters in cute or funny poses. If you so wish, we could depict Donald Duck breaking bridges, toy tanks, wooden soldiers, etc., with a mallet, which would put over your idea and be more in line with our medium. Or, if you have any other ideas that might be worked out in the Disney manner, we should be glad to have them. In any event, please let us know if we can help you further on this.[157]

Alderdice, who had been promoted to Major in the interim, must have liked Caldwell's suggestion because the final design did, in fact, feature Donald Duck swinging a hammer, destroying a bridge in the process, which carried a train loaded with swastika-adorned toy soldiers, a tank, and supplies. While one leather patch imprinted with the design has been located, it's not known if that patch is one-of-a-kind or how the design was ultimately used by the OSS.

One of the most recognizable military insignia designed during the war, and whose creation is often attributed to the Disney Studio, was in fact not designed by Disney artists. There has been much confusion surrounding the Navy's Construction Battalion "Seabee" insignia. The design, which features a flying bee carrying a gun and construction tools in his hands, has often been attributed to Walt Disney. While an image exists of Walt Disney holding either a piece of artwork or photograph featuring the bee design, Walt Disney and his artists had no role in the image's creation.

The originator of the Seabee emblem was Frank Iafrate, a Rhode Island School of Design dropout. Coincidentally, Iafrate was interested in working in the Disney Studio animation department, but when his dream of working at Disney's failed to materialize, Iafrate put his artistic talent to work at local bars drawing caricatures of the patrons. The twenty-two year old soon tired of the bar scene and successfully applied for a file clerk job at the Naval Air Station, Quonset Point, Rhode Island.

Iafrate earned extra money on the side drawing caricatures of base personnel. According to Iafrate, in early 1942, "… a Lieutenant came in. [He] had heard of my cartooning and asked me if I could produce a 'Disney Type' insignia that would identify and represent this new Battalion."[158]

---

157 Courtesy Les Hughes.

158 Seabeesmuseum.com

Iafrate's first design attempt featured a beaver, the rationale being the animals were industrious workers. He scrapped the logo when he discovered beavers turn tail and run when frightened—not quite the rugged, fighting image the Lieutenant was looking for.

Iafrate then hit upon the idea of using a bee, because he felt the bee represented, "The busy worker...who doesn't bother you...unless you bother him, at which point he comes back with a sharp sting. This was the way of the Construction Battalions."[159] The bee wore a Navy tar hat, carried a gun to show he was a fighter, and construction tools to show he was a builder. Iafrate gave the bee the rank of a Third Class Petty Officer and the insignia of the Navy Civil Engineer's Corps.

The initial Seabee design was encircled by the letter "Q", which represented the Battalion's base under construction at the Quonset Point Naval Air Station. The letter "Q" was replaced with a hawser of rope to give the design national appeal. Iafrate was also credited with inventing the unit's homonym: Construction Battalion = CB = Seabee.

Iafrate said: "The insignia took about three hours on a Sunday afternoon. The next morning I showed it to the officer in charge, who showed it to the Captain, who sent it off to Washington."[160] Admiral Ben Moreell, Chief, Bureau of Yards and Docks, Chief of Civil Engineers, approved the design for use in a nationwide recruiting campaign. Another design submitted at the same time featuring a muscular, helmeted, bare-chested sailor with a sledgehammer also gained some popularity.

For his role in creating the logo, the Secretary of the Navy awarded Frank Iafrate the Distinguished Public Service Award in 1949. Iafrate actually enlisted as a Seabee in the 1950s and was later honorably discharged with the rank of Chief Petty Officer.

While the Studio may not have created the original emblem, several Seabee units including the 24th, 60th, 78th, and 133rd, received Disney-designed Seabee images, while the men at Camp Hueneme received a stylized female Seabee named "Phoebe".

Walt Disney encouraged all of his staff to contribute ideas for insignia. The February 21, 1941, issue of *The Bulletin* reported:

> As official requests for insignia designs are being made more and more frequently by U.S. army forces, artillery battalions, and air squadrons, Walt today announced a Studio-wide competition to

---

[159] Seabeesmuseum.com

[160] Seabeesmuseum.com

the designing of all future service insignia requests. Aside from the pride of having rangy booted officers build espirit de corps around an insignia drafted by Disney men, or the knowledge that one's sketch is painted on pursuit ships, there is no reward.

First two insignia problems to be announced are: design for the 37th Pursuit Squadron at Hamilton Field. [The] squadron asks that the design be simple, in good taste, lucid, and suggests the inclusion of a machine-gun in the sketch, though this is not vital.

[The second design is] for Battery A, 98th Field Artillery Battalion, Fort Lewis, Washington. Battery A is a mule pack organization and suggests inclusion of a donkey character.

All insignia ideas submitted must observe the following:

- No numbers may be used in accordance to a War Department ruling.
- No stock characters may be used, Donald, Mickey, etc., according to a War Department ruling. It is permissible to alter them slightly, to draw a duck or a mouse for example.
- Insignias should be simple and designed for insertion within a circle. They may convey the purpose of the service for which they are intended. Example: an eagle wearing boxing gloves and doing a power dive submitted for a dive-bombing squadron.

All sketch ideas should be submitted to Hazel Garner, [an Administrative Assistant in the Publicity Department], where they will be judged by a committee.[161]

A follow-up article printed in the February 28, 1941, *The Bulletin* reported:

While design sketches for U.S. defense service insignia were already being submitted by studio personnel, an additional request has been received this week from the air corps. Newly organized 62nd Pursuit Squadron, based at Savannah, Georgia, has solicited an emblem with pursuit punch. This request supplements others now in studio competition.[162]

As the war progressed, Disney combat insignia began to be promoted and featured in newspapers across the country. The front page of the July 5, 1942, issue of *The Milwaukee Journal Roto Section* contained a half-page layout of Disney war-related illustrations. The article was similar to many such articles appearing in newspapers and magazines across America during the war. These stories gave the Studio positive

---

161 Author's collection.

162 Author's collection.

publicity, and showcased one of the many patriotic missions Walt Disney was involved with. One can assume insignia requests sent to the Studio increased when stateside servicemen saw the related stories in print. The newspaper article read:

> Donald and Pals, All Patriots
>
> Enlisted for the duration! That applies to Donald Duck and his pals at the Walt Disney Studios, where Donald and the rest are doing their part to win the war.
>
> Nearly three-quarters of the entire Disney production is going into war work, what with patriotic films along the lines of *The New Spirit*, shown at income tax time with Donald Duck, patriot, as the star. Besides, dozens of military units have asked for Disney designed insignia. Five artists work on them full time. There have also been five pictures for the Canadian war effort and the studio is making 20 shorts, combining animation, "live-action" and models for the United States Navy.

A total of nine insignia were depicted in the article, including Ninth Naval District; 3rd Weather Squadron; 205th Coast Artillery; Flying Tigers; Section Base, 11th Naval District; 36th Military Police; 6th Reconnaissance Squadron; 27th Signal Construction Battalion; and the 134th Medical Regiment. The newspaper layout was drawn by Hank Porter and also included three images from *The New Spirit* and one illustration from the Canadian bond film *Thrifty Pig*.

In September 1942, the *New York Times* reported:

> Already some of the Disney designs have gone through the smoke of battle. A ferocious bulldog in Marine uniform faced the Japanese as the emblem of the First Battalion of Marines, and the enemy at Subic Bay felt the sting of the rampant mosquito riding a torpedo as the mascot of the Navy's fleet of PT boats.

The aforementioned Marine Corps design was created in January 1942 for the 1st Defense Battalion, Fleet Marine Force, and featured a bulldog wading through the surf with cannon tucked under his arm.

Hank Porter and his fellow artists created approximately 75 designs for the Marines. One Marine Corps fighter squadron that had received a Disney-designed emblem even went so far as to send Walt Disney a propeller from a downed Japanese airplane as a Christmas present.[163] When queried, The Walt Disney Company Archives had no such artifact listed in their inventory.

---

163 *The Billings Gazette*, December 24, 1943.

In November 1942, a *New York Times Magazine* reporter wrote:

> ...as America mobilized and new armed units were set-up, hundreds of them turned to the Disney Studio for humorous emblems...typical of the reception they get was a letter from Brigadier General S.B. Buckner, commanding the Alaska Defense Forces. General Buckner wrote: "Since the arrival of the insignia all the seals in the Bering Sea have been out on the ice pack balancing "D's" on their noses, sneering at polar bears and expanding their chests."

A full-page color spread featuring 13 Disney-designed insignia appeared in the January 3, 1943, issue of the *St. Louis Dispatch*:

> Walt Disney's comic art is being widely utilized in the serious business of war. Many military units have adopted insignia specially designed for them in the studios, which produce the famous movie cartoons. Canadian and Fighting French, as well as United States Army, Navy and Marine units have asked for and received these designs.
>
> Whether a drawing marks an aviation squadron, an artillery battery or a cavalry outfit, it is a characteristic piece of Disney work, representing in a fancifully humorous way the function of that particular organization.
>
> In most of the devices the central figure is an animal, and two of the best known Disney cartoon characters, Pluto and Donald Duck, are included in this special military gallery, selections of which are shown on this page.

The article pictured Disney-designed insignia for a variety of units: USS *Albemarle* Aerological Office; 120th Bomber Reconnaissance Squadron RCAF; 125th Observation Squadron; 66th Quartermaster Battalion; 482nd Aviation Ordnance Company; 5th Corps Area Station Hospital; 3rd Coast Artillery, Battery K; 82nd Bombardment Squadron; Second Scout Company, Second Marine Division; Free French Information Service; 92nd Reconnaissance Squadron; 381st School Squadron; and the 73rd Evacuation Hospital.

In June 1942, the Japanese invaded the Aleutian Islands, making it the first and only American territory to be seized during the war. One year later, the Japanese were forced to retreat. Feeling that the insignia of the Alaska Defense Forces needed updating to represent the change from a defensive to offensive role, the unit requested and received an updated Disney emblem. The new design featured a snarling, helmeted polar bear.

Over the course of the war, other Disney designs were also updated. The Jacksonville Naval Air Station requested and received a new emblem in July 1943. The unit's second insignia, created in May 1941, pictured Donald as a duckling seated in a split, airborne eggshell. This design typified the unit's student cadets. When the role of the unit changed from a primary flight school to the training school headquarters for Navy and Marine "top guns," it was decided a new insignia was needed to reflect this change.

JAX became the Headquarters, Naval Air Operational Training Command, and on July 22, 1943, the base newsletter, *JAX Air News*, ran a story detailing the reason behind the design's update:

> Rear Admiral A.B. Cook, Chief of N.A.O.T., and Captain S.J. Michael, Commandant, have approved the adoption of a new official insignia for the Jacksonville Naval Air Station.
>
> Donald Duck, the Station's mascot on the old insignia used in the days when aviation cadets trained here, is still the mascot on the new emblem, but he's a changed man. He's now a full-fledged fightin' pilot now and he wears the cap and gown of a graduate operational flier.
>
> Donald, as he's characterized on the Station insignia, is a belligerent chap with a grim-visage and a bellicose glint in his eye that bodes no good for the Axis. Machine gun in hand, cloaked in the cap and gown of a graduate flier with ensign's stripe on his shoulder boards and a vision of Hirohito in his gun-sight, Donald will make his debut on the Station soon.
>
> Yes indeed, Donald has progressed since he first appeared on the Station insignia clothed only in an eggshell. Pictured as a blushing duckling then, he was seated in a split, air-borne eggshell, which typified the Station's student cadets in aviation training at the time.
>
> The revamped Station insignia today illustrates the change of activity here in the past year. As Headquarters for Naval and Marine commissioned officers operational training, the station now sports the fastest and deadliest Navy planes and most skilled instructors in the world. Before it became an operational training base, Jacksonville was dedicated to primary flight instruction for aviation cadets fresh from pre-flight schools.
>
> Many of the earlier cadets who first sprouted wings here have won their spurs in action on the world's battle map. Vice-Admiral Aubrey W. Fitch...recently cabled as follows: "Operational trained Navy and Marine Corps pilots arriving [in] this area are demonstrating a high order of ability as combat pilots." And so it came to pass that Donald the Duck grew up with the Station and today he's a full-fledged flyer, as depicted in the new insignia.
>
> The idea for the design of the Station insignia was originated by Robert A Fees, AMM3c, of Delaware, Ohio, staff artist for the *JAX*

> *Air News*. Fees submitted his design during Station-wide competition last month and his caricature was selected.
>
> Fees' drawing was then forwarded to the Walt Disney Studios, which hold a copyright on the original Donald Duck. The Disney Studio made minor alterations in Fees' work and gave the Station permission to use it. The official Station insignia bears the distinctive Walt Disney copyright.
>
> Admiral Cook plans to have a 12-inch square copy of the new Station insignia in Technicolor, framed and placed on the wall in his office along with the insignias of other stations in his command.[164]

The main base, base hospital, a Marine Corps complement, and the base cadet's mess all issued matchbooks that included a cover image of the updated design. The design was also used in the station's civilian employee booklet, was imprinted on stationary, and was used on the front cover of a photo album sold to station personnel.

As requests for insignia continued to stream into the Studio, a concern surfaced. The initial contract sent with the artwork stated that Walt Disney was presenting the insignia to the unit "with the stipulation that it will not be exploited for profit or for commercial sale to service personnel". Disney's merchandising representative, Kay Kamen, became alarmed when he learned some stationary companies were producing large quantities of letterhead featuring Disney designs to sell to servicemen. Because of this, the licensing agreement was revised to read in part: "...before you permit any profit-making civilian firms to reproduce the insignia in any form for commercial sale to the service personnel, such firms or individuals must obtain a license from Kay Kamen." See Appendix V for the full content of these letters.

By all accounts, the men in units that received a Disney-designed emblem wore their new crests with pride. Lt. Colonel Dan Sjodin was the Commanding Officer of the 831st Bombardment Squadron. He remembered the impact his unit's Disney-designed insignia had on the men under his command:

> We were designated a brand new unit. We had no insignia. We got to talking one day. Captain Rau [Sjodin's Executive Officer] asked, "Do you think Walt Disney would go ahead and make a patch for us? I'll write to him." He wrote to Walt Disney and got a letter back: "What is your mission? What kind of aircraft do you have?' Captain Rau told him: 'B-24 bombers."

---

164 Author's collection.

> By golly [Disney] came up with Timothy Mouse on the wings of a B-24 tossing a bomb. We were so darned proud of that. We went to Omaha and had 500 of those made up on leather. We passed it on to each of the men and the officers and they sure were happy. It was such a moral[e] boost to have a nice insignia. We were the first squadron that had a squadron insignia. It made our outfit tops.
>
> The other squadrons, those guys would walk by our guys and you could tell they saw that insignia and said, "I wish the hell I had one." The word got around fast. It didn't take long for the word to circulate.[165]

Walt Disney also commented on the morale-building effect an insignia could provide to the men in a unit:

> It seems that the designs find a lot of favor because they have a tendency to knit a squadron or a battalion of whatever organization they may be drawn for, closer together. The group is just a group until there is something to pin it together and then it becomes a real machine. Other groups challenge it and they too get into a fine competitive spirit.
>
> The design represents the same thing today that the red "kerchiefs" worn by General Custer's Seventh Cavalry did in the Civil War and later in Indian fighting. The General wore one, soon everyone was wearing one. The men were proud of the scarves, held those who wore them equal, and boasted that they could lick any outfit of similar size in the world.
>
> That's the kind of spirit, which we need today. If the designs can help foster it, there'll be designs.[166]

With a total cost of approximately $30,000, Walt Disney's insignia contribution was substantial. Each design cost an average $25 each to produce. "Never mind what the job is costing us. That isn't important," was Walt's attitude.[167] Patriotic words from a man whose Studio spend almost the entire war in debt—as high as $1.2 million in 1942.

Walt Disney felt passionately about his Studio's insignia contribution. The requests came from the men and women who had shared their childhood with Disney: they watched his films, joined their local theater's Mickey Mouse Club, read the newsstand *Mickey Mouse Magazine*, and invested their allowances in his character merchandise. The insignia weren't a government project, but rather an undertaking

---

165 Interview with author.

166 *Flying*, April 1942.

167 *Flying*, April 1942.

of a more personal nature. Walt reflected: "They'd sometimes send in telling us what they wanted, they didn't know where to go to get it...we did it all for them for nothing...we took care of them...because you can hardly turn them down, how can you?"[168]

The spirit of the Disney organization towards the men and women requesting insignia designs was summed up by Walt Disney and Hank Porter in 1942: "Let them write and tell us what they want and we'll do our part. They're certainly doing theirs and we are more than glad to pitch in with them, even in our small way."[169] And write they did.

Besides letting his artists act on insignia requests that came in to the Studio, Walt Disney also had his artists create designs based on requests addressed to him personally that he'd received through the mail.

On September 13, 1943, an intriguing request for a unique design landed on Walt Disney's desk. Included with that day's correspondence was a letter from someone named Kate Brown, and accompanying the letter was a postcard sent to her by her boyfriend, Robert Bishop. The letter contained an interesting request and the postcard was unlike any other Walt Disney had seen previously.

Kate Brown's boyfriend was Captain Robert H. Bishop of the United States Army Air Force. Brown and Bishop had met at Camp Croft, South Carolina. The postcard from Bishop was dated July 1943 and had originated at Stalag Luft III, a German prisoner of war camp situated near the town of Sagan, Poland. The camp was one of several built to hold captured Allied aircrew.

Four months earlier, on May 14, 1943, three flight crew from the 67th Bombardment Squadron assembled for a briefing at their base in the southeast corner of England. The day's target was the Krupp Submarine Works at Kiel, Germany. Pilot 1st Lieutenant Robert I. Brown's crew would fly this sortie. Brown usually piloted the bomber *Suzy Q*, but for this mission Brown's crew would fly a replacement B-24 named *Miss Delores*. Captain Bishop, a veteran of 19 missions, would be the bombardier.

Just after bombs away, *Miss Delores* was hit by flak in the nose section. The bomber faded from formation, was attacked by enemy

---

168 Pete Martin interview courtesy Diane Disney Miller.

169 *Flying*, April 1942.

aircraft, and was shot down. The other two 67th bombers on this mission were also downed.

The crew bailed over Kiel Bay. Captain Bishop splashed down and was rescued by a fishing trawler. All crew with the exception of three survived the attack. The day's mission resulted in the first of two Distinguished Unit Citations for the 44th Bombardment Group. (A second was awarded to the Group in August 1943 for a raid on the oilfields at Ploesti.) After his capture, Captain Bishop was incarcerated at Stalag Luft III. There is no record of Bishop's activities in the camp or even which barracks he was housed in.

Emmet E. Cook Sr. enlisted in the Cadet Air Corps in 1940 and signed on with the Royal Canadian Air Force in 1941. With America's entry into the war, he was called back to the U.S. Army Air Force before he could report to Canada. Cook served as a Bombardier aboard a B-17F named *Holey Joe*.

On March 22, 1943, Cook and his fellow crew were assigned to a replacement B-17 named *Junior*. The crew's regular bomber, *Holey Joe*, was grounded with mechanical problems. The day's mission was a raid on the harbor at Palermo, Italy. Cook recalled: "Our crew was with the 352nd Squadron of the 301st Bomb Group flying out of North Africa. [The raid] on shipping at the Palermo, Sicily Harbor…was my 32nd mission. Several ammo ships were blown out of the harbor."[170]

Junior and several of her crew would not survive the raid on Palermo. The B-17 was hit by flak. The bomber's left wing caught fire and eventually tore off, sending the plane into a spin. Five men including the pilot, co-pilot, engineer, radio operator, and ball turret gunner were trapped and perished in the crash. Emmet was able to bail out. "[I] had a rough landing in cactus as large as Texas cactus. [I] was captured by six goat herders, one with a gun. [They were] all very scared. The older one with [the] gun spoke broken English. He acted very nervous and scared. Later that evening they turned me over to the military."[171] The other two survivors included the waist gunner and the navigator.

Cook was incarcerated at Stalag Luft III, taking up residence in Block 108 in the North Compound. "I was impressed how well the

---

170 Interview with the author.

171 Interview with the author.

senior RAF officers and USAAF officers were organized. I played on the championship softball team [and] did a lot of oil painting and cartooning in books. [I] ran about five miles every day, weather permitting, around the circuit. [I] stayed busy and in top physical condition despite the lack of food."[172]

The young bombardier eventually joined the Camp's Escape Committee and helped plan what would later be known as the "Great Escape". Cook recalled: "[My duties were to] map the camp and locate blind sports for gardens and a place to dispose of sand [from the tunnels.] [I] stayed busy working with Flight Lieutenant Brian Evans on maps. I thought [the escape] was a very dangerous idea and had it not been for an air raid that night in Berlin, causing the light to go out in the tunnel, the British would have emptied the camp. But, as it turned out, [the air raid] may have saved many lives."[173]

In his spare time, Cook dabbled with watercolor paints and pencil crayons. Putting his artistic talents to work, Cook drew an emblem that would fast become the camp's unofficial insignia. The design featured Donald Duck in jail and the caption "I Wanted Wings". "I really don't remember [how the design came about.] I always enjoyed Disney's cartoons, especially Donald Duck. I suppose it was the frustration in Donald's expressions. Believe me, there were many frustrated airmen at Luft III. Around May or June of 1943, I first drew the 'I Wanted Wings'."[174]

The design captured the emotions of fellow prisoners, and, as the cartoon circulated throughout the camp, many POWs approached Cook asking him to draw the Donald design for them. "They loved it. Many wanted me to draw it on a postcard so they could send it home. I drew it on letters that they sent home to their family. I soon had many requests to draw the same picture in other [POW] logbooks. I drew it in many logbooks. I also did one in oil [paint] on a piece of Khaki pants...that I sewed to my British jacket. [I drew] some 50 I suppose. [I] did a lot of postcards that the Kriegies sent home. I was told the German censors also enjoyed them. [I] was glad to do it."[175]

---

172 Interview with the author.

173 Interview with the author.

174 Interview with the author.

175 Interview with the author.

Four months later, Walt Disney held a letter and a postcard bearing the Donald Duck Stalag Luft III illustration in his hands. He was intrigued by the image of Donald Duck in uniform behind bars—the image Cook originally conceived and which Bishop copied onto a postcard that he sent to his girlfriend. Captain Bishop had penned a note on the postcard:

> Dearest—One picture is worth a thousand words...I would like to have some of these made as insignia to wear on jackets with W. Disneys o.k. —Love Bob.[176]

The postcard was dated July 23, 1943. In the accompanying letter, Miss Brown wrote:

> Dear Mr. Disney.
>
> I am enclosing a card from Captain Robert H. Bishop who is a prisoner of war in Germany...I think the card is self-explanatory. I know what he wants but hardly know how to go about having it done—if it is even possible. I will appreciate any information or help that you can give me.[177]

Seventeen days later, Walt Disney penned a response:

> I am having the ensigne [sic] drawn up now and when completed I am going to have four-dozen made up in cloth for the captain. It will take at least two weeks to get them and I will have them forwarded to you unless you think they should be sent direct to Captain Bishop. In that event we would have to get his complete address.
>
> There is such an interesting angle to it that I am wondering if you or Captain Bishop would have any objection to us giving the story...to the press. It is after all a very human interest angle.[178]

On October 8, Miss Brown wrote to Disney saying she was thrilled:

> I appreciated your letter so very much and think what you are doing is the most wonderful thing that I've ever heard. I sent your letter and the card on to the Bishops—they were quite thrilled. I also mailed a copy of your letter on to Captain Bishop so he will know the insignias are on the way—it will give him something to look forward to. However, if you do give it to the press—I wish you would use his parent's name.
>
> As for the mailing, I hardly know what to say. All packages to prisoners of war must have an official label—these are issued to the next of kin every two months and permit an eleven-pound package. All

---

176 *Popular Mechanics*, May 1944.

177 Courtesy The Walt Disney Company Archives.

178 Courtesy The Walt Disney Company Archives.

this goes through the Red Cross. The next package will leave about the 10th of November...if you will forward your package to me, I will send it on. Would it be asking too much to have you send me two of the insignias? I would like to keep one as a souvenir and I'm sure his mother would want one.

I'm sure that Captain Bishop and all the boys at the camp will appreciate your kindness more than they can ever say. They have so much time on their hands that to have one of their dreams fulfilled will certainly help their morale. Just to know that the people here at home are still with them will mean so much.[179]

The story eventually appeared in two publications. A Knoxville newspaper ran the following article:

> We are bound to feel that a fellow with a sense of humor like Capt. Robert H. Bishop...will come out of that German prison camp still grinning. Look at the sketch...that comic strip character so familiar to everybody and, poor fellow, so sad he looks sitting there and peeping through the bars. The...insignia will be mailed to Capt. Bishop, and he and fellow prisoners probably will knock their German prison guards goggle-eyed [sic] by wearing them.[180]

The story also appeared in the May 1944 issue of *Popular Mechanics*. The article pictured a copy of Bishop's original postcard and the refined image created by Disney artists.

In 1943, Walt Disney embarked on a tour of Latin America on behalf of the Office of the Coordinator of Inter-American Affairs. The purpose of the trip was to reverse the tide of pro-Axis sentiment that was sweeping the region. Disney produced several movies as a result of this trip, including 14 public service films and two features. In his absence, Joe Reddy, Director of Publicity at the Studio, wrote Miss Brown with disappointing news:

> Since Mr. Disney has been in Mexico City...it is up to me to inform you of a little disappointment with regards to the insignia for Capt. Bishop. The only place in town turning out these insignias for wear on uniforms has so many government contracts we have found it utterly impossible to have them made. It would take so long that we are hopeful the war in Germany may be over before we could get them (that's a nice thought, anyway). I am airmailing the original drawing to you, which can be sent to Capt. Bishop. It might be possible the boys can make their own—perhaps it would help them to pass

---

179 Courtesy The Walt Disney Company Archives.

180 Courtesy The Walt Disney Company Archives.

their time away if only they can get the necessary materials. Walt will be as disappointed as you are but rather than have you miss the shipping date...I thought it best we send the drawing right to you.[181]

Five days later, Miss Brown wrote to Joe Reddy acknowledging receipt of the artwork:

> I appreciated your letter so very much. The original is so nice and I'm sure that Captain Bishop will like it. I am having some photo static copies made and I think we will send one of those...to see if it goes through before [sending] the original—it is so nice that I would hate for anything to happen to it.
>
> I work for the Soil Conservation Service in Spartanburg, S.C. I had to show the original to my boss, Head of Personnel Division, and he suggested having the copies made. Mr. Orsini, Head of the Regional Cartographic Division is making the copies. That Division is doing war work...Mr. Orsini called and said there was a man in his office from Camp Croft...who had offered to do some buttons. I let him go ahead, thinking whatever they may be, that the boys might like them as a second choice. I hope this is with your approval. If not, wire me collect and I will have them destroyed.
>
> I must confess that I was disappointed—I can imagine how the insignias would look now, after seeing the original, and I know they would have been more than what Bob was expecting. I certainly do appreciate and thank both you and Mr. Disney for all you have done — and I know all the boys will thank you too. At least they will know that we did all we could for them and that should help their morale. Please thank Mr. Disney for me personally. I think it is wonderful the way you helped me. Maybe soon—as you say—the boys will be here to thank you again in person.[182]

Many "I Wanted Wings" images survived the war. Most known examples are found in the YMCA diaries of Stalag Luft III inmates. The prisoner-drawn variations very closely resemble the design refined by Disney artists.

While Emmet Cook reproduced the image on numerous occasions, other artistic prisoners illustrated their own diaries and postcards with the Donald Duck design. Several variations of the design exist: Donald dressed in his cartoon clothes, a flight suit, and jail attire. Most POWs incorporated their prison serial number into the design. Few if any of these items have made their way into private hands. The

---

181 Courtesy The Walt Disney Company Archives.

182 Courtesy The Walt Disney Company Archives.

design has since been imprinted on souvenir items distributed at various ex-POW reunions, including towels, hand cloths, and tee shirts.

Besides being drawn and painted by POWs at Stalag Luft III, the Donald Duck "I Wanted Wings" design also found its way onto at least two aircraft. Lieutenant Albert A. Knafeltz flew a P-47D with the 62nd Fighter Squadron, attached to the 56th Fighter Group, providing air cover for the 8th Air Force. Lt. Knafeltz had the design painted on the cowling of his fighter—serial #42-26298. According to the Air Force Historical Research Agency, the fighter was manufactured by Republic Aviation and delivered on April 4, 1944. The P-47 went to Newark, New Jersey, where it was sent by ship to England on April 11, 1944, and assigned to the Eighth Air Force. Lt. Knafeltz's P-47 was dropped from inventory as salvage due to battle damage on September 19, 1944.

A photograph also exists that shows the design on an olive-drab B-24J at Watton Airfield (the 3rd Service Air Depot where Liberators that couldn't be repaired in the field were sent). The design appears to have been painted on a piece of armor plate that was added to 8th Air Force B-24s. This particular photo surfaced in an internet auction. The successful bidder was told: "The person owning the album was Staff Sergeant Harry Ward of Ogdensburg, Pennsylvania, and he was in aircraft maintenance."[183]

One can only speculate that Stalag Luft III POWs included the Donald Duck image on postcards or letters sent to men in the aforementioned P-47 or B-24 squadrons, where it was admired and then painted on the planes. Regardless, the story of the creation of the Stalag Luft III Donald Duck "I Wanted Wings" insignia is one of the most fascinating insignia stories of World War II.

Another request, just as intriguing as the Luft III postcard, arrived at the Studio on January 10, 1944. This time the note had been written by a young teenager living an ocean away from Walt Disney's Hollywood studio.

The letter originated from New South Wales, Australia, and had taken 41 days to cross the Pacific Ocean. This correspondence was different from almost all of the others that arrived at the Studio on a daily basis: this letter was written by a young member of the Australian Air League, an organization that promoted good

---

183 Email correspondence with author.

citizenship, teamwork, and self-reliance, as well as flying skills, to young cadets. The letter from Kevin Dawson read:

> I am a Drum-major of a youth organization. There are 6,000 boys in the League and they learn the principles of flying. Since the American Airmen have been in Australia, I have seen some very novel insignias on their flying jackets. Many of the boys in [my] company…have said how much they would like to have an insignia and I was hoping if it were not too much trouble, would you please design for us an insignia, which we could use for our very own?[184]

Despite all the pressure he was under at the Studio—the evaporation of overseas revenue and the pressing deadlines and minimal budgets associated with government work—Walt Disney took the time to have an insignia designed for the youngster, who was thousands of miles away on another continent. Walt Disney must have been impressed with the youngster's letter, as a design was completed and in the return mail later the same month. The Hank Porter creation featured a smaller kangaroo jumping over a larger one.

According to Squadron Lieutenant Brian Grinter, a current member of the League since the age of ten, "Approximately 25,000 members [both boys and girls] trained in the first five years up to the beginning of World War Two. When Australia joined other Commonwealth countries in declaring war in 1939, over 5,000 Air League volunteers joined Australia's armed services. The role of the Air League changed and then became the Air Training Corps, responsible for training young adults for military service."[185] The first AAL training squadron opened in New South Wales in January 1935 with 30 cadets. By 1942, 26,000 boys had been trained in aviation and 125 squadrons operated in three states.

While it's unknown as to how the emblem was eventually used, or the disposition of the original artwork, the insignia was reproduced on a patch celebrating the unit's 60th anniversary.

As the war drew to a close, the number of requests submitted to the Studio slowly dwindled. In 1945, Porter created a design for the Commander, Carrier Division 24, who was in charge of Operation Magic Carpet, the repatriation of American military personnel from the Pacific at the war's conclusion.

---

184 Courtesy The Walt Disney Company Archives.

185 Email correspondence with author.

Operation Magic Carpet consisted of a fleet ships that transported literally tens-of-thousands of Army, Army Air Force, and Navy personnel back home to the United States after Japan's surrender.

The insignia Porter created for this important mission featured Donald Duck dressed as a sultan, wearing a turban in the colors of the American flag, and Donald's three nephews, Huey, Dewey, and Louie, wearing the uniforms of the three branches of the military. The nephews have happy expressions on their faces, imitating, no doubt, the expressions of grateful servicemen as they realized they had survived the war and were now going home.

As an interesting side note to this design, Donald's turban featured two gold stars, which signified the rank of Rear Admiral, Upper Half.

As a sign of support to those service personnel who had been hurt and disabled during the war, Disney had Porter created an emblem for the Disabled American Veterans (DAV) organization. The DAV was established shortly after the end of World War I as an advocate of disabled veterans and their families, widowed spouses, and orphans. Porter's design featured the letters "DAV" caricatured as a human, sitting in a wheelchair, and holding a crutch under his left arm. This design was just another example of how strongly Disney felt towards those who had served their country.

Besides Studio-produced designs, servicemen used Disney characters in their unit emblems with neither the input from, nor the permission of, the Studio. Dozens of designs were created featuring crudely drawn Studio characters by servicemen in the field wanting a reminder of home.

And while American units requested official Disney designs or created their own, they were not the only ones to use Walt Disney's characters in their military emblems. A design featuring Donald Duck was introduced in France in 1937 when the French bought approximately 300 P-36 fighters from Curtiss, an American aircraft manufacturer. A cloisonné pin based on the design was worn by pilots who ferried the fighters to the French airbase located at Chartres, south of Paris. The image also made its way onto the fuselage of at least one P-36.

Mickey Mouse was also the mascot of choice for several Axis units, proving the worldwide appeal of Disney's characters was very real, especially amongst the Germans. Several photos from the war show various Mickey Mouse designs painted on the sides of German bombers and fighter planes. One U-boat even sported a Mickey illustration on the side of the submarine's conning tower.

Disney military insignia became so popular with the service men and women they represented, the designs soon began appearing on all nature of items, including stamp albums, gummed stamps, matchbooks, posters, shoulder patches, decals, pin-back buttons, mugs, glasses, plaques, ash trays, stationary, envelopes, writing instruments, programs, menus, Christmas cards, iron-on transfers, ceramic tiles, and playing cards.

Because public interest in Disney insignia was so great, Hearst Publications offered a series of 250 gummed and perforated insignia stamps and five related stamp albums to the general public. In February 1942, the *Los Angeles Examiner* published the first stamp album. Each album cost 15 cents and contained spaces for 50 designs. The April 18, 1942, *San Antonio Light* included a so-called "insignia column" with instructions on how readers could go about ordering the colorful stamps:

> Every day, a black-and-white copy of a combat insignia stamp will be published in *The Light*. These copies may be exchanged, absolutely free, for authentic, full-color insignia stamps. Clip and save 10, any 10 of these black-and-white copies from *The Light*. Send them, together with a stamped self-addressed envelope, to Combat Insignia Stamps, San Antonio Light, Broadway at Fifth, San Antonio, Texas, and you will receive, in return, the first series of combat insignia stamps, numbers 1 to 10. Combat insignia stamps will be issued in five series of 10 stamps each.

The first stamp album focused on Army Air Force and Navy emblems, while the other four albums pictured a variety of insignia representing all branches of the military. Most of the newspapers in the Hearst chain carried this circulation-boosting promotion. Despite the fact 62 percent of the stamps in the series represented Disney designs, the Studio received no licensing fees.

Besides the Hearst insignia stamp albums, a booklet was also offered by Western Air Lines (WAL). Western's tri-fold album contained room for the first 50 gummed stamps issued by Hearst. As well, much of the text found in the WAL folder was lifted from the first Hearst stamp album.

The WAL album is printed on both sides and when opened measures 16 by 18 inches. The folder's front and back covers featured reproductions of 24 Disney insignia designs. While there is no copyright printed on the folder, the item was advertised in newspapers as early as the spring of 1942:

> 50 educational U.S. Air squadron insignia stamps plus a handy pocket album.
>
> Know the battle emblems adopted by our Army, Navy, and Marine fliers. Next time you buy an air ticket, (regardless of destination) ask for these full-color limited edition Air Squadron insignia stamps, including the famous Disney designs. Now available at all Western Air Line ticket offices.[186]

At least two units also produced their own gummed stamps. Destroyer tender AD-40 (Pluto) and the Marine Corps' 1st Defense Battalion (gorilla) distributed stamps, many of which ended up being glued to mailing envelopes sent home to loved ones. The 533rd Engineer Boat and Shore Regiment (bullfrog) produced an ink stamp of their design, which was also impressed onto the outside of mailing envelopes.

Copies of Disney insignia designs were made available to the British public. Beginning with the September 11, 1943, issue, the British *Mickey Mouse Weekly* newspaper contained an illustration of a military emblem on the front cover: "This week you will find the mirth-making emblem which has been designed for a branch of the National Fire Service somewhere in England. This quaint little figure fashioned from a fireman's hose shows us that we can be business-like and efficient, even though we can still enjoy a good laugh." This particular design was created at the Studio in July 1942. The last issue of the *Mickey Mouse Weekly* to feature an illustration of a Disney-designed insignia stamp on the cover was the November 11, 1944, issue.

Next to the insignia stamps, the most common merchandise featuring Disney insignia are matchbooks. The Diamond Match Company sent a letter requesting permission to use Disney insignia on a matchbook cover for a Naval Supply Depot. The Studio replied: "Ok to fill orders from Navy sources, but not for general sale in retail stores." The design featured Donald Duck carrying a huge pack of supplies on his back.

Two series of matchbooks were produced for the general public under license to the National Match Company of New York. One set

---

186 *The Montana Standard Butte*, April 22, 1942.

of 20 was printed by the Maryland Match Company for the National Match Company. The designs in this series were produced in blue and red atop a yellow background. The unit's name appeared under the design. A point-of-purchase display sign for these matchbooks was available to retailers. The set was also sold in a grouping of 12, packaged in a box that carried a 1943 copyright and advertised the fact the matchbooks were "Walt Disney Designed". These particular matchbooks were printed in both a matte and glossy finish.

The second series of matchbooks was produced by D.D. Bean & Sons for the National Match Company and was comprised of 48 covers. These matchbooks reproduced Disney-designed insignia in blue and red atop a gray background. The back of the cover featured an ad for Pepsi-Cola. It is estimated that over one million of the Pepsi/Disney covers were distributed across the U.S. through the Whelan and United chain of retail stores.

Besides the two sets of matchbooks, many units had covers produced for their own military organizations. At least two dozen different covers featuring Disney insignia are known to exist. These range from a flying school cover that features the Aeronca Grasshopper, a war contractor logo Disney artists designed in November 1942, to covers printed for various warships, fighter squadrons, and naval air stations.

During the war the Universal Match Corporation of St. Louis hit upon a novel idea: they began printing match covers twice the standard size. The inside of the cover was designed as a postcard, which could be mailed to a loved one once the matches were used.

W.L. Stensgaard & Associates, a Disney licensee based in Chicago, produced a stunning series of Disney-themed insignia posters for use on the home front. The company's 1942 brochure pictured the full line of 54 posters that were sold to retail establishments. The posters were available in either horizontal or vertical format, and were sold individually or in panels showcasing several different designs. Some of the sets measured 15 inches tall by 60 inches long.

The brochure stated the designs were:

> Reproduced in nine rich oil colors on heavy, durable special comura (commercial mural) paper stock. Comura decorations are easy to handle. Can be cut to fit almost any desired space...thus affording many varieties of effective individual treatments. Can be appliquéd to any surface.

>These insignia were designed by Walt Disney for the War Department and are the insignia for the units of service they represent. They are used on the airplanes, tanks, or equipment and in many other ways. Members of each unit are very proud of their respective insignia. They represent youth, action and stamina and in colorful designs they interpret the type of classification of unit.
>
>Show them effectively in your windows and interior. They are new and people will be anxious to see them. They will also help you in selling more bonds and stamps and they will attract more attention to your displays. [187]

Display suggestions listed in the brochure included: "In the men's or boy's departments, at the entrance to a special serviceman's gift department, at a bond or savings stamp booth, on a display stand, column, ledge, or in a window display." The brochure goes on to call the designs "educational, inspiring and patriotic".

Disney artist Hank Porter relished the job of creating combat insignia. When the war ended, he used his talents to produce comic and story-book illustrations, presentation art, and material used in some of America's most well-known magazines. By all accounts, though, one of the jobs he enjoyed the most during his time at the Studio was creating insignia art for military personnel serving in Allied units around the world. Maxine said her father enjoyed this part of his career immensely:

>He loved cartooning. He had control of ...the insignia. He could do anything he wanted for these people and they all loved it. He did a lot of illustrations for books too but those were illustrations based on set characters from the movies. [Designing insignia] was his one big thing where he could shine.[188]

Because no clear licensing records relating to insignia-related items exist at the Walt Disney Archives, new and never-before seen insignia collectibles surface with regularity. What is clear is that, while Walt Disney was not too concerned about the merchandising of his insignia creations, his licensing representative Kay Kamen and his corporate lawyer Gunther Lessing were. It appears Walt Disney was more concerned with accommodating the numerous requests of the men and women battling the enemy on the frontlines than

---

187 Courtesy the collection of Dennis Books.

188 Interview with the author.

he was with earning royalties. This was in line with his philosophy as it related to the insignia designs:

> "How could you turn them down?" Walt said. "[The insignia] meant a lot to the men who were fighting and they didn't know who else to go to.[189] I had to do it. Those kids grew up on Mickey Mouse. I owed it to them."[190]

Insignia and Military-related Collectibles

IN001 Insignia trade cards. 1943. 3½ x 2¼

Each colorful card pictures two Disney-designed insignia on a bright yellow background. The text on the reverse side of each card gives a brief description of the pictured designs. All of the cards have rounded, playing card-type edges, and some of the cards are marked "© Walt Disney Productions" on the reverse. There are nine known cards in the set. The cards were distributed by the Leaf Gum Company of Chicago, Illinois, and were manufactured for or licensed by Whitman, a publishing company known mainly for its line of Disney children's storybooks.

IN001a Insignia trade cards. 1943. 3½ x 2¼
Eagle Squadron RAF and the 3rd Reconnaissance Troop.

IN001b Insignia trade cards. 1943. 3½ x 2¼
445th School Squadron and the Air Base Detachment.

IN001c Insignia trade cards. 1943. 3½ x 2¼
503rd Parachute Battalion and the First Ferrying Squadron.

IN001d Insignia trade cards. 1943. 3½ x 2¼
The Flying Tiger and the 57th Signal Battalion.

IN001e Insignia trade cards. 1943. 3½ x 2¼
Submarine Base and the United States Mosquito Fleet.

IN001f Insignia trade cards. 1943. 3½ x 2¼

---

189 Miller, Diane Disney, (as told to Pete Martin). *The Story of Walt Disney.* Dell Publishing Co., NY, 1959. p.182.

190 Thomas, Bob. *Walt Disney. An American Original.* Simon and Schuster, NY, 1976. p.179.

1st Defense Battalion and the Jackson Air Base.

IN001g Insignia trade cards. 1943. 3½ x 2¼
774th Tank Destroyer Battalion and the 21st Bombardment Squadron.

IN001h Insignia trade cards. 1943. 3½ x 2¼
13th Armored Division and the 751st Tank Battalion.

IN001i Insignia trade cards. 1943. 3½ x 2¼
67th Bombardment Squadron and the 56th Pursuit Group.

IN002 Insignia stamp albums. 1942.
These albums originally sold for 15 cents each. Disney artists drew almost all of the insignia images found on the gummed stamps, which were to be stuck inside the albums. The gummed insignia stamps were free for the asking. Black-and white versions of the stamps were clipped from a newspaper's insignia stamp column and were redeemed through the mail for a color copy of the same stamp. Each album holds 50 stamps. Hearst newspapers running the insignia stamp album promotion often printed the name of their newspaper at the top of the album's front cover.

IN002a Insignia stamp album. 1942.
Volume One: 16 Disney designs. Cover pictures the emblem for the 45th Army Air Base.

IN002b Insignia stamp album. 1942.
Volume Two: 50 Disney designs. Cover pictures the Mosquito Fleet emblem.

IN002c Insignia stamp album. 1942.
Volume Three: 44 Disney designs. Cover pictures the Flying Tigers emblem.

IN002d Insignia stamp album. 1942.
Volume Four: 46 Disney designs. Cover pictures the emblem for the 28th Composite Group, 1st Headquarters Squadron.

IN002e Insignia stamp album. 1942.
Series 2, Volume One: one Disney design.

IN002f Insignia stamp album. 1942. 11¼ x 8¼
Detail from the mailing envelope the albums were mailed in. The front of the envelope features a large illustration of the insignia for the 62nd Pursuit Squadron. This is the only envelope known to exist so it's unknown whether other newspapers used the same format to mail out their albums.

IN003 Boxed set of insignia stamp albums. 1942.

This boxed set contains all four insignia stamp albums. The box lid is illustrated with copies of the insignia stamps. A label on the box top reads: "A War Library collection of combat insignia. A living drama of United States and United Nations fighting organizations illustrated by their own colored postamps. This collection will be priceless in years to come. Four volumes. Each volume contains 50 different insignia of air, land and sea fighting units and the story of each. Designs are by Walt Disney, Walter Lantz, Pat Sullivan, George McManus, and other famous artists." This boxed set originally retailed for $1.00.

IN004 Gummed insignia stamp. Circa 1945. 2 x 1½

This gummed stamp was sold to men serving aboard the destroyer tender AD-40. The stamps would be affixed to mailing envelopes.

IN005 Western Air Lines insignia album. 1942. 16 x 18

Western's tri-fold album contained room for the first 50 gummed stamps issued by the Hearst newspaper chain. Much of the text found in the WAL folder was lifted from the first Hearst stamp album. The WAL album is printed on both sides and when opened measures 16 by 18 inches. The folder's front and back covers feature reproductions of 24 full or partial Disney insignia designs. While there is no copyright notice printed on the folder, the item was advertised in newspapers as early as the spring of 1942.

IN006 Insignia patches.

When a Disney-designed insignia was created and sent to the requestor, men in the unit often had patches made of their design. Patch construction included silkscreen on felt, decal on leather, stitched leather pieces, or paint on leather.

IN006a Insignia patch.

47th Bombardment Squadron. *Dumbo* crow.

IN006b Insignia patch.

451st Bombardment Squadron. Frog holding a bomb.

IN006c Insignia patch.

349th Bombardment Squadron. (Unauthorized design.) Mickey throws bombs from a flying Pluto.

IN006d Insignia patch.

452nd Bombardment Squadron. *Dumbo* crow.

IN006e Insignia patch.

56th Pursuit Squadron. Cardinal dressed as a policeman.

IN006f Insignia patch.
602nd Bombardment Squadron. Goofy.

IN006g Insignia patch.
603rd Bombardment Squadron. Peg Leg Pete.

IN006h Insignia patch.
Squadron 16, War Eagle Field, Civilian Pilot Training Squadron. Pelican.

IN006i Insignia patch.
Page Military Academy. Donald and his nephews.

IN006j Insignia patch.
Maintenance Engineers. Lampwick from *Pinocchio*.

IN006k Insignia patch.
Torpedo Squadron 2. Max Hare.

IN006l Insignia patch.
Marine Scout Bombing Squadron 133. Bulldog.

IN006m Insignia patch.
Patrol Bombing Squadron 122. Big Bad Wolf with bomb and telescope.

IN006n Insignia patch.
831st Bombardment Squadron. Timothy Mouse dropping bombs from atop a B-24.

IN006o Insignia patch.
389th Bombardment Group (H), 565th Bombardment Squadron, Group Automatic Flight Control Equipment Department. The robot character depicted on this patch can be found in the Donald Duck short cartoon *Modern Inventions*.

IN006p Insignia patch.
86th Chemical Mortar Battalion, 1st Platoon, A Company. Flower holds a mortar.

IN006q Insignia patch.
503rd Parachute Infantry Regiment. Parachuting cat.

IN006r Insignia patch.
515th Parachute Infantry Regiment. Parachuting Little Wolf.

IN006s Insignia patch.
958th Engineer Aviation (Topographic) Company. Gideon from *Pinocchio*.

IN006t Insignia patch.
98th Field Artillery Battalion. Braying donkey.

IN006u Insignia patch.
981st Field Artillery Battalion. Growling grizzly bear head.

IN006v Insignia patch.
646th Medical Collecting Company. St. Bernard.

IN006w Insignia patch.
275th Armored Field Artillery Battalion. Jiminy Cricket as a knight.

IN006x Insignia patch.
68th Tank Battalion. Boxing turtle.

IN006y Insignia patch.
758th Railway Shop Battalion. Jiminy Cricket fixing a broken train.

IN006z Insignia patch.
Alaska Defense Command. Seal balancing letters on his nose.

IN006aa Insignia patch.
3013th Engineer Maintenance Company. Lampwick from *Pinocchio*.

IN006bb Insignia patch.
The illustration on this one-of-a-kind patch was created by Emmet Cook, while he was a prisoner-of-war (POW) in the German detention camp Stalag Luft III. Emmet drew the original design on a postcard, which he mailed home to his mother in June 1943. He then drew the same illustration in his YMCA diary and later created the patch, which was made using oil paints and a piece of fabric taken from a pair of khaki-colored serviceman's pants. The number "944" seen on the right side of the patch signifies Emmet's German-issued POW identification number. Donald behind jail bars.

Other insignia patches include:
- 21st Bombardment Squadron. Bee with bomb held over his head.
- 67th Bombardment Squadron. Pelican.
- 77th Bombardment Squadron. Little Hiawatha.
- 449th Bombardment Squadron. African native.
- 16th Fighter Squadron. Dumbo Crow.
- Walnut Ridge Flying School. Donald.
- Yuma Army Air Field. Coyote.
- 10th Emergency Rescue Boat Squadron. Donald Duck in a rescue boat.

- Royal Canadian Air Force Flying Training School. Bambi
- Royal Canadian Air Force No. 10 Service Flying Training School. Donald Duck.

IN007 Iron-on heat transfers. Circa 1942. 3 x 5

These heat transfers feature Disney-designed insignia images. Two versions are available: one with and one without background scenery. Most of the tissue transfer papers are marked "© 1942 P.P. Co." and some have the "© WDP" logo as well. The P.P. Co. marking may be in reference to the Postamp Publishing Company, a Disney licensee in California that produced insignia stamps from 1942 through 1944. There may have been as many as 38 different Disney designs in the series, as the tissues seem to be sequentially numbered.

The transfers were distributed by the Bobin Sales Company of Chicago. The envelope in which the transfers were sold stated: "Aircraft Insignia. The spirit of American flying youth! These hot iron insignia transfers identify some of the most famous squadrons in the U.S. Air Forces. They are known throughout the world for their outstanding records and daring feats. Wear them proudly. You'll be the leader of your gang."

Known Disney designs include the following:

IN007a Iron-on heat transfer. Circa 1942. 3 x 5
Jacksonville Naval Air Station. Flying squirrel.

IN007b Iron-on heat transfer. Circa 1942. 3 x 5
67th, 68th, 69th Pursuit Squadrons. Boxing rooster.

IN007c Iron-on heat transfer. Circa 1942. 3 x 5
62nd Fighter Squadron. Boxing bulldog.

IN007d Iron-on heat transfer. Circa 1942. 3 x 5
Royal Air Force Eagle Squadron. Boxing eagle.

IN007e Iron-on heat transfer. Circa 1942. 3 x 5
108th Observation Squadron. Cardinal with telescope.

IN007f Iron-on heat transfer. Circa 1942. 3 x 5
15th Observation Squadron. Bee with binoculars.

IN007g Iron-on heat transfer. Circa 1942. 3 x 5
72nd Fighter Squadron. Little Hiawatha.

IN007h Iron-on heat transfer. Circa 1942. 3 x 5
79th Bombardment Squadron. Bug with a spear.

IN007i Iron-on heat transfer. Circa 1942. 3 x 5
Naval Air Station Hutchinson. Note the plane Jiminy Cricket is in trails an anchor, which signifies a Navy connection.

IN007j Iron-on heat transfer. Circa 1942. 3 x 5
16th Bombardment Wing. Horse chewing hay.

IN007k Iron-on heat transfer. Circa 1942. 3 x 5
Fighter Squadron 7 (stationed aboard CV-7 USS *Wasp*). Boxing wasp. This design was the first official Disney-designed insignia. The design was created on May 20, 1939.

Other iron-on heat transfers include:
- 503rd Parachute Battalion.
- 45th Pursuit Squadron.
- Marine Fighting Squadron 22.
- Torpedo Squadron VT-2.
- Fighting Squadron VF-42.
- Scouting Squadron VS-6.
- 23rd Pursuit Squadron.
- 6th Reconnaissance Squadron.
- 27th Observation Squadron.
- 6th Bombardment Squadron.
- 306th Bombardment Squadron.
- 29th Bombardment Squadron.
- 383rd Bombardment Squadron.
- 11th Anti-Submarine Squadron.
- 97th Fighter Squadron.

IN008 W.L. Stensgaard and Associates insignia poster brochure. 1942. 8½ x 11
This brochure was published by the same company that produced the Donald Duck Victory Garden sign. The brochure, "Insignia of Our Fighting Units, Symbols of Victory", includes the images of all 54 posters the company produced. The brochure opens to a huge 25½ by 21. The posters were sold in either a horizontal or vertical format and could be purchased individually or in sets.

IN008a W.L. Stensgaard and Associates insignia poster.
Example of four posters offered in the brochure.

IN008b W.L. Stensgaard and Associates insignia poster.
40th Bombardment Group (Medium). Example of a poster offered in the brochure.

IN008c W.L. Stensgaard and Associates insignia poster.
202nd Coast Artillery (Anti-Aircraft), Truck Drivers, Battery B. Example of a poster offered in the brochure.

IN008d W.L. Stensgaard and Associates insignia poster.
16th Infantry Anti-Tank Company. Example of a poster offered in the brochure.

IN008e W.L. Stensgaard and Associates insignia poster.
22nd Pursuit Squadron. Example of a poster offered in the brochure.

IN008f W.L. Stensgaard and Associates insignia poster.
Alaska Defense Force. Example of a poster offered in the brochure.

IN008g W.L. Stensgaard and Associates insignia poster.
Aviation Cadets, Jacksonville Naval Air Station. Example of a poster offered in the brochure.

IN008h W.L. Stensgaard and Associates insignia poster.
45th Air Base Squadron. Example of a poster offered in the brochure.

IN008i W.L. Stensgaard and Associates insignia poster.
Headquarters Battery, 1st Battalion, 133rd Field Artillery. Example of a poster offered in the brochure.

IN008j W.L. Stensgaard and Associates insignia poster.
67th Pursuit Squadron. Example of a poster offered in the brochure.

IN009 Naval Air Station, Jacksonville Florida drinking glass. 5½ inches tall
Imprinted with the image of the unit's Disney-designed insignia: Donald Duck in an eggshell.

IN010 St. Simon's Island Naval Air Station drinking glass. 5 ½ inches tall.
Imprinted with an unauthorized image of the base insignia: Donald Duck piloting an airplane.

IN011 503rd Parachute Infantry drinking glass. 5½ inches tall
Imprinted with the image of the unit's Disney-designed insignia: a parachuting cat.

IN012 Utility Squadron 3 drinking glass. 5½ inches tall
Imprinted with the image of the unit's Disney-designed insignia: Pluto atop a cloud.

IN013 Koppitz Victory Beer bottle. 7 inches tall

Brown-colored glass beer bottle from the Koppitz Melchers Detroit brewery. This bottle has a label that measures approximately 3½ x 4 inches. The Disney-designed insignia for the so-called "Mosquito Fleet" of patrol torpedo boats is reproduced on the label. The caption on the label reads: "Mosquito Fleet Emblem by Disney shows Uncle Sam has wartime sense of humor. Other emblems are brightly emblazoned on shirts, tanks, trucks and planes. Buy U.S. Defense Stamps and Bonds."

IN013a Koppitz Victory Beer bottle label detail.

Beer bottle label detail. The Mosquito Fleet emblem was the second insignia design created at the Disney Studio. This emblem dates to March 1940.

IN014a Koppitz Victory Beer bottle labels. 3½ x 3¾

Three Disney-designed insignia reproduced in red, white, blue, and black: Alaska Defense Force, 69th Quartermaster Battalion, and the Ellington Field Bombardment Training Unit.

IN014b Koppitz Victory Beer bottle labels. 3½ x 3¾

Three Disney-designed insignia reproduced in red, white, and black: 45th Air Base Squadron, 62nd Pursuit Squadron, and the Jacksonville Air Station.

IN015 13th Armored Division yearbook. 1945.

This hardcover yearbook-type publication chronicles the division's march across Western Europe and features the "black cat" Disney-designed insignia on an inside page.

IN016 USNR Midshipmen's School yearbook. 1943.

This hardcover yearbook-type publication was created for the school's first graduating class. An inside page illustration was titled "Midshipmen's Day".

IN017 Marine Corps Air Station El Toro yearbook. 1947.

This hardcover yearbook-type publication showcases some of the air station's staff and history. The yearbook's cover shows an embossed reproduction of the unit's Disney-designed insignia: a flying bull.

IN018 78th Naval Construction Battalion yearbook. Circa 1945.

This hardcover yearbook-type publication chronicles the unit's history. This Seabee unit was commissioned February 9, 1943, and served extensively in the South Pacific. One page pictures a color reproduction of a stylized Seabee and a female named Phoebe, both of which were designed by Disney artist Hank Porter.

IN019 133rd Naval Construction Battalion yearbook. 1945.

This hardcover yearbook-type publication chronicles the unit's history.

This Seabee unit was attached to the 4th Marine Division. The front cover is embossed with gold printing and the multicolor shield which displays the "Construimus Batuimus" Navy logo. Page six features the unit's Disney-designed Seabee insignia.

IN020 U.S. Navy Hospital Number 8 Battalion yearbook. Circa 1945.
This hardcover yearbook-type publication chronicles the unit's history. The front cover pictures the unit's Disney-designed insignia: Donald Duck carrying medical supplies. This medical unit was stationed on Guadalcanal for part of the war.

IN021 VF-2 Navy Fighting Squadron Two yearbook. 1945.
Hardcover yearbook-type publication details the squadron's history. The front cover features an embossed image of the unit's Disney-designed combat insignia: an agitated dragon shredding a Japanese flag.

IN022 CL-53 USS *San Diego* yearbook. Circa 1945.
Hardcover yearbook-type publication details the history of this light cruiser, which was the first Allied warship to enter Tokyo Bay at the end of hostilities. The inside front cover features an image of the ship's Disney-designed insignia: Panchito firing his pistols into the air.

IN023 Oriental Odyssey of Air Group Two yearbook. Circa 1946.
Hardcover yearbook-type publication details the squadron's history. An inside page features the unit's Disney-designed combat insignia: Max Hare riding a bomb.

IN024 Class 45-1B, Childress Army Air Field yearbook. Circa 1945.
Hardcover yearbook-type publication contains information on this bomber training school. An inside page features the unit's Disney-designed combat insignia: a stork from *Dumbo* with a baby in diapers who has a bomb in his hand.

IN025 533rd Engineer Boat and Shore Regiment yearbook. Circa 1945.
Hardcover yearbook-type publication contains information on the regiment. An inside page features the unit's Disney-designed insignia: a frog that has an axe and a bomb in his hands, a knife in his mouth, and a rifle slung over his back.

IN026 60th Naval Construction Battalion yearbook. Circa 1945.
Hardcover yearbook-type publication chronicles the unit's history. This Seabee unit served in the South Pacific in and around New Guinea and New Caledonia. The front cover pictures the unit's Disney-designed insignia: a stylized Seabee kicking a can that has the words "Can Do" spilling out of it.

IN027 Second Air Force camouflage poster. Circa 1942. 16 x 22

This poster pictures an angry Donald Duck, reminding combat personnel that their military position could be betrayed if they didn't keep the surrounding area clear of refuse and personal belongings.

IN028 Eleventh Armored Division booklet. 1944. 11 x 8½

This 32-page softcover booklet details the history of the division while in training at Fort Polk. The back cover pictures an illustration of Peg Leg Pete and Donald Duck dressed in ancient Roman attire. Pete barks out orders to the duck, who is painting a shell casing.

IN029 13th Armored Division history book. Circa 1943.

Softcover publication loaded with photographs and text detailing the unit's early history. Page six pictures the three men who thought of the Division's "black cat" nickname, posing with the Disney illustration of the unit's insignia. The back cover features a color photo of the unit's commanding officer posing with the same Disney illustration.

IN030 13th Armored Division theatrical program. July 1943.

This program was produced for a musical show written and performed by servicemen in the division. The show ran two nights at a theater in Marysville, California, and twice on the base. A local newspaper stated: "If the 13th Armored Division can take the Germans and Japs like it took Marysville last night, the war will be over. The soldiers of Camp Beale can play as well as they fight, and they do both superbly." The Division's training program prevented a longer run of the show and more than 1,000 were turned away from the town's box office.

IN031 13th Armored Division Christmas card. 1945.

Front cover features the division's Disney-designed "black cat" insignia. The inside printed salutation reads, "Merry Christmas and a Happy New Year. 13th Armored Division. Camp Beale, California."

IN032 13th Armored Division Christmas card. Circa 1945.

This variation features the unit's Disney-designed cat insignia wearing a Santa Claus cap on its head and a red ribbon tied to its tail.

IN033 USS *Bunker Hill* Christmas card. 6¼ x 3¼

This greeting card is illustrated with the unit's Disney-designed insignia: Donald Duck carrying a rifle and pitchfork. The cover reads "A Very Merry Christmas, from the USS *Bunker Hill*" and features an illustration of the aircraft carrier. The inside contains a printed message: "Wishing you the blessings of the season and Victory in the New Year", and features an illustration of the monument located at Bunker Hill.

IN034 USS *Housatonic* Christmas postcard. 1943. 4 x 6

The front side of this heavy stock postcard features the ship's Disney-designed insignia: an octopus.

IN035 Naval Supply Depot Oakland Christmas card. Circa 1943. 6½ x 8¾

The inside of this card features Donald Duck laden with every conceivable type of supply: from mops and pans to rifles and ammunition.

IN036 84th Station Hospital Christmas card. Circa 1945. 8½ x 11

This heavy stock card has an illustration created by a serviceman in the unit. The design features Pluto with his front paws resting on a helmet bearing the insignia of Axis powers.

IN037 U.S. Navy Dry Docks Christmas card. Christmas 1943.

This greeting card is illustrated with the unit's Disney-designed insignia: the Three Little Pigs dressed as Navy doctors performing surgery in an operating room on a "sick/disabled" ship.

IN038 Naval Air Station Roosevelt Christmas card. Circa 1944.

The front of this greeting card pictures Goofy eating a Christmas turkey.

IN039 AD-17 USS *Piedmont* Christmas card.

This greeting card is illustrated with the unit's Disney-designed insignia: Doc repairing a ship.

IN040 60th Naval Construction Battalion postcard. 4 x 6

This postcard features the unit's Disney-designed Seabee insignia: a Seabee kicking a can with his left foot. The words "Can Do" spill out of the can. A rolled paper in the bee's hand reads "Tokio [sic] highway" and is meant to represent blueprints. The caption on the back of the postcard reads: "Known as the can do organization, this bee typifies their spirit—proving it's possible to construct anything, anywhere, anytime."

IN041 Royal Air Force Eagle Squadron, envelope. 6¼ x 4

This top left corner of this blue-colored envelope is illustrated with an imprint of the squadron's Disney-designed insignia: a boxing eagle. An American serving in the unit mailed the envelope to the First National Bank in Wichita, Kansas. The envelope is dated October 9, 1941.

IN042 60th Naval Construction Battalion envelope. 1944.

This envelope has been addressed to someone living in Waterloo, Iowa, and bears the postmark "U.S. Navy August 31, 1944". The envelope has an illustration of the unit's Disney-designed insignia on the left front side.

IN043 Naval Air Station, Hutchinson, Kansas, envelope. 1944. 6½ x 3¾

This envelope bears a 2 x 2¼ imprint of the unit's Disney-designed insignia: Jiminy Cricket flying an airplane. The envelope is postmarked "September 20, 1944 U.S. Navy".

IN044 1st Defense Battalion envelope. 1943. 6¼ x 4

This envelope has a 2½ by 2½ gummed colored sticker attached in the lower left corner picturing the unit's Disney-designed insignia: a gorilla. A Sergeant in the H & S Battery mailed this letter to someone with the same last name in Columbus, Kansas. The envelope bears a postmark dated February 16, 1943, and also a "Passed by Naval Censor" stamp.

IN045 114th Infantry, F Company, envelope. 1942. 6¼ x 4

The envelope bears an imprint of the unit's Disney-designed insignia: a charging grasshopper.

IN046 533rd Engineer Boat and Shore Regiment envelope. 1945. 6½ x 4

The envelope's lower-front right corner is imprinted with an ink stamp of the unit's Disney-designed insignia: a frog that has an axe and a bomb in his hands, a knife in his mouth, and a rifle slung over his back.

IN047 Prisoner of War postcard. June 8, 1943. 4 x 6

This German-issued postcard was sent by Emmet Cook to his mother upon his internment in Stalag Luft III, a German detention camp made famous by the so-called "Great Escape". Emmet created the Donald Duck illustration found on front of the postcard. The design was adapted by other prisoners and quickly became the camp's unofficial insignia. Another POW, Robert Bishop, copied the design onto a postcard, which he sent to his girlfriend Kate Brown. Brown sent that postcard to Walt Disney asking the Hollywood producer if it was possible to make leather patches of the design. Disney asked artist Hank Porter to clean up the drawing, which was then sent to Brown's girlfriend. The war ended before the art could be used in any manner.

IN048 789th AAA AW Battalion postcard. 1943. 4 x 6

The front of this postcard features the unit's emblem: a vulture with a spear shot through its mid-section. This crest is unique from the standpoint of the emblem being the only Disney insignia design that shows the subject matter in the process of being killed.

IN049 USS *Sennett* heavy stock card. 9½ x 7

This card was either sold or given to crew serving aboard the submarine. The card's colored illustration features the sub's Disney-designed insignia: a Sennett wearing a tar cap about to swallow a merchant ship.

IN050 *Knots 'N Fathoms*, November 1944.

The cover of this publication features a special insignia created for the graduating class of the University of Colorado's Naval Reserve Officer Training Corps. The Ugly Duckling is the character that was used.

IN051 *Army Transportation Journal*, April 1945.

The cover pictures the Disney-designed *Dumbo* stork insignia for the Los Angeles Port of Embarkation. During the war, all American ports remained under civilian control. This magazine was a monthly publication of The Army Transport Association, a private organization founded in October 1944.

IN052 *Leatherneck*, July 1943.

Cover depicts the head of a bulldog, drawn by Disney artists. The magazine includes a two-page article that features 10 Disney-designed Marine Corps insignia.

IN053 *The Maintenance Engineer*, January 1945.

The cover of this publication features the engineer's Disney-designed insignia: Lampwick from *Pinocchio*.

IN054 *USCG Patrol*, March 1943.

Magazine cover features the insignia for the Coast Guard's so-called Corsair Fleet: Donald Duck dressed as a pirate.

IN055 *Slipstream*, February 20, 1942.

The cover of this publication shows the Cal Aero Academy insignia: a mother eagle about to teach her baby eaglet how to fly. An inside acknowledgement reads: "To Walt Disney, a genius as great to our era as Shakespeare was to his, we tip our wings for the Eagle Cover of this issue. We are honored with this corking cartoon symbolic of our first 'solo" designed by the Walt Disney staff especially for the Cal Aero detachment and for this issue of the *Slipstream*. We thank Lt. Don Brown for his assistance in obtaining it for us."

IN056 Graduation Banquet menu, Class XIV—MAC OCS. 1943. 4½ x 7¼

This menu was produced for the graduating class, Camp Barkeley Training Camp, Medical Administrative Corps, Officer Candidate School. The camp graduated 12,406 candidates from July 1942 to March 1945. The menu's front cover features an illustration of Bugs Bunny, while the back cover features an unauthorized drawing of Donald Duck—the use of Walt Disney's characters on unit publications is an indication of how popular these characters were with the men and women serving their country.

IN057 47th Air Depot Group menu. September 7, 1944.
Menu card for the Group's anniversary dinner. The front of the card pictures the unit's Disney-designed insignia: a winged elephant wearing a turban with a sledgehammer in its trunk and a wrench under its feet.

IN058 USS *Andromeda* menu. 1945.
July 4, 1945, menu features the ship's Disney-designed insignia: the Ugly Duckling.

IN059 USS *Pelias* menu. 1944.
Thanksgiving Day 1944 menu features the submarine's Disney-designed insignia: a mermaid affectionately known as Polly.

IN060 USS *Pelias* war bond ticket. 1945.
This sweepstakes ticket stub for a war bond lottery is imprinted with the submarine's Disney-designed insignia.

IN061 USS *Pelias* Domain of Neptunus Rex certificate. July 1942.
This certificate was given to sailors after they participated in a hazing ritual when they crossed the Equator. This certificate features a great image of the submarine's Disney-designed insignia

IN062 USS *Pelias* newsletter. November 23, 1944.
This Thanksgiving Day on-board newsletter features the submarine's Disney-designed insignia in the masthead.

IN063 USS *Pelias* souvenir program. 1945.
The program's front cover features the submarine's Disney-designed mermaid. The program was distributed on September 6, 1945, which was the submarine's "Third Anniversary Open House Day".

IN064 AD-17 USS *Piedmont* menu. 1945.
Thanksgiving menu features an image of Doc, who was chosen as the ship's mascot. Doc remained the ship's mascot through to the end of the Vietnam War.

IN065 AD-17 USS *Piedmont* newsletter. 1945.
Masthead features the ship's Disney-designed insignia: Doc.

IN066 603d Bombardment Squadron menu. 1943.
The inside front cover of this Thanksgiving Day menu pictures the unit's Disney-designed insignia: Peg Leg Pete wearing a flight helmet and chewing on the fin of a bomb cigar.

IN067 Cardboard standee. 8 x 10

Die-cut cardboard countertop standee. Jiminy Cricket, dressed in military uniform, holds a sign that reads: "Soldier. Wasted food prolongs the war. Eat your fill. Don't take more."

IN068 *Wing Tips.* 1943. 4 x 6
This handbook of the Aviation Cadet Regiment of the United States Naval Reserve contains all the information a new cadet would have to know. The 142-page book has over 36 amateur illustrations of Donald Duck. Page 126 pictures the unit's Disney-designed insignia: Donald Duck seated in a half eggshell.

IN069 Naval Aviation Cadet yearbook. 1941.
This 200-page yearbook pictures cadets and instructors stationed at the Jacksonville and Pensacola Naval Air Stations. The yearbook's cover pictures Donald in dress uniform, while several inside pages picture him in a half eggshell design.

IN070 Navy Relief Society. 1941. 9 x 12
This souvenir booklet commemorated the Jacksonville Naval Air Station's one-year anniversary, and was dedicated to the Navy Relief Society. The proceeds from the sale of the booklet and advertising space therein were donated entirely to the charitable cause. The Society collected funds and provided relief for widows, minor orphan children, and mothers of deceased officers and enlisted men of the regular Navy, Marine Corps, and Naval and Marine Reservists on active duty. The Station's Disney-designed insignia was featured on page two: Donald in a half-eggshell. Several poorly-executed non-Disney Donald illustrations are scattered throughout the inside pages.

IN071 Guide to U.S. Army Insignia and Decorations. 1942.
This 62-page hardcover book pictures numerous Army insignia. The book was published by Whitman. A section titled "Special Unit Insignia" pictures several Disney designs.

IN072 Jefferson Barracks Officer's Club booklet. February 1944. 9½ x 6
This booklet lists the names of the officers and their home state. The back cover features an illustration of a bee whose flight pattern spells out a capital letter "J".

IN073 3rd Engineer Special Brigade booklet. 1943. 5¾ x 9
This 32-page booklet documents some of the unit's accomplishments. There are numerous black-and-white photographs and drawings that show battlefield scenes, amphibious landings, sporting events, parties, presentations, and award ceremonies. The last page featured four Disney-designed insignia.

IN074 Naval Air Gunners School. 6½ x 10¼

This folder was used to hold writing paper or perhaps class notes for those attending the base gunnery school. It is marked: "US Naval Air Gunners School. Jacksonville, Florida. Ship's Service Department. Price 25 cents." An unauthorized Donald Duck illustration is featured on the cover.

IN075 47th Portable Hospital theater-made silk square. 1944. 11 x 13

This item was made in-theater. The piece of silk features a beautiful embroidered image of the unit's official Disney-designed insignia: Donald Duck with an IV bottle slung from his rifle.

IN076 1330th Army Air Force Base Unit newsletter. July 6, 1945.

The upper left corner of the cover of this mimeographed newsletter features the unit's Disney-designed insignia: Donald as a swami gazing into a crystal ball.

IN077 USS *Booth* newsletter. September 22, 1945.

The cover of this mimeographed newsletter, titled *The Assassin*, features the unit's Disney-designed insignia: Donald about to smash a submarine periscope with a wooden mallet.

IN078 USS *Anthedon* newsletter. 1945. 6¾ x 9½

This eight-page newsletter was published on the ship's first anniversary. The cover pictures an illustration of the ship's Disney-designed insignia: a hornet. Besides containing general news stories, the newsletter includes a description of the ship's emblem: "Last July, Walt Disney was asked to design an insignia for the ship. He said...we'd have to wait since he had 300 similar requests. He heard that the USS *Anthedon* had been affectionately called the 'Green Hornet', because of the green and black camouflage she used to wear. Thank you Walt Disney, we like it very much."

IN079 USNR Aviation Base, Hutchinson, Kansas. Newsletter. December 24, 1942.

During the war, this base went from being a USNRAB to a USN Air Station. The bi-weekly base newsletter was called the *HAB"IT"*. Volume one, number five, featured the base Disney-designed insignia on the front cover: Jiminy Cricket in an airplane that has an anchor trailing behind it. The 20-page issue marked the first appearance of the insignia.

IN080 56th Signal Battalion anniversary booklet. February 1, 1945. 6½ x 8¼

"4th Anniversary, 56th Signal BN Debit Verbum Transire." The back cover includes the notation: "Walt Disney, Reproduced by 668th Engr. Co." The inside front cover reads: "The rabbit on the back cover was drawn for this organization upon request by Walt Disney, and given by him to the Battalion to use on the trucks when so permitted. There is no other organization with this symbol. As you will note, the stars surrounding the rabbit total eleven, five above and six below to designate the 56th." This insignia was created by Disney artist Van Kaufman in the winter of 1941.

IN081 Victorville Army Air Field newsletter. July 1, 1944.
The front cover of this 16-page magazine-style newsletter pictures the base insignia: Donald Duck looking through a bombsight.

IN082 Naval Air Station Jacksonville civilian employee's booklet. 1945. 4 x 5¼
This 39-page booklet reprints illustrations created by Disney artist Tom Oreb that were originally used in a 1943 Disney employee booklet titled *The ROPES at Disney's*. The information contained in the Jacksonville booklet pertains to civilian staff employed on the base. The cover of the booklet features an illustration of an updated combat insignia created for the base in 1943.

IN083 Operation Magic Carpet poster. 1945. 11½ x 18
This poster was distributed to Navy personnel associated with Operation Magic Carpet—a military operation that saw the repatriation of American service personnel from bases in the Pacific Theater back to the U.S.A.

IN084 Insignia decals.
Many units had decals produced with their unit's Disney insignia design. These decals were applied to all manner of equipment as a sign of pride and brotherhood.

IN084a Insignia decal.
S.C.R.A.M. The acronym in the illustration stood for Ship Construction Repair and Maintenance. Beaver repairing a ship.

IN084b Insignia decal.
Yuma Army Air Field. Coyote firing a .50-caliber machine gun.

IN084c Insignia decal.
628th Tank Destroyer Battalion. Cat attacking a tank with an axe.

IN084d Insignia decal.
Victorville Army Air Field. Donald operating a camera.

IN084e Insignia decal.
247th Anti-Aircraft Artillery Searchlight battalion. Owl from *Bambi* with searchlight eyes.

IN084f Insignia decal.
Navy Bomb Disposal School. Max Hare disarms a bomb.

IN084g Insignia decal.
Naval Air Station Jacksonville. Donald Duck in an eggshell.
Other insignia decals include:
- 88th Ordnance. Pluto holding a wrench in his mouth.
- 3341st Quartermaster Truck Company. *Dumbo* Crow driving a jeep.
- 62nd Fighter Squadron. Bulldog with boxing gloves.
- USS *Argus*. Dog with anchor in the background.
- VMF-321 (Marine Corps). Devil cat atop cloud, rocket in one hand, bomb in other.
- North American Aviation, Flight Test Department. Donald Duck riding an eagle.
- VBF-9. Panchito firing pistols.
- 549th Bombardment Squadron. Devil riding a bomb.

IN085 Insignia letterhead.
Many units had their Disney-designed insignia printed on stationary.

IN085a Insignia letterhead.
Naval Air Station Jacksonville. Donald in a half eggshell.

IN085b Insignia letterhead.
Small Craft Training Center, Roosevelt Island. Saluting seahorse.

IN085c Insignia letterhead.
U.S. Navy Section Base, San Pedro. Seal fishing a mine out of the water.

IN085d Insignia letterhead.
Second Fair Wing Photo Unit. (This emblem may be a loose adaptation of the dwarf Dopey.)

IN085e Insignia letterhead.
USS *Jason* (AR-8). Happy repairs a ship.

IN085f Insignia letterhead.
USS *Mercy* (AH-8). Snow White tends to Dopey.

IN085g Insignia letterhead.
13th Armored Division. Bad luck symbols.

IN085h Insignia letterhead.

61st Signal Battalion. Donald sends smoke signals.

IN085i Insignia letterhead.
Sub Chaser Training School, Miami. (Unauthorized design.) Donald shoots a .50 caliber machine-gun.

IN085j Insignia letterhead.
Yuma Army Air Field. Coyote fires a .50 caliber machine-gun.

IN085k Insignia letterhead.
663rd Engineer Topographic Company. Goofy with surveying equipment.

IN085l Insignia letterhead.
Fighter Squadron 19, Satan's Kittens. Cat on a thunder bolt.

IN085m Insignia letterhead.
U.S. Army Hospital Ship *Republic*. 234th Ship Complement. Bugs in a helmet.

IN085n Insignia letterhead.
Jacksonville Top Gun School. Donald with .50 caliber machine-gun.

IN085o Insignia letterhead.
56th Armored Infantry Regiment. Knight on a tricycle.

IN085p Insignia letterhead.
10th AAF Emergency Rescue Boat Squadron. Donald captains a rescue boat.
Other insignia letterhead include:
- Jacksonville NAS. Donald in a half eggshell. (Variation with gold colored printing.)
- 114th Infantry, Company F. Charging cricket.
- 60th Naval Construction Battalion. Seabee.

IN086 Sheriff's Annual Show of 1943. 6 x 9
This multi-page program for the Los Angeles County Sheriff's Relief Association pictures Jiminy Cricket on the front cover in the role of an auxiliary policeman. Proceeds from the benefit were given to sick and disabled members and to the families of deceased deputies. In 1943 there were 238 Los Angeles Sheriffs serving in the armed forces.

IN087 Sheriff's Annual Show of 1944. 6 x 9
This item is identical to IN069 except the program references the comic team of Bud Abbot and Lou Costello on the front cover.

IN088 Insignia Photographs.

These photos were either taken by an official photographer associated with the base or unit, by someone serving in the unit.

IN088a Insignia photograph. 8 x 10
Naval Reserve Aviation Base Floyd Bennet. A member of the squadron poses beside his Curtis O2C-1 Helldiver aircraft. This unauthorized design was created in October 1931. The patch on Ensign Conway's jacket and the design on his plane's fuselage represent the first use of a Disney character in a combat insignia. Several planes from this squadron were hired by RKO and were used in the filming of *King Kong*. These planes were filmed attacking the giant ape and shooting him down from atop the Empire State Building.

IN088b Insignia photograph. 9½ x 7¼
Mosquito Fleet insignia. Associated Press Wire photograph dated May 9, 1942. The slug on the image reads: "New York, May 8. 'Is that my dad?' Nineteen-months [sic] old Joan Bulkeley looks a little wary as her dad, Lieut. John D. Bulkeley, hero of the Philippine torpedo boat successes, gets better acquainted in the nursery of their Long Island city home. Between the 'skeeter' boat skipper and his wife is tacked up on wall insignia designed for torpedo boats by Walt Disney." The image on the nursery wall has been altered slightly—the mosquito looks to be riding a depth-charge as opposed to a torpedo, which was depicted in the original design.

IN088c Insignia photograph. 3½ x 5
66th Quartermaster Battalion. Monkey repairs an engine. Marked on reverse with "Passed by base censor".

IN088d Insignia photograph. 3½ x 3¼
Aircraft Carrier Training Group. Pacific. Goofy flies a dilapidated plane.

IN088e Insignia photograph. 7½ x 9
5th Tow Target Squadron. Pedro the airplane towing a target sock riddled with bullets.

IN088f Insignia photograph. 8 x 10
Air Corps Basic Flying School, Cochrane Field. A frustrated Goofy sits in the pilot's seat, while an exasperated Donald Duck shouts into a microphone. Marked on the reverse with: "Army Air Corps. Official Photo. Photographic Section. Cochrane Field, Georgia."

IN088g Insignia photograph. 3 x 4
20th Photo Mapping Squadron, 4th Photo Group. Dumbo holding a camera in his trunk.

IN088h Insignia photograph. 5 x 4

499th Bombardment Group, 897th Bombardment Squadron. "The Big Stick". A caveman carrying a large club. The caveman in this design was based on one of the characters found in the Floyd Gottfredson Mickey Mouse newspaper strip, *Cave-Man Island*.

IN088i Insignia photograph. 4 x 5
469th Bombardment Group, 799th Bombardment Squadron. Thumper riding a bomb.

IN088j Insignia photograph. 2½ x 4½
Landing Craft Repair Base No. 2. The unit's wooden Christmas tree is pictured outside of the base church. A sign to the right of the cut-out tree features the unit's mascot: Goofy repairing a broken propeller on a landing craft.

IN088k Insignia photograph. 8 x 10
Gray Field Air Base. A serviceman poses outside of the unit's headquarters' building. A sign visible over his left shoulder features the unit's Disney insignia: a bee holding various tools in its hands.

Other insignia photographs include:
- VS-36. 2¼ x 3¼ Dopey diving through the air holding a camera.
- 41st Bombardment Squadron. 3 x 3 Bird saluting with a bomb under its wing. Disney insignia artist George Goepper at his desk with the finished illustration for the unit on his drawing board.
- 60th Naval Construction Battalion. 4 x 4 Seabee kicking a can.
- 60th Naval Construction Battalion. 4 x 4 formal photo of 23 of the unit's officers with the original art prominently displayed in the front row. Marked on reverse with "Passed by Naval Censor".

IN089 Lockheed factory insignia photographs. Circa 1942. Each measures 4¾ x 3¾
Planes rolling off the production line at Lockheed were painted with Disney characters by one of Lockheed's employees, with Walt Disney's permission. Mickey Mouse and Donald Duck were used extensively in little vignettes, many of which contained racist overtones. Many of these designs were painted over by men in the field, who were afraid that any wreckage from planes shot down and found by the enemy would incite rage and lead to dire consequences for the survivors. The cover of the May 22, 1942, issue of *The Lockheed-Vega Star*, a Lockheed employee newsletter, featured an image of Donald with an axe in his hands and the caption: "Let me have a quack at 'em!"

IN090 Pepsi Cola insignia matchbooks. 1942. 1½ x 4½
A set of 48 matchbooks were distributed during the war throughout the United States by Pepsi Cola. The matches were manufactured by the

National Match Company in New York and were published by DD Bean and Company of Jaffrey, New Hampshire. An estimated one-million matchbooks were distributed through the Whelan and United retail chain. Each case of 2,500 matchbooks usually contained several different designs. There is no record in the Disney Archives of a license being granted to either Pepsi-Cola or the two companies involved with the production of the matchbooks. Appendix IV contains a complete listing of all the matchbooks in this set.

IN091 Yellow series unit insignia matchbooks. 1943. 1½ x 4½
There are 20 matchbooks in this series. The matchbooks were manufactured by the Maryland Match Company for the National Match Company and were available with either a glossy or matte finish. The matchbooks were printed with a yellow background. The front cover pictures a Disney-designed insignia printed in red, white, and blue. The name of the unit was printed on the back cover. Many of the designs in this series were also reproduced on the Pepsi-Cola matchbooks. See Appendix IV for a complete listing of all the matchbooks in this set.

IN091a Yellow series unit insignia matchbooks. 1943. 1½ x 4½
751st Tank Battalion, 56th Pursuit Squadron, 58th Pursuit Squadron.

IN091b Yellow series unit insignia matchbooks. 1943. 1½ x 4½
7th Bombardment Squadron, 26th Material Squadron, Alaska Defense Force.

IN091c Yellow series unit insignia matchbooks. 1943. 1½ x 4½
62nd Pursuit Squadron, 47th School Squadron, 251st Coast Artillery.

IN091d Yellow series unit insignia matchbooks. 1943. 1½ x 4½
Utility Squadron, U.S. Naval Reserve, Women's Ambulance and Defense Corps of America.

IN091e Yellow series unit insignia matchbooks. 1943. 1½ x 4½
45th Pursuit Squadron, U.S. Mosquito Fleet, 40th Bombardment Group.

IN091f Yellow series unit insignia matchbooks. 1943. 1½ x 4½
46th Bombardment Group, 133rd Field Artillery, U.S.S. *Blue*.

IN091g Yellow series unit insignia matchbooks. 1943. 1½ x 4½
23rd Pursuit Squadron, 165th Field Artillery.

IN092 Yellow series unit insignia matchbooks box. 1943. 6 x 4
This cardboard box held 12 of the yellow series matchbooks (IN091). The front of the box is marked: "Safety Match Books. Walt Disney Designed. Insignia for the U.S. Armed Forces." The reverse of the box is marked:

"Manufactured by The National Match Company. Copyright 1943. Walt Disney Productions."

IN093 Yellow series unit insignia matchbooks display sign. 1943.
This die-cut cardboard sign was a countertop point-of-sale display promoting the yellow series matchbooks.

IN094 Universal Match Corporation, St. Louis. 3 x 4½
Because of paper rationing, these matchbooks were also used as postcards. They are twice the width of a normal matchbook.

IN094a Universal Match Corporation, St. Louis. 3 x 4½
Naval Air Station, Olathe, Kansas. Indian riding a hawk.

IN094b Universal Match Corporation, St. Louis. 3 x 4½
Naval Air Station Hutchinson, Kansas. Jiminy Cricket.

IN094c Universal Match Corporation, St. Louis. 3 x 4½
Army Air Base, Casper, Wyoming. Donald.

IN094d Universal Match Corporation, St. Louis. 3 x 4½
Naval Air Operational Training Command, Jacksonville, Florida. Donald.

IN094e Universal Match Corporation, St. Louis. 3 x 4½
Searchlight Maintenance Detachment. (Unauthorized Donald Duck design.)

IN094f Universal Match Corporation, St. Louis. 3 x 4½
Naval Air Station, Minneapolis, Minnesota. Penguin on skis.

IN094g Universal Match Corporation, St. Louis. 3 x 4½
First Motion Picture Unit (created by Disney artist Van Kaufman while serving in the unit). Cartoon cameraman in an airplane. (While not a Disney design, this image was created by Disney artist Van Kaufman. Many Hollywood artists, including several from the Disney Studio, served with this unit during the war.)
Other matchboxes include:
- Naval Air Station, Jacksonville. Donald sitting in a half eggshell.
- Naval Air Station, Jacksonville. Donald (updated design).
- Naval Hospital, Jacksonville. Donald (updated design).

IN095 Miscellaneous matchbook covers, various manufacturers, various dates.
These covers were produced for men in the listed units.

IN095a Miscellaneous matchbook cover.
Naval Air Station, Jacksonville, Marine Corps. Donald.

IN095b Miscellaneous matchbook cover.
USS *Dionysus* (AR-21). Goofy.

IN095c Miscellaneous matchbook cover.
USS *Mindoro* (CVE-120), circa 1946. Minnie.

IN095d Miscellaneous matchbook cover.
USS *Piedmont* (AD-17). Doc.

IN095e Miscellaneous matchbook cover.
U.S. Navy Section Base, San Pedro, California. Seal.

IN095f Miscellaneous matchbook cover.
Small Craft Training Center, Roosevelt Island. Seahorse.

IN095g Miscellaneous matchbook cover.
Publications Department, Raritan Arsenal. Parrot.

IN095h Miscellaneous matchbook cover.
FASRON 110, (Fleet Air Service Squadron), Pacific Fleet. Donald.

IN095i Miscellaneous matchbook cover.
Naval Air Station, Livermore. Donald.

IN095j Miscellaneous matchbook cover.
Marine Corps Air Station, El Toro. Flying bull.

IN095k Miscellaneous matchbook cover.
Naval Air Station Anacostia. Donald.
Other matchbox covers include:
- Naval Air Station, Jacksonville. Aviation Cadets Mess. Donald sitting in an eggshell.
- Jacksonville Naval Air Operational Training Command. Donald (updated design).
- Naval Hospital, Jacksonville. Donald (updated design).
- Naval Supply Center, Oakland. Donald.
- Naval Reserve Aviation Base, Atlanta, Georgia. Donald.
- U.S. Army Signal Corps, Langley Field, Virginia. Bee.
- Motor Torpedo Boat Squadron Training Center, Melville, Rhode Island. Mosquito.

- Naval Air Station, Minneapolis, Minnesota. Penguin on skis.
- Naval Air Station Hutchinson, Kansas. Donald.

IN096 Mickey Mouse Weekly.
This newspaper comic-style publication was published in England. The first issue to feature a Disney insignia on the cover was the September 11, 1943, edition. The last insignia image appeared on the cover of the November 11, 1944, issue.

IN096a Mickey Mouse Weekly.
September 11, 1943. National Fire Service. Stylized hose.

IN096b Mickey Mouse Weekly.
September 25, 1943. Flying Instructors No. 15, Royal Air Force. Thumper points at airplane.

IN096c Mickey Mouse Weekly.
October 23, 1943. 1224th Air Training Corps Squadron, B Flight, Royal Air Force. Jiminy Cricket.

IN096d Mickey Mouse Weekly.
November 6, 1943. Home Guard Mess. Pluto.

IN096e Mickey Mouse Weekly.
November 20, 1943. Free French, Royal Air Force. Jiminy Cricket with butterfly net.

IN096f Mickey Mouse Weekly.
December 18, 1943. Marine Section, Royal Canadian Air Force. Monkey in a boat.

IN096g Mickey Mouse Weekly.
January 1, 1944. 1079th Squadron, A Flight, Royal Air Force. Diving eagle.

IN096h Mickey Mouse Weekly.
January 15, 1944. Free French, Royal Air Force. Donald pulling a Hitler-headed worm from French soil.

IN096i Mickey Mouse Weekly.
February 12, 1944. Royal Canadian Air Force Station, Dartmouth, Nova Scotia. Fencing cat.

IN096j Mickey Mouse Weekly.
February 26, 1944. 66th Quartermaster Battalion. Monkey fixing an engine.

IN096k Mickey Mouse Weekly.

March 11, 1944. 482nd Ordnance Company, (AVN) Bomb Division. Bulldog with sack of bombs.

Other issues include:
- October 9, 1943. HMS *Oxlip*.
- November 20, 1943. Royal Air Force Free French.
- February 26, 1944. 66th Quartermaster Battalion, Iceland.

IN097 *What is Propaganda?* July 1944.

This 48-page War Department Education Manual (EM-2) was published as part of the so-called G.I. Roundtable Series by the United States War Department. The front cover features an illustration of Donald Duck, while the inside pages feature several other Donald illustrations and numerous caricatures of Hitler and Mussolini. The booklet's frontispiece states: "G.I. Roundtable pamphlets provide material which orientation and education officers may use in conducting group discussions or forums as part of an off-duty education program."

IN098 Coast Guard Infantry Drill booklet. Circa 1943. 6 x 8

This 24-page soft-cover booklet covers proper drill procedures as well as a manual of arms. The booklet is profusely illustrated with images of Bugs Bunny as the Drill Instructor and Mickey Mouse, Donald Duck, and a host of other non-descript cartoon characters trying to do what the rabbit is ordering, sometimes with comical consequences. The booklet was created by a non-Disney artist for G.B. Gelly, Captain, USCG, Captain of the Port, Los Angeles.

IN099 *Alternating Current*. Circa 1943. 5¼ x 8¼

The 121-page soft-cover manual was created for men attending the U.S. Navy's Submarine Chaser Training Command, Miami, Florida. The manual explores alternating current theory and contains a plethora of information on related alternators, transformers, and electric motors. The cover features a non-Disney illustration of Donald Duck and his three nephews.

IN100 *Direct Current*. Circa 1943. 7¾ x 10¼

This 176-page soft-cover manual was created for men attending the U.S. Navy's Submarine Chaser Training Command, Miami, Florida. The manual explores the theory of magnetism and electricity. The cover features a non-Disney illustration of Donald Duck and his three nephews.

IN101 Entertainment for Servicemen in Miami. Circa 1943. 5½ x 9

This 16-page soft-cover booklet was given to servicemen attending the Sub Chaser Training Center in Miami, Florida. The booklet contained numerous entries for sports, entertainment, and community-related activities. The cover and inside pages feature a non-Disney illustration of Donald Duck.

IN102 *Digest*, December 1945.

This magazine was produced for the U.S. Navy Airborne Electronics Division. The cover design was created for the Airborne Coordinating Group, Naval Research Lab, Washington, D.C. If you look closely at the artwork you will notice Donald and Goofy are looking through stereo-view glasses at a head-and-shoulders illustration of an attractive lady, who bears a striking resemblance to one of the Centaurettes from *Fantasia*.

IN103 Easter card. 1943. 5¼ x 5¼

This Hallmark Easter card was created for loved ones to send to their sweethearts serving in the military.

IN104 Pasadena Area Station Hospital, December 25, 1943 program. 9 x 12¼

This large-sized program's cover features an illustration of Donald as Santa about to go down a chimney. Smoke from the chimney spells out the words, "Christmas Dinner".

IN105 Jacksonville Naval Air Station photo album. Circa 1943.

The blue-colored, hardcover book held black-colored pages on which photographs could be affixed. The album's cover features the station's Disney-designed insignia.

CHAPTER 5
Propaganda and Training Films

"Mickey Mouse and his pals, including the Big Bad Wolf with a Hitler mustache and a swastika arm band, are going all out in their efforts to help win the war. The studios of Walt Disney actually are making more buy-bond films, pay-taxes films, fire-gun films, and recognize...plane films than they are old-line cartoons for laughs alone." —The Coshocton Tribune, January 25, 1942.

In May 1941, a bitter strike gripped the Disney Studio. At the invitation of Nelson Rockefeller, head of the Office of the Co-Coordinator of Inter-American Affairs (CIAA), Walt Disney left the hostile situation behind and embarked on a tour of South America. Rockefeller told Disney: "Your pictures are popular down there and there's a Nazi influence you can help offset if you'd go down and meet people."[191]

The CIAA's mandate was to strengthen ties between the U.S. and Latin America. Pro-Nazi sentiment was running high in several South American countries, and the CIAA was looking for a way to counter this potential hemispheric threat. Part of the CIAA's strategy was to inundate the region with American entertainment and educational films. Nelson Rockefeller felt Walt Disney could provide some of the product his agency was looking for.

Disney Production Manager Robert Carr sent a lengthy memo to the CIAA outlining "ideas for more Walt Disney films for South American release". The document cataloged 49 subjects:

> Animation, being a magical medium, has profound potentialities for evoking sentiment and awe. "Ave Maria" in *Fantasia* was only a beginning. We should make full use of this quality in many of the "big" subjects suggested, creating a deeply religious feeling, and associating this with political ideals. We can have beautiful and reverent

---
191 Miller, Diane Disney, (as told to Pete Martin). *The Story of Walt Disney*. Dell Publishing Co., NY, 1959. p.166.

scenes in which The Christ of the Andes is seen in the background, or a huge cross fills the sky; or more subtly, when the voice, the music, and the artist's style of painting suggests a religious atmosphere... as when we see the Spirit of Pan American, or of Victory, standing behind our weapons. This will put over certain ideas impossible to present otherwise.

The 49 subjects presented in this report will require the use of every known animation technique—and some as yet unknown. However, the important thing is not so much how certain inconceivable visualizations will be accomplished, but rather to make certain that the subjects chosen are politically right.

A wide-range of propaganda films were covered in Section VI of the memo. Titles included *We Have More Food*; *We Have More Men*; *We Have More Steel*; *We Are in the Right*; *All for One, One for All*; *Wings of Victory*; *Hemisphere Defense*; and *Hitler the Anti-Christ*.

Section XIV of the memo covered "The Creation of New Symbols" and stated in part: "Above all, we—The Rockefeller Committee and the Disney studio—must CREATE SYMBOLS." The memo listed, as an example, "Pan Americana", who was described as a "noble female figure, bearing a torch and a cross, subtly suggesting both the Virgin Mary and the Goddess of Liberty".

With a government offer of financial guarantees for the production of several shorts, Walt Disney, his wife Lillian, and 16 handpicked Studio artists departed Los Angeles for South America on August 17, 1941. Rio de Janeiro was the first big city the group visited. Disney was the guest of honor at a dinner hosted by the Brazilian President, and while in Rio the artists visited galleries, zoos, and nightclubs gathering information on the area's culture and customs.

After spending three weeks in Brazil, the group moved on to Argentina. In Buenos Aires, the hotel provided the artists with a mini-studio located on the rooftop garden. From Argentina the group visited Chile for one week and then the crew split into two: several of the artists visited Peru, Bolivia, and Mexico, while Walt Disney and several others sailed back to New York City through the Panama Canal on a 15-day cruise.

Two feature-length films were produced as a result of the South American visit: *Saludos Amigos* and *The Three Caballeros*. Some of the live-action segments in *Saludos Amigos* were shot by Disney himself with his 16mm camera. Both films were successful at the box office.

As a further part of the CIAA contract, the Studio produced several educational and health films for the South American market. One of the first educational films to be completed was *The Grain That Built a Hemisphere*. This film looked at the history of corn and corn-based products, and like the Canadian bonds films, used previously released footage—in this case, sequences were recycled from *The New Spirit, The Spirit of '43, Bambi,* and *Farmyard Symphony*.

The first Studio-produced CIAA health film was *The Winged Scourge*. This film examined ways of combating mosquitoes and the disease they carried. Disney artists called upon the services of the Dwarfs from *Snow White* to help them illustrate their point. All new animation was created for the film, as none of the existing sequences from *Snow White* were deemed suitable.

At a story meeting for *The Winged Scourge*, Walt Disney emphasized the serious side of the film:

> The film is basically to tell people how to get rid of mosquitoes. The only reason to bring in the Dwarfs is to add a little interest. When you begin to get into gags and impossible things, you're not accomplishing the job we're supposed to. The ideas as I saw it was we'd talk the picture and after you've explained everything...to get relief...we'd go into the operation of the thing, pep up the ending by taking seven ordinary citizens...we take each Dwarf and he goes about his work as it's supposed to be done. Maybe it's Dopey spreading the oil...let him be cute but don't go into these gags. Where you'd get your interest, we'd throw in music. Nothing to laugh at beat hell, but something to lighten it. It's a serious problem but we are showing how simple it is. Even Dopey can do it.[192]

According to a story in the April 17, 1945, issue of *Look* magazine, members of the British government were so impressed with *The Winged Scourge* they "ordered 65 prints of the film for distribution in India during the monsoon season, when mosquitoes are most prevalent there...it is estimated the picture will eventually be seen by...36,000,000 persons".

Other films completed for the CIAA included *Hookworm, Cleanliness Brings Health, Defense Against Invasion, Insects as Carriers of Disease, The Human Body, How Disease Travels, Infant Care, Tuberculosis, What Is Disease, Planning For Good Eating, Environmental Sanitation,* and *Water: Friend or Enemy*.

---

192 *Fortune*, August 1942.

The Studio released five anti-Nazi propaganda films in 1943. The Studio's Publicity Department referred to these films as "psychological productions"[193] and they included *Reason and Emotion, Chicken Little, Education For Death, Der Fuehrer's Face*, and *Victory Through Air Power*. The CIAA helped finance the first four films.

The film *Reason and Emotion* satired Nazi regimentation. The film's main characters were an intellect named Reason and a caveman named Emotion. This film was the least successful of all of Disney's propaganda films. Addressing the main theme of the film, artists Joe Grant and Dick Huemer wrote: "If the German people had not allowed themselves to be overwhelmed by the diabolical Nazi appeals to their primitive emotions and had only permitted their reasoning powers full sway, there probably would be no Nazi party."[194]

Chicken Little was a twist on the childhood nursery tale of the same name, except in Disney's version a Nazi fox ate all the barnyard animals. The moral of the cartoon was "...to show the deadly effect upon our war effort of loose wagging tongues...*Chicken Little*...a perfect example of the horrors that can happen through the spreading of false information".[195]

In the film, the evil Foxey Loxey whispered to Chicken Little that the sky was falling. To back up his claim, Foxey tore a star from an astrological ad on a billboard and dropped it on Chicken Little's head. As Chicken Little spread the rumor throughout the coup, Cocky Locky, the leader of the roost, tried to discount the story.

Foxey Loxey then started another rumor saying Cocky Locky had lost his leadership skills and that Chicken Little should become the new leader. With panic now running rampant through the coop, all the animals left the safety of the poultry pen and followed Chicken Little to a nearby cave, where Foxey Loxey ate them.

Chicken Little ended with the villainous Foxey Loxey reclining on a rock, licking a wishbone. As the narrator said, "Hey, wait a minute. This isn't right. That's not the way it ends in my book.", Foxey Loxey retorted, "Oh yah. Well don't believe everything you read brother."

---

193 Shale, Richard. *Donald Duck Joins Up*. Diss. U. of Michigan, 1982. Ann Arbor: UMI. p. 63.

194 *Dispatch from Disney's*, 1943 Disney employee newsletter.

195 *Dispatch from Disney's*, 1943 Disney employee newsletter.

The original script called for Foxey Loxey to be holding a copy of Adolf Hitler's *Mein Kampf*, but this was deleted from the film. Instead, Foxey Loxey is seen smoking a cigar while playing with Chicken Little's yo-yo. The camera fades out on a book he is leaning against titled, *Psychology*.

Education for Death was based on the 1941 book written by Gregor Ziemer titled, *Education for Death: The Making of a Nazi*. Disney's film followed the life of a German boy from birth to manhood, his indoctrination into the Nazi fold, and his ultimate death in combat. The film showed how Nazis took control of a German life right from the moment of birth when parents were told what to name their newborn. As he grew older, little Hans, the film's subject, fell ill. His mother received a visit from the Gestapo telling her not to fuss over the child, as sickness was a weakness.

In school, Hans and his classmates studied natural history. As part of their teachings, the children witnessed a fox eating a rabbit. As other children applauded the actions of the fox, Hans sympathized with the rabbit. Hans was rebuked by his teacher and after being reprimanded quickly gave the correct response: "I hate the rabbit. The rabbit is weak. He is no Nazi rabbit."

The film ended with Hans marching off to war as a member of the Hitler Youth. The group of marching children turned into a group of marching soldiers, which then transformed into a graveyard of crosses.

Education for Death contained a humorous sequence, which the artists titled "Fairy Tales of the New Order". This segment contained a caricature of Hitler as "Prince Charming", who awakened a rather robust, blonde-haired "Sleeping Beauty" named "Germania". As Wagner's "Ride of the Valkyrie"s played in the background, Hitler loaded the overweight Germania onto his horse, which staggered under the immense load.

Recalling his work on the "Fairy Tales of the New Order" sequence, Director Gerry Geronimi said: "We had quite a time animating expressions to fit the furious gutturals of the German dialog. We had to call in German speaking actors to sit for the artists. The real fun came when our own Ollie Wallace modeled for Hitler as a knight and he spoke a hodgepodge which was his conception of the Nazi tongue."[196]

---

196 *Dispatch from Disney's*, 1943 Disney employee newsletter.

Education for Death was released in some cities alongside RKO's film *Hitler's Children*, the live-action feature based on Zeimer's book.

One of the funniest and least serious of all the Disney propaganda films was *Der Fuehrer's Face*. The story was originally written as the plot for Disney's first income tax film, with the title *Donald Duck in Nutziland*, but the song, which was released in advance of the film, was such a huge hit, Disney changed the film's title to that of the song. The film starred Donald Duck and won the Studio an Academy Award for the Best Cartoon Short Subject in 1943.

Commenting on the use of Donald as the film's hero, artists Joe Grant and Dick Huemer wrote: "...we feel that a public character such as Donald Duck, writhing rebelliously in the clutches of the Nazis, will bring the situation home to every man, woman and child in this country...for Donald belongs to them like a member of their own family. They will end up hating Hitler twenty times more than if they had gone through the same ordeal with some curly-haired hero who is, after all, merely another movie actor."[197]

The film opened with a military band marching around Donald's neighborhood. The band featured the caricatured likenesses of Hirohito, Mussolini, and Goering. The entire opening sequence had a Nazi theme: fences, telephone poles, shrubs, a windmill, and even the clouds had a swastika design.

The film's next sequence pictured Donald Duck sound asleep. Donald was awakened by a swastika alarm clock, and, as he struggled from bed, he saluted pictures of the Axis leaders. For breakfast, he treated himself to a coffee bean dipped in water and a whiff of bacon and egg aroma sprayed from a spritzer. Donald topped off his meal with a piece of bread cut from a loaf with a saw.

Next, Donald trundled off to a munitions factory where he worked "48 hours a day for the Fuehrer" assembling bombs and bullets. Interspersed with the ammunition on the conveyor belt were pictures of Hitler, which Donald had to salute. As his workday continued, Donald was treated to a vacation. A canvas alpine backdrop was lowered into place and Donald underwent an intense calisthenics workout that contorted his body into swastika designs. With the vacation over, the narrator announced: "By special decree, you have been selected to work overtime."

---

[197] *Dispatch from Disney's*, 1943 Disney employee newsletter.

Donald returned to work and as the ammunition and pictures of Hitler passed at an ever-increasing speed on the conveyor belt, our poor hero suffered a nervous breakdown. In his nightmare Donald became the shell casings and was pounded on by a caricatured Adolf Hitler. Donald then woke up at home and "heiled" the shadow of an outstretched arm on his wall. When he realized the shadow was really the arm of a small, decorative Statue of Liberty sitting on his windowsill, Donald ran to the window, hugged the statue, and happily exclaimed: "Am I glad to be a citizen of the United States of America." The film ended with a caricature of Hitler's face being hit by an over-ripe tomato.

One of the film's highlights was the theme song, *Der Fuehrer's Face*, written by Disney composer Oliver G. Wallace. Wallace was born in London, England, on August 6, 1887. At some early point in his life, Wallace and his family journeyed across the Atlantic Ocean to Canada, where they traveled across the continent and settled on the West Coast.

Wallace began his musical career playing piano for live vaudeville shows—a teenaged Wallace moved from the province of British Columbia to Washington State, where he found work playing the piano during the showing of silent films.

In 1908, the Dream Theatre in Seattle, Washington, became the first theatre in the United States to have an organ. The opening day organist was none other than Oliver G. Wallace, whose reputation as an organist by that time had became legendary. Wallace played the organ at various theatres in the Pacific Northwest, including the Clemmer Columbia Theater in Seattle. On April 7, 1912, the *Seattle Times* reported:

"On either side of the proscenium arch...will be placed the pipes of the massive organ, which will be one of the finest on the coast. Oliver G. Wallace, recognized as a genius in the interpretation of photoplays on the pipe organ, will be the player."

A 1955 Studio biography quoted Wallace as saying: "I got my first job playing for vaudeville and single reels in 1906. Believe me, you had to be snappy with your invention to keep up with the shadows in those early flickers." The biography further stated: "Highlights of his career as a theatre accompanist include inaugurating the nation's first theatre organ in Seattle...and playing for Sid Grauman in Los Angeles' famed Rialto." Wallace also played the Broadway Theatre in

Portland, Oregon, before being transferred back to Seattle where he played a Hope-Jones "unit orchestra" organ at the Liberty Theatre.

During his time as a theatre organist, Wallace teamed up with Seattle-born composer and church leader Harold Weeks to write "Hindustan", a love song that became Wallace's first successful composition. According to the *Der Fuehrer's Face* campaign manual: "Writing popular songs isn't a new thing for Oliver Wallace. 'Hindustan', which he composed during the period of World War I, sold more than 1,000,000 copies and is one of the all time All-American popular tunes." In the 1930s, Wallace moved to Hollywood, where he wrote musical scores for motion pictures at Columbia and later Universal Studios.

Wallace began his career at The Walt Disney Studios on February 1, 1938, joining musician Frank Churchill as a Studio composer. The earliest Disney film Wallace worked on was the Mickey Mouse short *Mickey's Amateurs*, which was released on April 17, 1937. His work on the film was un-credited.

Wallace remembered being asked by Walt Disney to compose a song for *Der Fuehrer's Face* one afternoon:

> Walt encountered me in the hall and gave me a rush order. "Ollie, I want a serious song, but it's got to be funny." The further information that it was going to be for a picture telling Donald Duck's adventures in Naziland didn't help very much. "What do you mean?" I asked. "Suppose the Germans are singing it," Walt offered. "To them it's serious, to us it's funny." Walt walked away. I stood in the hall. Once more I was on the spot.[198]

Wallace said he wrote the chorus while riding his bicycle to the grocery store with his wife. Half-an-hour later, the song was finished. At the Studio the next day, Wallace recounted:

> I sang it all over the place. The sound brought Walt out into the hall. "Let's hear it," Walt said. I stalled. "Orchestration...there's a funny sound in it...can't be made without an instrument...has to be practiced." The truth is, I didn't know what Walt would think of a highly robust Bronx cheer. Could such a sound be used in a Disney picture? "Let's hear it," Walt said. I let loose. Walt laughed. The rest is history.[199]

According to the *Der Fuehrer's Face* campaign manual, Wallace had "two daughters, Martha, fifteen-and-a-half years old, and Mary,

---

198 *Dispatch from Disney's*, 1943 Disney employee newsletter.

199 *Dispatch from Disney's*, 1943 Disney employee newsletter.

seventeen-and-a-half. They are typical high-school youngsters, more interested in Boogie Woogie than in Bach, and what is more, they are Wallace's worst critics. He tried the song on them and they got such a bang out of it that Wallace knew the song was in."[200]

The song was recorded by Lindley Armstrong "Spike" Jones, the son of a Southern Pacific Railroad employee. Jones acquired his nickname because people thought the youngster was as thin as a railroad spike.

Jones received his first musical instrument, a drum set, when he was 11 years old. The set sparked what would eventually become a lifelong passion for making music. In the 1930s, Jones performed with the Victor Young Band, and for a time, Jones also performed with legendary singer Del Porter. From 1937 to 1942, Jones was a member of the John Scott Trotter Orchestra.

Jones teamed with fellow musicians George Rock, Mickey Katz, Doodles Weaver, and Red Ingle to form Spike Jones and his City Slickers. At the pinnacle of his career, Jones' group was composed of 16 musicians. An article in the November 3, 1942 issue of the *New York Post Magazine* referred to Jones as "the music master of a little group of jazz musicians". Jones' trademark was to parody the day's popular songs.

Jones recorded *Der Fuehrer's Face* on July 28, 1942, in Hollywood. The song was released on the "B" side of a Bluebird 78 rpm record (B-11586) in September 1942. A limited number of preview pressings were distributed to radio stations around the United States, and in a matter of weeks the song was the rage of the airwaves—*Der Fuehrer's Face* spent 16 weeks on the charts climbing as high as number three.

New York radio personality Martin Block played the song on his *Make Believe Ballroom* program. The song became an immediate sensation after Block played the song for the first time. The station received literally hundreds of phone calls asking him to play *Der Fuehrer's Face* again. Block used the song as a vehicle to sell War Bonds—he offered a free copy of the record to anyone who pledged a $50 bond.

Block's promotion was so successful that "…in two days…the song had earned $60,000 for Uncle Sam…Bluebird was $350,000 behind in…orders and Southern Music, which published the sheet music…reported they had sold 15,000 copies of the song. Restraints on the performance of the song had to be made…in order to permit

---

200 *Der Fuehrer's Face*, publicity campaign manual. p.4.

the record makers and music publishers the opportunity to catch-up with the avalanche of orders that had poured in."[201]

The record label credits Carl Grayson as the singer. The label also lists Willie Spicer on the "birdaphone", the musical instrument that was used to make the razzing sound. Willie Spicer was not a member of the band—as a matter of fact, the name was apparently made up just to make the label more attractive.

Over 1.5 million records were eventually sold and Southern Music reported they had "...sold 15,000 copies of the song, in a space of time comparative to that in which "Deep in the Heart of Texas" sold when it was first published, and that song broke existing records".[202]

The film's campaign manual reported sales of the song "have already reached such proportions, both as to sheet music and as to records, that the producers were forced at one time to restrain the performances of the song by bands in order to give the manufacturers the opportunity to catch up with accumulated orders".[203]

Theatre owners were encouraged to promote *Der Fuehrer's Face* through the use of the short's trademark Bronx cheer. The film's campaign manual suggested an effigy of Hitler be placed in the theatre lobby with its hand raised in salute. A placard was to be placed in front of the dummy encouraging patrons to give Hitler the raspberry. Another idea suggested that a dartboard target of Hitler's face be placed in the lobby. Filmgoers were given prizes based on where their dart stuck on the target. *Der Fuehrer's Face* was arguably the most popular war-related film produced by the Disney Studio.

Wallace's career at Disney's lasted over 25 years. Wallace composed music for almost 150 short cartoons and wrote music for several of Disney's animated features including *Dumbo, Cinderella, Alice in Wonderland, Lady and the Tramp,* and *Peter Pan,* as well as dozens of Disney television specials.

Wallace was nominated for five Academy Awards during his tenure at Disney's. In 1941, Wallace, along with fellow composer Frank Churchill, won the Oscar for Best Scoring of Musical Picture for their work on *Dumbo*. Wallace and fellow musician Paul J. Smith assumed

---

201 *Der Fuehrer's Face*, publicity campaign manual. p.4.

202 *Der Fuehrer's Face*, publicity campaign manual. p.4.

203 *Der Fuehrer's Face*, publicity campaign manual. p.4.

the responsibilities of composing the majority of music at the Studio in 1942, when fellow composers Frank Churchill committed suicide and Leigh Harline left to sign an exclusive contract with RKO.

The Studio's fifth propaganda film dealt with more serious subject matter. In 1942, Simon and Schuster published *Victory Through Air Power* written by Major Alexander de Seversky, a Russian-born ex-patriot. Born into nobility, Seversky survived the Russian Civil War and the partial loss of one leg when he was shot down during World War I. Seversky later emigrated to the United States where he excelled as a test pilot, inventor, businessman, and visionary who filed more than 360 patents. Seversky was awarded the Medal of Merit by President Harry Truman and served as a special consultant to the chiefs of staff of the Air Force. He became a U.S. citizen in 1927 and died in 1974.

Victory Through Air Power outlined Seversky's theory that the short, interior Axis supply routes had an advantage over the long, exterior Allied supply routes. Seversky advocated attacking the Axis industrial heartland with long-range, multi-gun bombers.

Disney acquired the rights to Seversky's book in the summer of 1942. An article in the August 1943 *Book of the Month Club News* reported: "Major Alexander de Seversky couldn't believe at first that Walt Disney had actually applied for the film rights to the book. When convinced that the offer was a genuine one, the author asked, 'Will he put Donald Duck and Mickey Mouse in it?'"

Disney approached government sources to see if they were interested in financing a film based on the book, but he soon found the book's anti-Navy stance was held in contempt by many of President Roosevelt's top advisors. Disney decided his Studio would produce the film with no government aid.

In addition to appearing in the live-action segments of the film to explain his theory, Seversky also acted as the film's technical advisor. In one instance, he queried columnist Louella Parsons on where he could purchase sequins. "Where can I get those fish scales ladies wear on their dresses?" he asked the Hollywood reporter.[204] Parsons wanted to know why he needed them. Seversky replied, "I'm making a miniature airplane and I need them for the nose."[205]

---

204 Hopper, Hedda. "Hollywood." *New York Daily News*. October 13, 1942.

205 Hopper, Hedda. "Hollywood." *New York Daily News*. October 13, 1942.

Seversky also created sketches and revised the script as events during the war proved his theory correct. Seversky had advocated the bombing of Axis hydroelectric dams in order to cripple the enemy's industrial base. Before the film was completed, Royal Air Force Lancaster bombers breached two of three hydroelectric dams near Germany's Ruhr industrial region. The July 14, 1943 *Motion Picture Daily* reported: "*Victory Through Air Power* is a direct and very startling parallel of the actual: the devastation created by the RAF when it blew up the Moehne and Eder dams in West Germany. Disney had drawn, colored, and photographed his footage over five months ago."

Prime Minister Winston Churchill viewed a copy of *Victory Through Air Power* and was impressed with Seversky's argument. During the Quebec Conference, Churchill asked President Roosevelt if he had ever seen Seversky's film. When Roosevelt responded no, Churchill had a print of the film flown in from New York. The two leaders viewed the film and Roosevelt was so impressed he ran the film the following day, this time with his Joint Chiefs of Staff in attendance.

At all of his meetings with military brass and at all of his lectures, Seversky repeated the phrase: "If we have twice the range, we will only have half as much fighting to do." Albert Lasker, a brilliant advertising executive who helped promote Seversky's theory and the film, turned Seversky's phrase into a succinct and marketable slogan: "The longer the range, the shorter the war."

Once the film was completed, Lasker promoted the feature in influential circles. His contacts included politicians, members of the military, newspaper editors, radio commentators, and Hollywood powerbrokers. On July 2, 1943, Lasker hosted a buffet dinner at the prestigious Waldorf Astoria hotel in New York, which was attended by over 1,700 guests including Walt Disney, Seversky, and most of New York's elite. The July 8, 1943, edition of *Motion Picture Daily* reported: "A screening of the new Disney production...will be held in conjunction with the supper." Lasker also paid $1,800 for the production of a special insert in the July 29, 1943, *New York Times* promoting the film. The insert was written by Jack Goodman, the head of advertising at Simon and Schuster, who were publishers of Seversky's book.

Victory Through Air Power took 14 months to complete and was released in July 1943. Theater owners were encouraged to sponsor "Miss Victory Through Air Power" contests, and children were encouraged to write essays on how victory through air power could be achieved.

Reviews for the film were mixed. *Parents Magazine* named the film the "Outstanding Picture of the Month for Family Audiences", though it is hard to imagine children sitting through the complex theory as explained by Seversky. The film's final scene is also quite terrifying and it's hard to imagine young children sitting through that sequence without experiencing some type of trauma: Allied bombers were shown leaving Alaska with their deadly cargo of bombs destined for Japan. An American eagle, representing the bombers, struck repeatedly at the head of an octopus, which represented Japan. When the octopus's head was destroyed, the tentacles slowly released their grip on the Pacific Islands. This scene summarized Seversky's theory— strike at the heart of the enemy instead of fighting for the outposts.

Besides propaganda films, the Disney Studio produced over 75 military training films. This is quite a feat considering Disney had previously only made two educational films. Walt's first educational short was *Tommy Tucker's Tooth*, produced in 1922 while he was in Kansas City, Missouri. The film was used to teach school children proper dental care. The second educational short was produced as a sequel four years later under the title *Clara Cleans Her Teeth*. Both films dealt with dental hygiene and were commissioned by Dr. Thomas McCrum.

The Studio's first foray into training films was of a non-military nature and was produced in March 1941 at Disney's own initiative and expense. Disney had contacted George Papen, a project engineer with Lockheed, wanting to know if the aircraft manufacturer would be interested in a training film dealing with aircraft production. Papen said yes, and the film, *Four Methods of Flush Riveting*, was used to train the flood of new Lockheed workers.

Although Disney lost money on the film, *Four Methods of Flush Riveting* was highly acclaimed. An April 1942 Studio memo stated: "Although praised highly by Washington officials, no agency of the U.S. government has yet found the funds or authority to make this urgently needed film available to American war industries—although many requests for the film have been received from all over the country."[206]

Disney's first military contract was with the U.S. Navy's Bureau of Aeronautics. A Navy representative had been in touch with the

---

[206] Shale, Richard. *Donald Duck Joins Up*. Diss. U. of Michigan, 1982. Ann Arbor: UMI. notes for Chapter Two. p.16.

Studio as early as November 1941. On December 8, 1941, the Studio was offered a contract to produce 20 training films on aircraft and warship identification. The series became known was WEFT, an acronym for Wings, Engine, Tail, and Fuselage.

The *Middlesborough Daily News* reproduced an account of how Disney was awarded his first military contract:

> At eight o'clock on the morning of Dec. 8, 1941, Walt Disney received a call from the Navy's Bureau of Aeronautics asking if he could turn out 20,000 feet of training film. "I'll turn out anything you want," said Walt. "Okay, you can start right away on aircraft identification pictures," was the reply. "But who is going to identify the aircraft for me?" asked Walt. "We'll have a man out there in a couple of hours," said the Navy. Walt Disney—and his studio—had been drafted.[207]

Just over two weeks later the *Greley Daily Tribune* ran the following story:

> Twenty-one single reel films to be used in training Navy outlooks, observers, and pilots to recognize instantly the nationality of warships and aircraft will be made by Walt Disney Productions.
>
> Lieut. J.C. Hutchinson, who will supervise the productions, said they not only will include actual photographs, but models and animated cartoons.[208]

Ub Iwerks was the most prolific animator to work at Disney's early Hyperion Avenue studio. Iwerks owned a one-third share of the fledgling company when he severed his ties with Disney in February 1930. Iwerks returned to the Disney Studio in 1940, shortly after his own studio failed. Because of his fascination with aviation, the history of flight, and model airplanes, Iwerks was assigned the task of writing most of the scripts for the WEFT series.

The WEFT contract marked the beginning of the Navy's wartime association with the Studio. On June 1, 1941 Walt Disney sent a letter to his contact, Chester Feitel, in Washington:

> Check and see that we get the highest priority on Navy Contracts. We are currently rated "A-one-D". We need highest priority possible if we are to push Navy work with speed requested of us.[209]

On July 3, 1941, Feitel wrote Disney's licensing rep Kay Kamen

---

207 *Middlesborough Daily News*, December 21, 1945.

208 *Greeley Daily Tribune*, December 24, 1941.

209 Courtesy the Paul Anderson archives.

indicating he was confident the Studio was going to be assigned a better priority rating on Navy contracts than the one Disney currently held:

> It looks like we are going to get another contract for a new series of WEFT identification films. This will enable us to keep our Studio unit going through 1943. We checked this with Commander Fraser who is working on the matter.[210]

Because of his valuable assistance in securing government contracts, and because of his many contacts in Washington, D.C., Disney wrote to Feitel on July 15, 1942, informing him he was trying to get him a deferment to work at the Studio. Feitel was officially hired by the company on September 21, 1942, although he worked for the company in some capacity before that date. Regardless, Disney's request for a deferral was denied—Feitel left the company on March 27, 1943, but returned as a Sales Consultant in December 1949, just two months after Kamen's untimely death in a plane crash.

An article in the February 1942 edition of the *Fitchburg Sentinel* gave an indication of the transformation that was now taking place at the Studio. The Walt Disney Studios was now making the transition to a war plant. Entertainment films would soon be supplanted by the production of government material:

> How the haunts of Mickey Mouse have changed! In Walt Disney's inking and painting department...that gave life to the most famous of animated cartoons, work now revolves around the unhumorous subject of spotting airplanes.[211]

By the spring of 1942, the Studio was fully involved with the production of films for the government. The March 1942 edition of *Flying* reported:

> Staff members have gone up in blimps to photograph submarines; they've haunted airports and air bases; they've ridden on aircraft carriers; they've gone aloft on simulated bombing missions; and they've flown in the fastest of planes...the Disney technique has advanced from the straight animated cartoon to productions involving cartoon characters, animated graphs and charts, and live characters.

On September 9, 1942, Kay Kamen wrote to Walt Disney regarding the Navy films being produced at the Studio:

---

210 Courtesy the Paul Anderson archives.

211 *Fitchburg Sentinel*, February 17, 1942. The article has a photograph of one woman holding a piece of art with airplanes on it, as Hutchinson and two other ladies looked on.

> In talking with Lt. Orchard and Hutchinson, it was indicated that the Navy intends that Disney shall produce nothing but Navy films in addition to our theatrical films—in other words, they expected to give you more commitments that would take up practically all of your production facilities.
>
> I met with Hutchinson…and told him that we were planning to do some things for the Treasury and that we were also planning to produce "Service and Maintenance" films for the aircraft and similar war industries. He said that was okay as they were extremely important too, but what he and Orchard were thinking of when they talked about getting all the Disney facilities for the Navy was that it was not necessary for us to make pictures like the Agriculture picture [*Food Will Win the War*].[212]

In 1942, the Studio produced a series of films for the Navy detailing aircraft production. Disney camera crews traveled to defense plants across the United States to gather footage:

> The first three months were spent in aircraft plants from Seattle to San Diego preparing the shooting script. The camera crew then followed and shot approximately 70,000 feet of aircraft production methods. The amount of footage, while impressive, is not as remarkable as the job the boys did in photographing the material in the midst of war production turmoil. It meant aircraft plant clearance for each Disney representative, cooperation of plant management, conferences with aeronautical engineers, and getting the job done with a minimum of interference with aircraft production.[213]

The July 13, 1943, issue of *Look* magazine reported on Disney's involvement with producing films for the military:

> War boots on, Walt Disney is now devoting much time to Army and Navy work; his bright down-to-fact film treatments have simplified many training problems of the armed forces.

By 1943, the last of the Navy's aircraft production films had been completed. Some of the titles included: *Aircraft Riveting, Bending and Curving, Blanking and Punching, Forming Methods, Heat Treating, Lofting and Layouts, Mock-up and Tooling,* and *Template Reproduction.*

Rules of the Nautical Road was completed for the Navy in 1943. The film was adapted from a book written by university professor Raymond Farwell. The topic dealt with traffic rules for ships. Because nautical rules are based on the position of red and green lights, which

---

212 Courtesy the Paul Anderson archives.

213 *Dispatch from Disney's*, 1943 Disney Studio employee newsletter.

distinguished port from starboard, most of this series was produced in color.

Rules of the Nautical Road began with a review of a 1917 naval disaster, which saw a freighter and military supply ship collide in the Canadian port of Halifax. The resulting explosion killed over 2,000 and injured over 20,000. The film had 26 parts and used a sliding cel technique, whereby the image from a single drawing was transferred to a cel, and this single cel was filmed moving across the associated background. This technique eliminated the cost of creating hundreds of drawings and their related celluloids. To stay within the Navy's budget, special effects, such as the ship's wake, were omitted.

Because of a housing shortage in the Burbank area, Farwell moved into Walt Disney's office suite, where he not only slept but also did his cooking and laundry. Farwell lived at the Studio for six months, until an apartment was found for him.[214]

Another important series of films completed for the Navy dealt with meteorology for pilots. Disney artists recreated the realistic weather conditions pilots would face in the field. Work on the series began in 1942 and finished two years later. Eleven films were produced under the general title "Aerology for Navy". Titles in the series included: *Icing Conditions*, *The Cold Front*, *The Warm Front*, and *Fog and Thunderstorms*.

On August 22, 1943, the *New York Herald Tribune* reported:

> The lucid and comprehensive style in which these films have been made accounts for the way they have been welcomed so enthusiastically by both Navy trainees and instructors.
>
> The artists at the Disney Studio in Burbank are literally cross-sectioning and tearing apart the various elements of the weather for education of flyers, making this film a visual textbook of the future for airmen the world over.
>
> Produced for the Naval Bureau of Aeronautics, the film will detail the inside workings of thunder, lightning storms, fog, ice, and in fact every element other than mechanical a pilot encounters after taking his ship off the ground. The study encompasses the experiences of more than one hundred of the greatest Allied Nations flyers, plus well-known civilian and commercial pilots, together with all accepted textbooks on this subject.

---

214 Shale, Richard. *Donald Duck Joins Up*. Diss. U. of Michigan, 1982. Ann Arbor: UMI. p.37.

At the war's conclusion, no fewer than 33 films had been commissioned for the Navy, making this branch of the armed forces the Studio's largest customer.

Besides the Navy, Studio artists produced training films for other branches of the military. A wide range of topics was eventually covered including torpedo tactics, chemical warfare, precision bombing, aircraft carrier landing techniques, electronics, camouflage, and glider training. Several complex and technical subjects were also covered by Disney artists, including the operation of the electronic supercharger, gyroscopic creep and precession in torpedoes, and the theory of simplex and phantom circuits.

Disney artists received clearance to work on several top-secret government projects including two titled *Fixed Gunnery and Fighter Tactics* and *High Level Precision Bombing*. As work began on these and other highly sensitive subjects, security at the Studio was tightened, and entry to units working on these films was severely restricted.

Besides the Navy films, Ub Iwerks also worked as a director on *Stop That Tank: The BOYS Anti-Tank Rifle*, a training film produced in 1942 at the request of the National Film Board of Canada. A July 28, 1941, letter to Walt Disney from John Grierson, the Commissioner of the National Film Board of Canada, indicated the Canadian training film would run 1,000 feet and have a budget of approximately $15,000.

Under the wordy headline, "Walt Disney Training Films Prove Final Banishment of Influences of the Disciples of Old-Style Doctrines and Instructional Methods", the *Lethbridge Herald* announced the collaboration:

> The high-water mark of modernity in Canadian training methods will be, of course, the arrival of the first film of a series from the Walt Disney studios. Even to have suggested such a startling innovation to any army a few years ago, would have required an exceedingly daring and strong-minded individual. It would have been considered as grotesque as the Disney characters which will shortly be cavorting in Canadian Army lecture huts—and teaching the fine points of new weapons and the tricks of new tactics while they do.
>
> The first Disney film to be included in the equipment of Canadian Army training centres discloses many methods of stopping tanks using guerilla tactics, and deals particularly with the proficiency and usefulness of the new [BOYS] anti-tank rifle, swiftly coming into general use. Some few hundred feet of film give detailed instruction on the care and handling of the rifle's mechanism, interspersed with

riotous scenes of Disney "tanks" in great pain as they are drilled in ambush. There is an [sic] hilarious medley of fun and information on tank-sniping. Animated cartoons disclose a tank's most sensitive and vulnerable joints and a score of "surprise" methods and ruses are revealed, whereby an actual panzerkraftwagen [sic] can be stopped.

Stop That Tank! also has value in disproving the fallacy that the new Canadian anti-tank rifle "kicked like a mule" and "couldn't stop a shadow". Army rumor had maligned the weapon, which has an astonishingly gentle recoil, and in facing tank attack can be both deadly and an enormous comfort to the defence.

The story of how the General Staff adopted animated cartoons to assist the training program alone reveals the new Canadian military mentality. An ex-Disney cartoonist, an Englishman who had been living in the United States, turned up in the ranks of the artillery in Petawawa. He had passed his elementary military tests and had already been spotted as unusually gifted. He had been selected for the artillery survey section when it was suggested that his talents could undoubtedly be utilized by headquarters because "[t]hey have imagination there now".

Imagination was immediately found, and the above comment substantiated. The great worth of films of that type in dramatizing army instruction was seen at once, and Sergeant Pete Page is now in Hollywood as Canadian military technical advisor on the cartoon films of the Disney series.[215]

This instructional film dealt with the operation of the BOYS MK 1 anti-tank gun, which had suffered a poor reputation following the disastrous battle at Dunkirk, France. Canadian military officials wanted to bolster the gun's reputation and called on Walt Disney to help. The short contained three minutes of humorous animation and 18 minutes of detailed instruction.

Stop That Tank contained one of the Studio's first caricatures of Hitler. The film's animated sequences were drawn by animators Ward Kimball and Fred Moore. The two artists injected their own brand of humor into the film: Canadian soldiers concealed in haystacks, a barnyard, and even a latrine fired the anti-gun at Hitler as he rode around the battlefield in a tank.

Besides directing the film, Ub put his knowledge of guns to use, animating the sequences involving the instructional portions of the film. These educational sequences contained detailed cross-sections,

---

215 *Lethbridge Herald*, November 1, 1941, author's collection.

microscopic, and exploded views explaining the gun's technical mechanisms. Ub "drew each mechanism of the MK 1 in minute detail, from the unusual recoil reducing chamber at the end of the barrel to the adjustable sights".[216]

The "x-ray animation" used in the training film could show the insides of weapons where no camera could penetrate—showing these detailed views would have been impossible using conventional live-action photography.

Because no one at the Studio had ever seen an anti-tank gun before, special arrangements were made to have one of the weapons shipped to Los Angeles so the animators would have a real model to refer to.

Since the production of military training films was a new venture, cost overruns were common and several government contracts had to be rewritten. The Studio lost money on several films including *Protection Against Chemical Warfare* and *Aircraft Carrier Mat Approaches and Landings*. Carl Nater, the Studio's Production Coordinator for military films said:

> This changeover in production at the Walt Disney Studio has brought a set of problems that is not frequently encountered in the average war plant. There was no radical changeover of heavy machinery or the installation of new dies and presses. It was a mental rather than physical adjustment. Studio personnel accustomed to working two to three years on one picture were suddenly requisitioned to produce a film in four to six months. The financial departments, accustomed to budgeting pictures for three-quarters-of-a-million to one-and-one-half-million dollars found themselves piecing out 12,000 and 15,000 dollars for production budgets.[217]

As military and government contracts were signed, several "key" departments at the Studio strained under the pressures of increased production and pressing deadlines. The Camera Department now worked 20 hours per day, six days a week. The four so-called "leftover" hours were used for servicing and maintaining the camera equipment.[218]

Units that worked on black-and-white films began using their own inkers and painters to help ease the bottleneck in the Ink and

---

216 Iwerks, Leslie, *The Hand Behind the Mouse*. Disney Editions, NY. p. 156.

217 Nater, Carl. *Walt Disney Studio—A War Plant*. Presented October 21, 1943.

218 *Dispatch from Disney's*, 1943 Disney Studio employee newsletter.

Paint Department. Artists in the Layout Department now dealt with complex technical and mechanical problems, while those in Special Effects had to find ways of combining live-action and animated photography. Carl Nater explained:

> Our Layout Department...found itself dealing with difficult and highly mechanical problems. In one particular instance, a squadron of 12 torpedo planes was making passes at an enemy ship. Each plane was moving independently of the others and it became necessary to make a separate camera exposure for each element in the scene—one for the ship, one for the wake of the ship, one for each plane, etc. On approximately 1,000 feet of animation we shot 18 exposures for each scene, thus actually increasing the shooting time for each scene 18 fold, plus the normal margin of error on retakes. We figured we had quite a headache.
>
> Before our Camera Department began with each of the 18 exposure scenes, layout men had to design the camera operation. Layout men... suddenly found themselves using slide rules to figure out camera moves calibrated at times to 1/100th of an inch.
>
> Our Special Effects Camera Department had to determine methods of achieving a marriage between real photography, animation photography, three-dimensional model work, and any other technique necessary to solve a given problem.[219]

Necessity soon forced many of the units to become intact within themselves, containing all the elements of production. Departments such as Story, Direction, Layout, Animation, Background, Checking, and Inking and Painting were often contained in a single unit. On many occasions, the only time a scene left a particular unit was when the sequence went to the Camera Department.[220]

The Studio's 1942 *Layout Manual* detailed the different methods production staff used to reduce the cost of production. There can be no doubt this manual was created as a reference guide for staff who were about to embark on a new direction—the production of films for the military. The profit margins on military films were small or non-existent, and the Studio needed to ensure staff produced the films under budget and on time. In the manual's forward Walt Disney wrote:

> In time of war, many things, like flying and medical science, make terrific strides. So it is with our own business, which, unfortunately,

---

219 Nater, Carl. *Walt Disney Studio—A War Plant*. Presented October 21, 1943.

220 *Dispatch from Disney's*, 1943 Disney Studio employee newsletter.

> is still saddled with the misnomer "cartoon". In the last year or so we've done comparatively little "cartoon" work, but a great deal of animated picture work.
>
> The technique of our business has changed. Our horizons have rolled back almost to infinity regarding the educational material we handle. [D]uring this transition period, [so] many new methods have been created to solve new problems that there is a danger many of these may become forgotten. Many simple, inexpensive ways have been evolved to achieve effects, which formerly were done by animation. In some instances the newer methods have proved even more effective visually. To preserve these in reference form is the purpose of this manual, for, to be of worthwhile value, a creative man must have at his fingertips every atom of information, past and present, which pertains to his job, and it's impossible for most of us to be that good without something to refer to.
>
> Shrewd, creative men will use these techniques as foundations for newer and more effective methods of creating the animated picture of the future.[221]

The manual looked at all facets of production: cameras, sliding cels, three-dimensional models, live action, film processes, exposure sheets, the process lab, rotoscope, stock material, and layout, and is a wealth of information pertaining to the Studio's production of war films. The manual made reference to cost-cutting measures in the preface:

> The examples in this manual are given merely to illustrate certain use of the facilities which we have at our command. With judgment, imagination, and ingenuity, these principles can be adapted to innumerable uses.
>
> In recording and illustrating them, it was not the intention to suggest that these are the only ways to get a particular effect; nor, even, in the event two versions are given, that one is better than the other. Either, or both, may be uneconomical, if not in layout man's time—then, perhaps in checking, ink and paint, or camera time—and ALL functions and their costs must be considered by the layout man. Saving his own time by laying out a scene that calls for a highly complicated end, and consequently costly shooting, is not economy. Nor is it good economy to put in large amounts of his own time in order to achieve a trick effect in an unimportant scene. Consider: are ripples on that water necessary? Must those trees really animate? Do they add to the

---

221 1942 *Layout Manual.* Walt Disney Studio. Courtesy the Paul Anderson archives.

PURPOSE of the scene? Can a sliding cel take the place of animation? Will it be more economical in checking and shooting time to use the 11-Field camera in place of the Multiplane Circular Disc?

Cost-Per-Foot [CPF] is a horrid phrase but it's got to be put up with, like hot spells and taxes. The suggestions in this manual should help keep old man CPF where he belongs—and still maintain the Disney quality which is our most vital asset.[222]

One way to cut costs was to minimize the use of animation. Several of the more interesting shortcuts detailed in the manual eliminated the need for animated sequences by substituting sliding cels, pivot cels, and three-dimensional models. The manual also gave an indication as to some of the complex layout problems artists had to contend with.

Training films allowed the military to show the same film with the same information to men in units scattered around the globe. Among the many training films produced at the Studio for the military was a series created with the assistance and knowledge of a bonafide war hero: James "Jimmy" Thach was the Squadron Commander of the "Fighting Three", which held the record of shooting down 54 Japanese planes against the loss of only three pilots, all in just two days of combat. Thach was one of many "war heroes" who came from active combat missions to advise Studio artists on the fine art of warfare.

A short essay written by Lt. Cmdr Thach regarding the series of films he was working on appeared in the Disney employee newsletter *Dispatch from Disney's*:

A Chinese philosopher once said: "One picture is worth a thousand words." If the same ratio were used in evaluating the Animated Training Films, the adage would become: "One 2000-foot movie is worth a million words." With the addition of sound, the ratio is even greater.

The Navy's Bureau of Aeronautics, realizing the value of the training film as an educational medium, has over 1,400 subjects in production. One of the more important of these, "The Jacksonville Project", has been assigned to Walt Disney Productions.

The value of this training film can be compared with the importance of the fighter pilot to modern warfare. The fighter plane, as a weapon, must insure successful offensive air operations and effect defenses against attacking enemy planes.

---

222   1942 *Layout Manual*. Walt Disney Studio. Courtesy the Paul Anderson archives.

> The Navy knows that control of the air depends upon the number and quality of the fighters put into the skies. The rapid progress of war makes it necessary to turn out fighter pilots quickly and efficiently. This is a big job for instructors, but it would be an even greater problem without the use of Training Films.
>
> Our bases are scattered throughout the world, but the use of Training Films brings the same information to each base. This makes it possible to organize teaching facts, so that every pilot will be given the benefit of intelligent instruction.
>
> These Animated Training Films are not based upon theories of armchair combatants, but contain factual information gained from experience in battle. They convey proper information to the student flyer through the use of simulated battle action. The enemy is presented to the student just as he will see him in actual combat. The value of this is obvious, for the student sees the conditions he is going to face, gets the feel of battle, but at the same time has the opportunity to study every possible method of combating the most complex problem presented. Training Films break down airplane maneuvers, open up enemy tactics, so that they can be carefully analyzed. Detail that could not otherwise be detected are brought fully into light.
>
> In the future, animated films will play an important part in our peacetime educational program. But to win this peace we must first send more and better fighter pilots into the sky. Walt Disney Productions' animated training film, "Jacksonville Project", will materially assist fighter pilots to get this job done, quickly and efficiently.[223]

The March 1945 edition of *Flying* reported:

> A veteran of Pacific fighting [has] returned to the United States. He had been at the head of one of the fightingest [sic] of Navy Squadrons. His name [is] J.C. Jimmy Thach, a Navy commander credited with training the famed "Butch" O'Hare and other aces and with the development of the "Thach weave", a new fighter technique. Enlisting Thach's experience, the Navy ordered 10 pictures on fighter tactics. The completed job was to run from 15,000 to 20,000 feet and to cover every phase of fighting.

The films were collectively known as the "Jacksonville Project, Production 2648". The official name for the series was "FIGHTER COMBAT TACTICS, MN84 A-I". Two films in the series were produced in color: MN84F and MN84G. Only six of the 10 films are currently known to exist. The list of fighter combat training films written and directed by Thach covered a range of topics:

---

223 *Dispatch from Disney's*. 1943 Disney Studio employee newsletter.

- MN84A: *Use of the Illuminated Gun Sight in Mixed Gunnery*
- MN84B: *Fundamental Gunnery Approaches*
- MN84C: *Snoopers and How to Blast 'em*
- MN84D: *Don't Kill Your Friends*
- MN84E: *Group Tactics Against Enemy Bombers*
- MN84F: *Offensive Tactics Against Enemy Fighters*
- MN84G: *Defensive Tactics Against Enemy Fighters*
- MN84H: *Escort Doctrine*
- MN84I: *Combat Patrol*
- MN84J: *Conclusion and Summary*

Ub Iwerks was the executive producer of the series. Dan Keefe directed the live-action segments involving Thach, who was at the Studio for the filming of at least one segment in January 1943 (this sequence was shot in a schoolroom setting created on one of the Studio sound stages). Animators on the series were Jack Atwood, Bob Carlson, Jim Davis, John Hench, Bill Layne, Lance Nolley, Art Scott, and Harvey Toombs.[224]

A Studio inter-office communication sent from Carl Nater, the Studio's production coordinator for military films, to Thach on July 21, 1943, reported the cost for three of the films in the Thach series:

> We have completed and delivered and have our final costs on three subjects in your series. Although the financial aspect is not your primary concern, we thought you might be interested in knowing the actual costs incurred on the first three subjects we have done.
>
> To get started on this series and receive our Letter of Intent we had to estimate what we thought they would run. It has been very gratifying to us to discover that the first three pictures have all been under the figures we submitted to the Bureau, and which they in turn authorized.[225]

The three films mentioned in the memo were *Use of the Illuminated Sight in Mixed Gunnery, Fundamental Gunnery Approaches;* and *Offensive Tactics Against Enemy Fighters*. The letter of intent estimated the films would cost $155,780.78. Actual production costs were $127,565.60,

---

[224] Email between Disney Archivist Dave Smith and Wayne Weiss, courtesy Wayne Weiss.

[225] Courtesy Wayne Weiss.

meaning these three films were under budget with a savings of $28,215.18.

The August 9, 1943, *Los Angeles Times* reported in part:

> Motion pictures are playing an important role in the victories being scored over the Japs in the air above the South Pacific. This was disclosed yesterday when Comdr. John S. (Jimmy) Thatch [sic] staff gunnery officer at the Navy base in Jacksonville Fla., said good-bye to the staff at the Walt Disney Studio, where he has been stationed nearly a year, since his return from a combat zone, supervising and narrating a series of training pictures for the Navy on fighter combat tactics.
>
> An advocate of fundamentals, he claims the "Fighting Three" won their battles before they left the carrier flight deck. The Navy Flyer-hero, considered one of the best strategy combat pilots in the world, stressed the high importance of training films in preparing our pilots for victorious aerial combat.

During the war, a cartoon character named Dilbert Groundloop was created by Captain Austin Doyle, USN, and Lt. Cdr. Robert Osborn, USNR. Dilbert came to symbolize the newly minted aviator who thought he knew everything. Osborn sent Thach an undated note written on Jacksonville Naval Air Station stationery congratulating him on one of the films in the series. The memo read: "Dilbert couldn't be better! And you fitted him in so smoothly. The film impresses me very much because it is clear and the images stick. Congratulations!"[226]

The Walt Disney Company owns no material related to the production of the films in this series. Being "confidential" in nature, all of the scripts, pre- and post-production art, and unused film were returned to the Navy.

As an interesting side-note, Thach was a critic of another wartime strategic initiative undertaken at the Disney Studio, namely Alexander de Seversky's theory of building long-range, multi-gun bombers. Seversky published his theory in book form under the title *Victory Through Air Power*. An article in the September 30, 1942, *Port Arthur News* reported in part:

> Lieut. Comdr. John S. Thach, a hero of the Battle of Midway asserted... the United States could "cut a path across the Pacific to Japan", with a well-balanced fleet spear-headed by aircraft carriers. "There is a popular theory that we can win this war in an easy way, that we can build a fleet of colossal bombers that will fly thousands of miles to

---

226 Courtesy Wayne Weiss.

bomb the enemy and return to wait for a message of surrender." On the contrary, Thach said the nation would have to win the war "the hard way, by sending carrier-based fighters and dive-bombers to gain and hold control of the air while occupation forces move in under such protection. With a properly balanced force (naval) we can cut a patch across the Pacific to Japan itself and cut it quickly, and make it stick."

The subject of Thach's new fighter tactic was also the subject of episode 110 of the CBS radio program *The First Line*, which was broadcast on March, 1944. Page one of a 25-page radio script lists Thach as a participant in the radio show, in which he discusses his new tactic without giving away top secret information.

As work on war-related films expanded at the Studio, the production of animated shorts fell drastically. This point was referenced in a pamphlet titled, *Motion Picture Industry in War-Time America 1943-1944*:

> That is why the public saw so few Disney shorts last year [1942]. Only nine were made against the normal annual output of 18 to 21. Educational and psychological films, along with the training pictures for Army and Navy, put Donald Duck and his pals in the background.[227]

In a February 1943 *New York Times* interview, Walt Disney commented:

> The war has taught us that people who won't read a book will look at a film. It's shown that you can take knowledge out of a dusty tome somewhere and wrap up the effort of many teachers in one can of film. You can show that film to any audience and 20 minutes later it has learned something—a new idea or an item of important information—and it at least has stimulated further interest in study.

This was an important concept, as Disney's training films were viewed by thousands of military personnel worldwide. Walt summed up the Studio's role in producing propaganda and training films when he wrote the following for a 1945 Princeton University publication:

> The pressure of the last four years has forced us all to scrutinize and put on trial the things we do, the way we do them, and the reason we do them.
>
> Under the urgency of our national crisis, we have been compelled to reject any move that had no purpose, any method that was cumbersome or slow, and to cast off any means that would not guarantee results. The watchword was to retain whatever was efficient...and to

---

227 Author's collection.

cast off whatever was not effective. The motion picture took a leading part in all phases of wartime education—propaganda and information as well as training. It explained and supported ideas, it showed with impartial fidelity the course of events, it made hidden phenomena visible, and it demonstrated the way to control them.[228]

Propaganda and Training Film Collectibles

PTF001 *Victory Through Air Power* press book (supplement). 1943. 14 x 24
This 17-page press book pictures all of the posters, lobby cards, and still photographs that could be ordered to promote the film. The publication also contains sample ads, promotional ideas, and a sample copy of a four-page newspaper comic book supplement.

PTF002 *Victory Through Air Power* poster. 1943. 27 x 40
Searchlights scan the sky and form the letter "V" for victory.

PTF003 *Victory Through Air Power* map. April 1943. 9 x 6 (envelope)
This envelope contains a large fold-out sheet featuring a color map of the world, which recipients could use to chart the course of the war. Info on the backside includes profiles of Allied and Axis planes, images of many combat and rank insignia, and details about the different materials used in the manufacture of aircraft.

PTF004 *Playthings*. June 1943.
Front cover features a Kay Kamen ad for *Victory Through Air Power*.

PTF005 *American Photography*. November 1943.
Front cover features an illustration from *Victory Through Air Power*.

PTF006 *Liberty*. July 31, 1943.
Front cover has a promotional illustration for *Victory Through Air Power*.

PTF007 *National Geographic*. November 1943.
This issue has a full-page ad for *Victory Through Air Power*. The illustration is based on the film's climactic ending that pitted the American eagle against the Japanese octopus.

---

[228] *The Public Opinion Quarterly*. Summer 1945, School of Public Affairs, Princeton University.

PTF008 *National Geographic.* January 1944.
This issue has a full-page ad for *Victory Through Air Power*. The illustration is based on the film's premise that the way to win the war was to strike at the heart of the enemy's industrial heartland.

PTF009 *Sunset.* January 1944.
Back cover has an ad for *Victory Through Air Power*. The illustration shows the development of bombs. The ad was sponsored by Adel, a wartime plane manufacturer.

PTF010 Unknown magazine. Circa 1943.
Full-page *Victory Through Air Power* ad. The illustration shows that the first flight carried out by the Wright brothers could have been made within the wingspan of a modern bomber.

PTF011 *Good Housekeeping.* July 1943.
This page was titled "Walt Disney's Pluto Wins a Victory Through Air Power". With the help of Mickey's two nephews and a kite, Pluto swoops down and steals a bone from his bulldog nemesis.

PTF012 *Der Fuehrer's Face* poster. 1943. 27 x 40
Donald throws an over-ripe tomato at Hitler's face.

PTF013 *Der Fuehrer's Face* 78 rpm Bluebird record. Circa 1942.
The music on this disc was recorded by Spike Jones and His City Slickers. Bluebird label #11586. The flip side has a song titled "Gee But It's Great to Meet a Friend".

PTF014 *Film Weekly*, August 5, 1943.
Full-page ad for *Der Fuehrer's Face*.

PTF015 *Der Fuehrer's Face* sheet music. Circa 1942.
Southern Music Company. The cover shows Donald Duck pitching a tomato at Hitler's face. The first printing contained a reference to the film's original title: *Donald Duck in Nutzi Land*. This reference was deleted in future printings. Disney artist Ward Kimball is believed to have created this artwork.

PTF016 *Song of the Eagle* sheet music. 1943. 9 x 12
Forster Music Publishers Inc. The front cover pictures an American eagle swooping down on a menacing Japanese octopus, and is marked: "From the Walt Disney motion picture *Victory Through Air Power*."

PTF017 *The Victory March* sheet music. 1942. 9 x 12
Southern Music Company. The front cover features over two dozen Disney characters marching with several signs and placards promoting war savings.

The identical illustration was also used on the front cover of the book of the same name, which was published by Random House in 1942. The sheet music is marked: "The Victory March song was written to aid the U.S. Treasury Department in the War Savings Campaign."

PTF018 *Yankee Doodle Spirit* sheet music. 1942. 9 x 12

Southern Music Company. The front cover pictures tanks and airplanes set against a background that looks like an American flag. An inset illustration features Donald Duck with American flags as pupils. The front cover is marked: "From the Walt Disney Motion Picture *The New Spirit* produced for the U.S. Treasury Department."

PTF019 " Hop on Your Pogo Stick" sheet music. 1943. 9 x 12

Southern Music Company. The front cover features Goofy bouncing on a pogo stick. This arrangement was used in the Goofy short cartoon *Victory Vehicles*. In the short, Goofy demonstrates various modes of transportation inspired by the war restrictions on automobile use.

PTF020 *Walt Disney Songs*. 1943. 9 x 12

This song folio contains music from six of Disney's wartime features. The format for each arrangement includes a photo of the sheet music or book cover the song was from, the song's lyrics, musical arrangement, and black-and-white promotional photographs from the book or movie.

PTF021 *Song Hits*. Volume 6, Number 6. November 1942.

This magazine published popular song hits of the day. This issue contains a two-page article titled: "Donald Duck—He works for Uncle Sam." The article lists the lyrics for three Donald Duck war-era cartoons: The Yankee Doodle Spirit from *The New Spirit*; Brazil from *Saludos Amigos*; and *Der Fuehrer's Face* from the film of the same name. Part of the related article's text reads: "Donald Duck, one of Hollywood's best loved personalities, is no slacker. He is doing as much for the war effort, if not more, than any other Disney character."

PTF022 *The New Spirit*, poster. 1942. 27 x 40

One-sheet theatre poster. This poster's illustration pictured a happy Donald Duck standing with his hands up by his chest. The poster advertised the film as a "Special Attraction".

PTF023 *The Spirit of '43*, poster. 1943. 27 x 40

One-sheet theatre poster. Donald Duck looks up at a sign that reads: "Income Tax Bureau. Welcome." This film was the second tax film produced by the Studio for the Treasury Department.

Epilog: Postwar

> "We learned a great deal during the war years when we were making instruction and technological films in which abstract and obscure things had to be made plain and quickly and exactly applicable to the men in the military service."[229] —Walt Disney

World War II had a profound effect on Walt Disney's Studio. With few exceptions, all of Disney's feature-length animated productions produced between 1940 and 1945 performed poorly at the box office. The release of *Pinocchio* occurred five months after the outbreak of war and coincided almost exactly with the Studio's loss of the overseas market. *Fantasia* was panned by critics as an "arts" movie, and both *Bambi* and *The Reluctant Dragon* had limited success.

The war impacted the Studio's bottom line. The fiscal year ending September 27, 1941, saw a deficit of almost $800,000. The fiscal year ending October 3, 1942, saw a loss of $191,000. In 1943, the Studio turned a profit which reduced the deficit to $785,000 from a high of just over $1.2 million the previous year. The fiscal year ending September 30, 1944, saw a profit of $486,000, while net income for the fiscal year ending September 29, 1945,was $351,000. The 1945 Annual Report reported:

> A general lessening of the Government's needs for training films enabled your company to devote substantially all of its facilities to the production of entertainment product during the past year. Eighteen short subjects [compared to 14 the year previous] were completed and delivered for release...the major portion of the Company's operation was devoted to work on two full-length feature pictures, *Make Mine Music* and *Uncle Remus* [later renamed *Song of the South*].

The cost and time involved in producing a full-length feature were prohibitive in the post-war years, so the Studio released several films composed of short segments linked together. The first films released after the end of the war included *Make Mine Music*, *Fun and Fancy Free*, *Melody Time*, and *The Adventures of Ichabod and Mr. Toad*.

---

229 *Wisdom*, Volume 32, December 1959.

Because Walt Disney was unable to withdraw funds from England (to stimulate the post-war economy, English lawmakers decreed any monies earned in their country had to be reinvested there), the Studio produced several live-action films in that country. These films included *Treasure Island*, *The Story of Robin Hood*, *The Sword and the Rose*, and *Rob Roy the Highland Rogue*.

Through his involvement in training and educational films, Walt Disney became convinced there was a market for non-fiction shorts. The first such film to come out of the Studio was a so-called "Good Neighbor" travelogue titled *The Amazon Awakens*. This film was produced in 1944 and took viewers on a live-action tour of the Amazon River basin.

Continuing on the theme of live-action nature films, Disney began producing a series of what he called True-Life Adventures. The first film was released in 1949 under the title *Seal Island*. This film chronicled the lives of seals off Pribilof Island in Alaska. The short ran 27 minutes in length and was filmed entirely in color. When RKO, the Studio's distributor, expressed little interest in wanting to handle the film, Walt Disney rented the Crown Theater in Pasadena, California, to prove there was a market for his newest endeavor. The movie was a box office success and went on to win an Academy Award for best two-reel documentary.

The success of Seal Island led to the production of several additional True-Life Adventures. The series covered everything from life in the Everglades, deserts, and prairies, to lions, beavers, bears, and water birds. Walt Disney discovered there was money to be made in producing live-action films where the animal actors drew no salary. The *Living Desert* cost Disney $300,000 to make and grossed over four million dollars.[230]

In 1943, over 90 percent of the footage the Studio produced was done under government contract.[231] During June of 1943, the Studio shipped 34,899 feet of film, which represented an all-time monthly high.[232] The end of the war meant the end of government contracts

---

230 *Time*, December 27, 1954.

231 Shale, Richard. *Donald Duck Joins Up*. Diss. U. of Michigan, 1982. Ann Arbor: UMI. p. 24.

232 *Motion Picture Daily*, July 13, 1943.

that had sustained the Studio. With the war's conclusion, private corporations approached the Studio wanting industrial films. By the end of 1946, eleven such films had been produced for companies like Westinghouse and Texaco.

Walt Disney also began to look at television as a source of revenue waiting to be exploited. In the 1944 company annual report, Disney wrote:

> We have been working hard on our postwar plans. We have thought a lot about television...television will need the same basic kind of entertainment the public has always demanded.

World War II challenged the artistic and financial resources of Walt Disney's Studio, but the challenge was met head-on. As the war progressed, the Studio became a genuine war plant, and just as Lockheed and other industrial companies produced valuable war material, so too did the Disney Studio.

The war provided Walt Disney with a chance to experiment, at government cost, with new ways of producing live-action and educational films. And although the profit margin on government-sponsored films was small, these contracts kept the Studio in business at a time when there was the threat it would have to close due to the economics of closed markets. Walt Disney said it best when he stated:

> It's hard to say good things about a war, but this is a tremendous opportunity to show what our medium can do. The hell with the six percent we could have made on our government work. Not many people get a chance like this to help both their country and themselves.[233]

As the war came to a conclusion, Walt Disney penned an article for the 1945 *Hollywood Reporter, Annual Edition*:

> As the curtain drops, obliterating the fire of war which has been consuming Europe and the conflagration in the Orient is being brought under control, an exciting future of the world at peace can be contemplated.
>
> It will be a world in which the motion picture is bound to play an important role.
>
> The industry's war-time experience in entertainment, educational, training, and propaganda fields guarantees its position in the days to come.

---

233 *Fortune*, August 1942.

The question naturally arises—just what participation the motion picture will take in the mental and (educational) reconstruction of that portion of the world sadly in need of new ideals and concepts.

Is the industry prepared to accept the challenge which undoubtedly will be hurled at it, to help mould the conditions which will be aimed to prevent world war three?

Every assurance that it can fulfill any task for which it is impressed is given by its war-time production record.

There will be disagreement, logically, on the best means of obtaining post war aims, so that no one person can project the integrated thoughts of the industry.

Yes, in the main, I believe our leaders are fundamentally agreed that the war has opened a whole new world for motion pictures...a world as fascinating as that chartered by Magellan and Columbus.

Our own war-time experiences have led us to reevaluate the entire future of the animated motion picture, with its flexibility of technique and scope."

And only three years after the war had ended, Walt Disney was already dreaming his next dream. In a hastily scribbled note in May 1948, Walt Disney made mention of plans for a "Mickey Mouse Park", which would eventually become known as Disneyland.[234]

---

234 Gordon, Price, and Mumford, David. *Disneyland. The Nickel Tour.* Camphor Tree Publishing. 2000. Santa Clarita, CA. p.11.

Walt Disney's Comics and Stories

Several issues of *Walt Disney's Comics and Stories* comic books featured a wartime theme on their cover. Several issues also contained reproductions of Disney-designed combat insignia on the inside front and back covers. Issues with six insignia designs usually had those images featured on the inside front cover, while issues with 12 designs had the images split evenly between the inside front and back cover pages.

May 1942
Cover: Donald Duck, dressed like Uncle Sam, holds defense stamps.

July 1942
Cover: Donald Duck in uniform marches with Pluto.

October 1942
This issue featured 12 insignia designs.

November 1942
This issue featured 12 insignia designs.

December 1942
This issue featured six insignia designs.

January 1943
This issue featured 10 insignia designs. A war bond ad was inserted into the space where two additional designs would have been placed.

March 1943
Cover: Pillbox Number Four. Donald's nephews playing war. This issue featured 12 insignia designs.

April 1943
Cover: Donald Duck stands in line with several other non-descript cartoon characters. Donald's three nephews have tunneled under the line and two of them have popped-up in front of Donald. A window at the front of the line is staffed by an owl. A sign over his head reads: "Buy war bonds and stamps."

July 1943

Cover: Donald is flying an airplane that has been attacked by a Gremlin. Donald holds a flyswatter in his right hand. There are four other Gremlins in the background, waiting to swoop down on Donald.

August 1943

This issue featured six insignia designs.

October 1943

This issue featured 12 insignia designs.

December 1943

This issue featured six insignia designs.

January 1944

This issue featured six insignia designs.

February 1944

This issue featured 12 insignia designs.

March 1944

This issue featured 12 insignia designs. Beginning with this issue, insignia designs were no longer printed on the inside front cover—all insignia designs were now featured on the inside back cover.

April 1944

This issue featured 12 insignia designs.

May 1944

Cover: Donald sits on a fence dressed in a cat costume with two other cats. Two shoes have been thrown at the trio. Donald's cart is filled with shoes. The sign on his cart reads: "Second Hand Shoes. NO Ration Points." This issue featured 12 insignia designs.

June 1944

This issue featured 12 insignia designs.

July 1944

Cover: Donald Duck, dressed like Uncle Sam, holds a $100 savings bond in his left hand and tips his hat with his right hand. This issue featured 12 insignia designs.

August 1944

This issue featured 12 insignia designs.

September 1944
This issue featured 12 insignia designs.

October 1944
This issue featured 12 insignia designs.

November 1944
This issue featured 12 insignia designs.

April 1945
This issue featured 12 insignia designs.

July 1945
The front cover of this issue had a Revolutionary War scene. The flag Mickey was carrying is illustrated with a message from several of America's leading warriors urging citizens to purchase more War Bonds. The message carried the facsimile signatures of the following:

Admiral William Leahy: President Roosevelt's personal advisor and Chief of Staff from 1942 onwards. He presided over meetings with the Joint Chiefs of Staff and acted as liaison between the Joint Chiefs and the President.

Admiral Chester Nimitz: Commander in Chief of the U.S. Pacific Fleet from December 17, 1941, to the war's conclusion. Nimitz commanded all battles in the Central Pacific and was a proponent of amphibious assaults. His flagship was the USS *Missouri* on whose deck General MacArthur accepted the formal Japanese surrender.

Admiral Ernest King: appointed Commander-in-Chief of U.S. Naval Forces when America entered the war. In 1942, he assumed the duties of the Chief of Naval Operations. He was also a member of the Joint Chiefs of Staff.

General Douglas MacArthur: a pre-war advisor to the Philippines government. MacArthur was recalled to active duty in July 1941, and less than one year later he was forced to retreat from the Philippines after Japanese troops invaded the island. MacArthur believed in "island-hopping", whereby enemy troop concentrations were avoided in favor of attacking smaller islands crucial to the enemy's supply line.

General Dwight David Eisenhower: assumed control of the Army Operations Branch in Washington, D.C., in 1942. Eisenhower commanded the Allied assault of French North Africa and later became the Supreme Allied Commander in Europe in charge of the Normandy landings. Eisenhower was elected President of the United States in 1952.

September 1945

This issue had the continuing series *Mickey Mouse and the War Orphans*.

Note that a Gremlins serial started in issue 34 (1943) and ended with issue 41 (1944). Issue 34 also contained a cut-out paper doll of the Gremlin Gus, while issue 35 contained a cut-out paper doll of the female Gremlin Fifinella.

Print Media: Magazines and Newspapers

Air Trails, July 1942
Aeronca airplane ad pictures the company's Disney-designed insignia and the *Mr. Grasshopper Wins His Wings* booklet.

American Cinematographers, May 1944
This issue contains an in-depth article titled: "Walt Disney Studio—A War Plant."

The American Legion, February 1943
Illustration titled "So you won't run, eh Adolf!" Disney artist Hank Porter created this piece of art, which features the American Eagle, Russian Bear, Chinese Dragon, and British Lion circling caricatures of Hitler, Mussolini, and Hirohito. Also pictured are Mickey Mouse standing atop a tank, Donald Duck atop an artillery cannon, and Goofy who is polishing a rifle. This illustration represents one of the few depictions of the Axis leaders as drawn by Disney artists.

American Photography, November 1943
The cover of this issue pictures a scene from the "History of Aviation" sequence which appeared in the film *Victory Through Air Power*.

The American Magazine, February 1944
Victory Through Air Power advertisement featuring Donald Duck.

The Analog, December 1944
The back cover of this magazine pictures the Disney-designed Treasury Department "Bonds for Babies" war savings certificate. The illustration's caption reads: "The perfect gift for a child."

Army Transportation Journal, April 1945
The cover pictures the Disney-designed *Dumbo* Stork insignia for the Los Angeles Port of Embarkation. During the war, all American ports remained under civilian control. This magazine was a monthly publication of The Army Transport Association, a private organization founded in October 1944.

Aviation, June 1942
This issue contains a full-page advertisement for Beech Aircraft's Disney-designed Beechcraft Busy Bee.

The Beech Log, October 20, 1944
This copy of Beech Aircraft's in-house employee publication features a one-page story illustrated with five Jiminy Cricket illustrations.

Bombs Away, July 1, 1944
Weekly magazine produced for servicemen stationed at the Victorville California Army Air Field. The cover features the Air Field's Disney-designed Donald Duck emblem.

Boston Daily Globe, July 21, 1943
Contains a review for *Victory Through Air Power*.

Christian Science Monitor, July 19, 1943
Contains a review for *Victory Through Air Power*.

Colliers, February 20, 1943
Aeronca Grasshopper ad.

Commonwealth, August 6, 1943
Article titled "Winged Victory".

Coronet, September 1942
"Donald Duck Goes to War." This seven-page article contains illustrations from the Canadian anti-tank training film, and a colorful gatefold that pictures "Walt Disney's Volunteer Army" that was created by artist Hank Porter.

Coronet, November 1943
"Walt Disney's Chicken Little."

Cosmopolitan, December 1942
Gremlins story illustrated by Disney artists.

Cosmopolitan, January 1944
Victory Through Air Power ad.

Cue, July 17, 1943
Review for *Victory Through Air Power*.

Daily Worker, July 21, 1943
Negative review for *Victory Through Air Power*.

Detroit Free Press Magazine, January 9, 1944
Cover and two inside pages promote the Goofy short *Victory Vehicles*. The article contains five illustrations that show alternate modes of transportation.

Discovery, May 1946
"Disney's Health Films."

Elks Magazine, June 1945
Published by the Elks Grand Lodge, this issue has an article titled "Professor Disney". The article contains illustrations from Disney's hygiene film, *Defense Against Invasion*.

Esquire, March 1943
"Disney—Our Secret Weapon." This article mentions the Canadian BOYS MK 1 anti-tank gun training film.

Family Circle, January 21, 1944
Cover pictures the Disney-designed insignia of the Women's Airforce Service Pilots. The accompanying article, "They Fly That Men May Fight", gives background information on the WASP, an all-woman unit of pilots who flew aircraft from factories to debarkation points.

Film Daily, July 13, 1943
Victory Through Air Power.

Film and Radio Discussion Guide, October 1943
This issue has a *Victory Through Air Power* illustration on the cover and also contains an article on the film.

Flying, July 1943
Article on the 319th Women Airforce Service Pilots training detachment.

Flying, March 1945
"Walt Disney's Animated War." This five-page article is illustrated with four photographs that picture various military officers at the Studio either standing in front of storyboards or holding three-dimensional models.

Flying, April 1942
Cover pictures a Disney-designed insignia.

Flying, March 1945
This issue has an article titled: "Walt Disney's Animated War."

Journal of Living, September 1943
Pictures the three Disney-designed Food Distribution Administration "good nutrition" posters.

Fortune, April 1942
"Hollywood in Uniform." Article contains a picture of Donald Duck.

Fortune, July 1942
Beechcraft ad mentions the Disney designed "badge of merit", an incentive award presented to productive employees.

Fortune, August 1942
"Walt Disney—Great Teacher." This spectacular nine-page article features over 130 black-and-white and color pictures for Disney war films including *Education for Death, Chicken Little, Food Will Win the War, Defense Against Invasion,* and *Donald Duck in Nutziland*, which was later renamed *Der Fuehrer's Face*. This issue contains one of the best period articles on the Studio's war effort.

Fortune, February 1944
Victory Through Air Power ad featuring Donald Duck.

The Gosport, July 1940
Naval Air Station publication with Donald Duck on the cover.

Harpers, April 1942
Donald Duck article.

Horticulture Illustrated, March 15, 1945
Advertisement for the *Victory Garden Green Thumb* record book with Mickey Mouse illustration on the cover.

The Inland Printer, May 1944
Cover illustration from *Victory Through Air Power*.

Journal of the Society of Motion Picture Engineers, March 1944
"Walt Disney Studio—A War Plant." This article was written by Studio staff member Carl Nater and was originally presented at the Engineer's Technical Conference in Hollywood, California, October 21, 1943.

Knots 'N Fathoms, November 1944
Cover depicts a saluting duck insignia. This magazine was published and distributed at the graduating ceremony of the University of Colorado Naval Reserve Officer Training Corps.

Leatherneck, July 1943
Cover depicts the head of a Marine bulldog drawn by Disney artist Hank Porter. The dog wears a white cap with Marine Corps insignia. The inside two-page article pictures 10 Disney Marine Corps insignia.

Liberty, October 19, 1940
Cover pictures Donald Duck driving his jalopy, which is adorned with American patriotic symbols. An eagle with two U.S. flags in its mouth is tied to the top of the radiator. Just 14 months after this magazine was published, the might of the eagle was unleashed as America was drawn into another world war.

Liberty, March 14, 1942
Cover pictures Mickey Mouse, Donald Duck, Pluto, Timothy Mouse, and Pluto filling out an income tax form. Mickey lists Hollywood as his home and Walt Disney as a dependent. The editorial page has a brief article on the "not a buck for Donald Duck" campaign being waged on Capitol Hill.

Liberty, July 31, 1943
Cover and accompanying page two article titled "Victory Through Air Power". The article is illustrated with 14 storyboard-type drawings.

Life, October 28, 1940
Two-page article on naval aviation insignia. Several were designed by Disney artists.

Life, May 26, 1941
Three-page article: "Speaking of Pictures, Disney Designs Army and Navy Insignia."

Life, March 16, 1942
The New Spirit—Disney's Tax Film. Three-page article featured one page of storyboards with Donald Duck. The other two pages pictured color pastel storyboards of inanimate objects brought to life in the film.

Life, August 24, 1942
This issue contained a one-page Book of the Month Club ad for the book *Victory Through Air Power*.

Life, August 31, 1942
"Walt Disney Goes to War." This 10-page article featured artwork from several Disney war films including *Stop That Tank, Aerology for Navy, Reason and Emotion,* and *Rules of the Nautical Road.*

***Life**, September 7, 1942*
Article titled "Speaking of Pictures...This is Scrap" contains a photograph of Walt Disney about to smash one of his ornamental lawn deer with a sledgehammer. Disney was promoting a scrap metal drive.

***Life**, September 21, 1942*
One-page Book-of-the-Month Club ad for *Victory Through Air Power*.

***Life**, November 2, 1942*
Three-page article titled "Disney's Song 'Der Fuehrer's Face' Razzes Nazis".

***Life**, December 14, 1942*
A Donald Duck insignia is featured on the nose of a plane.

***Life**, January 11, 1943*
One-page ad featuring the Disney-designed Aeronca insignia.

***Life**, February 1, 1943*
Three-page article examining *Education for Death*.

***Life**, May 31, 1943*
This issue contains a full-page Gremlins Lifesavers ad.

***Life**, July 19, 1943*
This issue contained a three-page article titled "*Victory Through Air Power*— Walt Disney Transforms Seversky's Book". This issue also contained a nine-page essay on the Women's Airforce Service Pilots. One photo showed a WASP pilot wearing a Fifinella patch.

***Look**, December 3, 1940*
Three-page article on *Fantasia*.

***Look**, March 10, 1942*
Four-page article titled "Donald Duck Pays His Income Tax".

***Look**, August 25, 1942*
Two-page article that examines the film *Food Will Win the War*.

***Look**, June 1, 1943*
One-page Gremlin Lifesavers ad.

***Look**, July 13, 1943*
Two-page article titled "Walt Disney Envisions Victory Through Air Power".

***Look**, April 17, 1945*
Five-page article titled "Walt Disney—Teacher For Tomorrow".

The Maintenance Engineer, January 1945
Cover pictures the unit's Disney-designed insignia: Lampwick from *Pinocchio*.

Motion Picture Daily, July 7, 1943
Review for *Victory Through Air Power*.

Motion Picture Industry in War-Time America, 1943-1944
This 47-page publication gives an overview of the state of the motion picture industry in America during the mid-point of World War II. The Disney Studio is mentioned several times.

Movie Radio Guide, October 17, 1942
"How Movies Can Best Aid the War Effort". This short article includes a picture of Walt Disney and two other celebrities standing in front of a radio microphone.

Movie Stars Parade, April 1943
This issue contains a one-page article on the Donald Duck short *Spirit of '43*.

Movieland, May 1943
"A Studio Goes To War".

Nation, July 3, 1943
Article on *Victory Through Air Power*.

National Geographic, November 1943
Issue contains a full-page color ad for *Victory Through Air Power* titled "Victory Through Air Power. Peace Through Air Power".

National Geographic, January 1944
Issue contains a full-page color ad for *Victory Through Air Power* titled "Blast the Hub and Smash the Wheel".

New Republic, September 6, 1943
Victory Through Air Power.

New York Herald Tribune, July 19, 1943
Review of *Victory Through Air Power*.

New York Times Magazine, January 11, 1942
"Disney Family of Cartoon Carrots".

New York Times Magazine, February 22, 1942
"Donald Duck Joins Up".

New York Times Magazine, November 15, 1942
"Disney's Troupe Goes to War".

New York Times Magazine, January 17, 1943
Education for Death.

New York Times Magazine, April 11, 1943
"The Gremlins Reform an RAF Fable".

New Yorker, July 17, 1943
Victory Through Air Power.

Newsweek, June 1, 1942
Article on California war production workers pictures the Disney-designed Beechcraft Busy Bee insignia.

Newsweek, September 7, 1942
"Plane Pixilators." (Gremlins article)

Newsweek, January 25, 1943
Saludos Amigo and Yankee Donald Duck.

Playthings, February 1942
A Kay Kamen *New Spirit* ad was featured on the front cover.

Playthings, May 1943
A Kay Kamen Gremlins ad appeared on the front cover.

Playthings, June 1943
A Kay Kamen *Victory Through Air Power* ad appeared on the front cover.

Playthings, August 1943
A Kay Kamen ad for the Goofy film *Victory Vehicles* appeared on the front cover.

Playthings, May 1945
A Kay Kamen war loan ad appeared on the front cover.

Popular Mechanics, November 3, 1942
"Donald in Nutziland Sired Der Fuehrer's Face."

Popular Mechanics Daily Picture Magazine, November 8, 1942
Article on *Education for Death.*

Popular Science, October 1942
"How An Anti-Tank Gun Works." This two-page article is illustrated with six pictures from the Canadian BOYS MK 1 anti-tank gun film, *Stop That Tank*.

Popular Science Monthly, September 1942
"Mickey and Donald Work For Victory." This two-page article contains photos of Walt and war-related conceptual artwork.

Popular Science Monthly, April 1944
Contains two pages of color illustrations featuring Disney-designed military insignia.

The Public Opinion Quarterly, Princeton University, Summer 1945
"Mickey as Professor." Short article written by Walt Disney.

Reader's Digest, September 1941
The Canadian edition has a back cover illustration for the Canadian war savings certificate folder.

Reader's Digest, July 1942
Victory Through Air Power.

Reel News, June 1942
"Walt Disney Goes to Washington."

Roto Magazine, September 27, 1942
This supplement was included in the *Courier Journal*. This particular issue has a short paragraph and accompanying photograph related to the Royal Air Force Eagle Squadron insignia.

Sacramento Bee, September 4, 1943
Front-page article announces that the Disney Studio has created mascots for the McClatchy media empire. "Gabby" was the chain's radio mascot, while "Scoopy" was the chain's newspaper mascot. Disney designed the characters in exchange for a $1,500 donation by McClatchy to the Army Relief Fund.

Saturday Evening Post, August 1942
Roald Dahl's *Gremlins* appears in print for the first time.

School Arts, September 1943
"Mickey Mouse and Donald Duck Join the Colors." This two-page article is illustrated with pictures from *Der Fuehrer's Face,* and *Education for Death.*

Slipstream, February 1942
Cover features the insignia of the Cal Aero Training Academy. The eaglet being thrown from the nest represented a new pilot's first solo flight.

Song Hits, November 1942
"Donald Duck Goes To Work For Uncle Sam."

Sunset, January 1944

Back cover has an ad for *Victory Through Air Power* showing the development of bombs. There is a small cartoon with Pluto with the text: "Pluto says sic 'em, lick 'em, buy more bonds." This ad was sponsored by Adel, a wartime plane manufacturer.

Theatre Arts, January 1943

"The Disney Studio at War." This ten-page article contains four illustrations from *Der Fuehrer's Face*.

This Week, July 5, 1942

This newspaper supplement of the *Boston Herald* has an article titled: "Walt Disney Goes to War." The article is illustrated with a photograph showing the Mickey Mouse gas mask. Several Disney insignia designs are also featured.

Tide, July 15, 1943

Contains a ½-page story on the publication *Mickey Mouse on the Home Front*.

TIME, December 22, 1941

"Hollywood to the Wars." This article mentions the U.S. Army Searchlight Battery stationed at the Disney Studio in Burbank and the fact that ammunition was being stored in the Studio parking lot.

TIME, August 17, 1942

"Teacher Disney."

TIME, February 9, 1942

The New Spirit income tax film.

TIME, June 15, 1942

Disney English educational films.

TIME, September 14, 1942

"Battle of Europe." Article mentions the Gremlins.

TIME, January 18, 1943

Education for Death.

TIME, July 12, 1943

Victory Through Air Power.

Toronto Star, January 23, 1941

The issue included a two-page insert pictures 12 insignia. Seven of the "Fighting Mascots" were drawn by Disney artists.

United States Army Recruiting News, March 1942
Article titled "Fun From the Clouds" contains an illustration of the 503rd Parachute Infantry Regiment's Disney-designed parachuting cat insignia.

U.S. Coast Guard Patrol, March 1943
Cover features Donald Duck as the mascot of the Corsair Fleet.

Variety, July 7, 1943
Victory Through Air Power.

APPENDIX I
Wartime and Military Short Films

Disney's wartime films include:

1941
- *The Thrifty Pig* (bond film, National Film Board of Canada)
- *Seven Wise Dwarves* (bond film, National Film Board of Canada)

1942
- *Aircraft Carrier Landing Signals* (Navy)
- *Aircraft Carrier Mat Approaches and Landings* (Navy)
- *All Together* (bond film, National Film Board of Canada)
- *Aircraft Riveting* (Navy)
- *Approaches and Landings* (Navy)
- *Battle of Britain* (Army)
- *Bending and Curving* (Navy)
- *Blanking and Punching* (Navy; no animation)
- *Donald's Decision* (bond film, National Film Board of Canada)
- *Forming Methods* (Navy)
- *Icing Conditions* (Navy)
- *Know Your Enemy—Germany* (Army)
- *The Nazi's Strike* (Army)
- *The New Spirit* (Treasury Department)
- *Out of the Frying Pan into the Firing Line* (Conservation Division of the War Production Board)
- *Prelude to War* (Army)
- *Protection Against Chemical Warfare* (Navy)
- *Stop that Tank* (BOYS MK 1 anti-tank film, National Film Board of Canada)

- *US Army Identification Series—WEFT* (Navy)
- *US Army Identification Series—WEFT and Warships* (Navy)

1943

- *Aeronca Project [Basic Maintenance of Primary Training Airplanes]* (Army and Aeronca)
- *Air Masses and Fronts* (Navy)
- *Air Transport Command* (Navy)
- *Aircraft Carrier Landing Qualifications* (Navy)
- *Aircraft Welding* (Navy)
- *The Aleutian Islands [Alaska Defense Command Project]* (Army)
- *Battle of China* (Army)
- *Battle of Russia* (Army)
- *Beechcraft Maintenance and Repair* (Beech Aircraft Corp. and Army)
- *British Torpedo Plane Tactics* (Navy)
- *C-1 Autopilot* (Part of an eleven-part series completed for the Army as part of the Minneapolis Honeywell Project. This title was composed of three films: "Basic Principles", "Control Panel", and "Servo Motor". The unit this film was created for also received a Disney-designed insignia.)
- *Carrier Rendezvous and Breakup* (Navy)
- *The Cold Front* (Navy)
- *Divide and Conquer* (Army)
- *Fast Company* (Army)
- *Fixed Gunnery and Fighter Tactics* (Navy)
- *Fog* (Navy)
- *Glider Training* (Army)
- *Heat Treating* (Navy)
- *High Level Precision Bombing* (Army)
- *Know Your Enemy—Japan* (Army)
- *Lofting and Layouts* (Navy)
- *The Mark 13-Modification I Aerial Torpedo* (Navy)

- *Mock-Up and Tooling* (Navy)
- *The Occluded Front* (Navy)
- *Rules of the Nautical Road* (Navy)
- *The Spirit of '43* (Treasury Department)
- *Substitutions and Conversion* (Army)
- *Template Reproduction* (Navy)
- *Thunderstorms* (Navy)
- *V.T.B. Pilot Training* (Navy)
- *The Warm Front* (Navy)

1944

- *Air Brakes, Principles of Operation* (Army)
- *Attack in the Pacific* (Office of War Information)
- *Automotive Electricity for Military Vehicles* (Army)
- *Basic Map Reading* (Army)
- *Battle of Cape Gloucester* (Army)
- *Carburetion, Basic Principles* (Army)
- *The Case of the Tremendous Trifle* (Army)
- *Electric Brakes, Principles of Operation* (Army)
- *The Equatorial Front* (Navy)
- *A Few Quick Facts #7 [Venereal Disease]* (Army)
- *Flying the Weather Map* (Navy)
- *Fundamentals of Artillery Weapons* (Army)
- *The Howgozit Chart* (Navy)
- Howitzer, 105mm M2A1 and Carriage M2, Principles of Operation (Army)
- *It's Your War, Too* (Army)
- *Operation and Maintenance of the Electronic Turbo Supercharger* (Army)
- *Theory of Simplex and Phantom Circuits* (Army)
- *Tuning Transmitters* (Army)
- *Two Down and One to Go* (Army)
- *Ward Care of Psychotic Patients* (Army)

- *Weather at War* (Navy)
- *Weather for the Navigator* (Navy)
- *Your Job in Germany* (Army)

1945
- *Another Chance [United Nations Peace Charter]* (Army)
- *Burma Campaign* (Army)
- *Dental Health* (Army)
- *On to Tokyo* (Army)
- *War Comes to America* (Army)

APPENDIX II
Walt Disney Gremlins Letter

This article originally appeared in a Royal Air Force Journal on November 16, 1942. The article was also reprinted in *Slipstream, A Royal Air Force Anthology* (1946), a collection of R.A.F. short stories.

As soon as the Air Ministry heard that I was about to do a Gremlin film, they asked me to write a short article expressing my views of Gremlins in general.

Now I don't think this is a fair request. Truthfully, I have no more idea of Gremlins that I have of fighter tactics or high level bombing. I can only go by what I hear.

I consider it one of the great misfortunes of my life that not being an air gunner, a pilot, or a navigator, I shall never be able to boast of having seen a Gremlin in person.

I shall never be able to discuss, as you men do, the deeper and more subtle points of Gremlin-lore, and suggest new methods of training them to behave. Unfortunately, I am not a Gremlinologist.

With every other film I've made, I've been able, in times of discussion, to stand up and shout "You're wrong!" and then proceed to back up my argument with detailed specifications regarding the size and color of the noses of the Seven Dwarfs, the shape of Pinocchio's hat or the length of Bambi's legs.

But in dealing with your Gremlins, I'll admit I'm at a loss. I can't even pretend that I've seen one, and I must get all of my information and instruction from the R.A.F. fliers themselves.

Numbers of them have passed through here and have come to see me and tried to help me. And from their careful descriptions I have tried to draw the Gremlin as he is actually seen by you in his various phases; on your machines in the air, and as you see him around the airdrome and in the mess.

No one realizes more than I the importance of these little men and the task I am undertaking.

So far I haven't a clue.

That's why I'm depending upon you men for all the gen [sic] I can possibly get about Gremlins. As you can see, I've even begun to pick up some of your language.

Naturally, I can't place the entire responsibility upon your shoulders, but I do wish you'd keep me informed of any new tactics and habits the Gremlins develop from time to time.

Do you suppose it would be possible to find one of the little fellows who could be spared and have him crated and shipped to California? I can assure you that he'll be treated with the utmost care and consideration at this end. We have a plentiful supply of used postage stamps of all vintages, which I understand is his staple diet, and he would be allowed the freedom of the Studio. Although I wouldn't be able to see him, I'm sure he'd serve as an excellent Technical Adviser.

Perhaps this is asking for the impossible, but I do intend to see that when the Gremlins reach the screen, they will be the same Gremlins that you men have flown with and lived with.

And if I should put up any blacks in this film due to lack of pukka gen, [sic] I do hope you won't tear me off a terrific strip.

Walt Disney

APPENDIX III
Gunther Lessing WASP Letter

This is a copy of the letter The Walt Disney Studio sent to the Women Airforce Service Pilots regarding the use of Fifinella as their insignia, after the unit was deactivated in December 1944. The letter and preceding paragraph appeared in an undated WASP newsletter, *The Fifinella Gazette*.

> Fifinella, the little winged pilot, is a symbol of our organization and all that we stand for. For creating her and giving us permission to use her, we thank Walt Disney. The following is a wire from Walt Disney, in connection with Fifi, which we thought you might be interested in reading:
>
> "This will serve as your authorization to use the name and insignia of Fifinella in connection with the post inactivation organization of the WASPs, which is tentatively titled the Order of Fifinella. The name and insigne may not be used for commercial purposes or in connection with any merchandising endeavors from which profit is derived without our specific permission in writing. Also, you will be obligated to append copyright notice to all publications.
>
> "Walt deems it an honor to be numbered among your members with the understanding that because of his many commitments he will be unable to take advice or assume any obligations unless specifically agreed to in each instance. I trust you will understand the valid reasons for these reservations.
>
> "We regret your organization's inactivation but you are entitled to rest on your laurels with the consciousness of a wonderful work wonderfully and efficiently performed during times of great stress.
>
> "Walt Disney Productions by Gunther R. Lessing, Vice-President"

Appendix IV
Matchbook Covers

The following list identifies the unit designations for the 48 Pepsi matchbooks that feature Disney-designed insignia.

- 751st Tank battalion
- 114th Field Artillery, Battery D
- 165th Field Artillery, Battery A
- 45th Air Base Squadron, 46th Base Group
- Patwing Support Force, Aviation Repair Unit 1
- 26th Material Squadron, 19th Air Base
- USS *Blue*
- 48th Pursuit Squadron
- 251st Coast Artillery
- 3rd Reconnaissance Squadron
- 6th Reconnaissance Squadron
- US Naval Reserve Aviation Base
- 46th Air Base
- 9th Field Artillery Battalion
- 56th Signal Battalion
- USS *Hornet*
- Jackson Air Base
- 206th Coast Artillery, Battery B
- 69th Quartermaster Battalion
- Interceptor Squadron
- 331st School Squadron
- Air Corps Training Detachment
- 2nd Signal Armored Battalion

- USS *Carolina*, Alternate Aviation Arm
- Women's Ambulance and Defense Corps of America
- 7th Bombardment Squadron
- 45th Bombardment Squadron
- 40th Bombardment Squadron
- 37th Pursuit Squadron
- US Naval Aviation Station, Aviation Cadets
- Primary Training Squadron 11-A
- 8th Air Corps, Area Service Command
- 55th School Squadron
- 114th Infantry, Company F
- 56th Pursuit Squadron
- 121st Air Corps Observation Squadron
- 134th Medical Regiment, 2nd Ambulance Battalion
- 503rd Parachute Battalion
- 1st Marine Brigade
- 46th Bombardment Group
- 42nd Bombardment Group, 75th Squadron
- 4th Field Artillery Battalion
- Utility Squadron #5
- 57th Signal Battalion
- Mosquito Fleet, Torpedo Boat Squadron
- 22nd Pursuit Squadron
- Air Base Detachment
- 72nd Quartermaster Battalion, Company A

The following 20 matchbooks were produced by the Maryland Match Company for the National Match Company. These matchbook covers were printed with a yellow-colored background and either a glossy or matte finish. The cover pictured an insignia printed in red, white, and blue. The name of the unit that was pictured on the cover was printed on the back cover.

- 45th Pursuit Squadron
- 23rd Pursuit Squadron
- 58th Pursuit Squadron
- Alaska Defense Force
- 47th School Squadron
- 133rd Field Artillery
- 62nd Pursuit Squadron
- 46th Bombardment Group
- Women's Ambulance and Defense Corps of America
- 165th Field Artillery
- USS *Blue*
- Utility Squadron #5
- 75th Mosquito Fleet, Torpedo Boat Squadron
- 251st Coast Artillery
- 751st Tank Battalion
- 56th Pursuit Squadron
- 7th Bombardment Squadron
- 40th Bombardment Group
- 26th Material Squadron
- US Naval Reserve Aviation Base

Appendix V
Insignia Licensing Agreements

When a unit received a Disney-designed insignia, a letter outlining the legal restrictions around the use of the design was sent with the original artwork to the person or the organization that requested the emblem.

The first version of the Studio's legal correspondence was revised in January 1942, when it was learned that companies were producing large quantities of stationery to sell to service personnel. The following is the first iteration. (Vernon Caldwell worked in the Studio's legal Department.)

> Walt Disney is happy to present this insignia to the [name of the unit] for unrestricted use within the armed forces of the United States.
>
> He is presenting this insigne to the [name of the unit] with the stipulation that it will not be exploited for profit or for commercial sales to service personnel. Any questions arising as to the authorization and usage of the insigne should be referred to Kay Kamen, Agent of Walt Disney Productions, 1270 Sixth Avenue, New York City.
>
> We hope the design will meet with your approval.
>
> Cordially,
> Walt Disney Productions
> Signed Vernon Caldwell

The revised letter contained more explicit information about licensing agreements.

> Walt Disney is happy to present this insigne to the [name of the unit] for unrestricted use within the armed forces of the United States with the stipulation that before you permit any profit-making civilian firms to reproduce this insigne in any form or for any commercial sale to service personnel, such firms or individuals must first obtain a license from Kay Kamen, Agent of Walt Disney Productions, at 1270 Sixth Avenue, New York City.

This condition applies only to private merchandise for sale and in no way affects your official use of this insigne on your standard equipment.

We hope this design will meet your approval.

Cordially,
Walt Disney Productions
Signed Vernon Caldwell

APPENDIX VI

Oskar Lebeck Letter: "Der Fuehrer's Face" Party Favor

This is the transcript of a letter from artist Oskar Lebeck to Eleanor Packer of Western Publishing. Packer was Western's comic book editor who liaised with various West Coast cartoon studios. In the letter, Lebeck is asking Packer to contact The Walt Disney Studios in regards to the production of a book and party favor based on the film Der Fuehrer's Face. Neither item was produced commercially.

> December 1, 1942
> From: Oskar Lebeck
> To: Eleanor Packer
>
> We worked out two dummies, one of Donald Duck's Schnitzelbank in book form and the other in a folded large sheet like a map, which people can pin up on the wall at a party. We are most excited about the folded sheet, perhaps since we can manufacture this much more quickly, and being a novelty item, it would probably sell many [more] copies than the book would.
>
> The situation is this now—that we have to get the Studio's okay for this item quickly. As you will see form the dummy, we are playing up the Schnitzelbank rhymes and use on each page two lines from *Der Fuehrer's Face* lyrics as a refrain on the bottom of the page. This item, we anticipate, might sell in million figures and would stimulate sales of the sheet music.
>
> Be sure to impress upon the Studio how much everybody out here likes the item. Somebody from the O.W.I. [Office of War Information] has a dummy of the Schitzelbank now and though we have not had his report yet on how various departments reacted to this item, he assured us that Washington will be very much interested in seeing this Schnitzelbank produced, especially at this time. He feels that up to now nothing has been done in way of propaganda that has equaled this item.
>
> Wire the Studio's okay to us. In the meantime, we are going ahead with the artwork and ideas, being certain that the Studio will give us their okay. The rhymes and drawings in this dummy are, of course, very rough and all will be revised. We will airmail tracings of the actual drawings of the Schnitzelbank rhymes to you for Studio okay before we go ahead making plates. We want to rush this job as much as possible so that we can put this thing out on the stands as quickly as possible.

APPENDIX VII
Community Singing Game: "Der Fuehrer's Face" Party Favor

The following is a transcript of a letter sent to Disney licensing representative Kay Kamen regarding a merchandising tie-in with *Der Fuehrer's Face*. No copies of the so-called "Community Singing Game" were ever produced.

> October 14, 1942
> From: Chester Feitel
> To: Kay Kamen
>
> Here is a merchandising possibility, which looks practical and interesting to me:
>
> Community Singing Game—*Der Fuehrer's Face*
>
> This game would be similar to the old fashioned Schnitzelbank and would consist of shade cloth or heavy treated paper imprinted in one color. It would also consist of several paper noisemakers which sound like the "Bronx Cheer" (the type of gadget now sold for party favors): noisemakers would also be made of paper so the suggested game could be made without too much trouble with priorities. We might also include a smaller sheet or card imprinted with a simplified version of the music—three or four bars specially arranged would be sufficient. This simplified version would be useful for anyone who cared to accompany the community singing on a piano or other instrument.
>
> Noisemakers would have additional uses. For example, Southern Music could see they were placed with orchestras, who in turn could place them on tables in restaurants and nightclubs, for use by guests when *Der Fuehrer's Face* was played. It might also be of interest to RKO for distribution in connection with the exhibition of the motion picture.
>
> Whitman could handle this and should want to do so, as the success of the song and the assured success of the picture would create a great automatic consumer demand. I think the irony of adapting the old German game Schitzelbank to ridicule Germany intensifies the appeal of this letter so I am supplying him with one.

I spent last evening with Nat Winecoff and he thought the possibilities were sensational and is, of course, more than eager to cooperate. If you agree, Nat suggests that you see the New York representative of Southern Music (is his name Ralph Peer?). Nat asked for a copy of this letter so I am supplying him with one.

I realize that we may seem to be a little late in getting started on this item but I do not think this is serious as the song will probably be a war classic and will be popular for the duration and long after; and the game will be used and enjoyed even longer. Will you let me know your reaction to this?

Regards,

CDF:R

APPENDIX VIII
A Message from Walt

From "The Annual Report for Employees of Walt Disney Productions" (December 31, 1945):

> The end of the war has given us the chance to go ahead with plans, which until now we could only think about. It has also confronted us with a number of problems.
>
> It's good to walk down the hall and welcome back so many of the fellows who spent years in the service. It's also good to have finished the training film program that absorbed practically all of our energies, and to get busy with the work of making entertainment pictures.
>
> We have many readjustments to make. Our re-conversion job consists of reorganizing our staff to include the experienced men whom we lost and who have now returned, of training others to provide for increased production, and to build up our inventory of stories in preparation and of pictures in work.
>
> This program will take time, work and sound thinking. Our people have the talent and skill to carry it out. I believe it can be done quickly and efficiently in proportion to the enthusiasm and the team work we can apply to it. All these qualities mean good pictures, and good pictures mean that our future is assured.
>
> We have a clear road ahead. Let's get under way.
>
> Walt Disney

APPENDIX IX
The World Is Our Marketplace

From a Disney press release entitled "The World Is Our Marketplace":

> Disney pictures are designed for a worldwide audience. They overcome differences of speech and customs that often handicap other motion pictures.
>
> During the war markets were greatly diminished. Our pictures did not play in many countries, which were open to us before. Our job now is to not only regain what was lost but to extend this activity to a full world-wide scope. That work is well under way.
>
> Our Distributor (RKO) and our own foreign offices are operating again with vigor and confidence. With improvement in conditions and communications, there is every chance that the pictures we make for world acceptance will soon enjoy full world distribution.
>
> There is now hardly a spot on the globe, which is not equipped to show pictures, nor where the inhabitants are not hungry to see them. In a condition like this, we have a definite advantage in that our product is universally known and appreciated.
>
> Our objective, briefly, is to insure [sic] complete international circulation of our pictures. Special plans are being made with our distributor to market in the former war-blocked countries that accumulation of fine pictures we have on hand, and which, almost without exception, are ideally suited for successful exhibition everywhere—such as *Pinocchio, Dumbo, Bambi, Fantasia*, and others, as well as a series of fine short subjects. To this end, translations are being made into the principal European and Oriental languages.
>
> This backlog of fine product, available for marketing in many territories yet untouched, is a great reserve of financial strength to help insure [sic] for our company a successful period ahead.

APPENDIX X
Mickey Mouse and the D-Day Password Puzzle

Many Disney reference books have stated the words "Mickey Mouse" were used as the password for the D-Day landings—the invasion by Allied forces that took place on the beaches of Normandy on June 6, 1944. My own book, *Toons At War*, initially made this inaccurate claim as well.

After exhaustive research conducted by others, the claim has been debunked. It has now been determined that "Mickey Mouse" was not the overall password for the June 6, 1944, invasion of France. A newspaper article uncovered by fellow Disney historian and researcher Michael Barrier appears to have unlocked the initial source for the claim, suggesting the phrase was actually used as a secret code at the unit level.

The following United Press story appeared in several post-invasion newspapers including the *New York Herald Tribune*, June 8, 1944; the *Charleston Daily Mail*, June 8, 1944; the *Uniontown Morning Herald*, June 6, 1944; and the *New York Post*, June 30, 1944.

Here is the *New York Post* version:

"Dear Mickey Mouse:

"How are you, old boy? How I'd like to see you again!"

"That's all the letter said," concluded Walt Disney. "Just that. It was from an American prisoner in Germany."

To Mr. Disney...this letter in a recent batch of Mickey's fan mail seemed to mean more than the news item that, on June 6, naval officers gathering for an invasion briefing at a port in southern England had to whisper "Mickey Mouse!" into the ear of the sentry before they could receive their orders. Naval officers gathering for invasion briefing at a southern port approached the sentry at the door and furtively whispered into his ear the password of admission: "Mickey Mouse."

The *Uniontown Morning Herald* reported:

With heroic, tragic stories of the invasion filling news columns, it is good to have from the beachhead stage some incident to lighten the stark drama. One such small dispatch tells of a naval unit, which used in preparation for D-Day the password "Mickey Mouse". It was not an inappropriate choice—to pick Walt Disney's lively and forever successful young rodent for a part in gnawing at the coast of France.

Acknowledgments

I originally published this book in 2000 under the title *Toons At War*. Since then, I've accumulated a lot of new information about The Walt Disney Studios' involvement in the war. Recently, I decided it was time to do a revision of the original book in order to share some of this new information with interested readers. That revision, complete with its new title, is what you're looking at right now.

I'd like to thank the following people for helping me out, both with the original publication and this revised edition.

I owe a big thank you to my friend Dennis Books of Seattle, Washington. Dennis and I have known each other for over 25 years. Dennis owns a phenomenal collection of vintage Disney memorabilia including almost 900 pieces of "Golden Age" art, and literally thousands of vintage three-dimensional figurines, story books, and various pieces of rare ephemera. Dennis has been collecting for over 40 years. Not only is his collection one of the best, but Dennis has also visited with and interviewed many Disney legends. His knowledge of animation art and the early history of The Walt Disney Studios is amazing. Besides 1930s Disney collectibles, Dennis also owns a large collection of Disney WW II-related memorabilia and reference material, which he graciously granted me access to while writing this book.

Another big thank you goes to my friend Sam Grabarski, who has supported my research and interest in this chapter of The Walt Disney Studios for around 10 years. Sam owns a large collection of original Disney-themed insignia patches and original Disney insignia art.

Thanks are also due to the following:

Michael Barrier, a researcher I hold in very high esteem. Michael began interviewing animation greats back in the 1960s. Michael gathered important information at a time when no one else was doing the same, and, thanks to Michael, a lot of important material has been gathered and recorded that would have been otherwise lost. I highly recommend Michael's two books: *Hollywood Cartoons: American Animation in its Golden Age* and *The Animated Man: A Life of Walt Disney*. Michael's musings can also be found on his website, MichaelBarrier.com.

Paul Anderson, editor of the now defunct *Persistence of Vision*, and proprietor of the new online resource *Disney History Institute*. Back in 1999, Paul gave me unfettered access to his own archive of material, which is second only to The Walt Disney Company Archives. I am grateful for his assistance and for the access he granted to his collection of research material.

Didier Ghez, who edits the invaluable *Walt's People* series for Theme Park Press. These books contain interviews with past and present Disney employees and are an important addition to the realm of Disney history. Didier also maintains a blog at disneybooks.blogspot.com, where he shares a wide range of historical information related to The Walt Disney Company.

Jeff Pepper, who runs an excellent Disney history site at 2719Hyperion.com. Jeff is the person who thought of my book's new title: *Service With Character*.

Jim Korkis, another researcher I hold in high regard. Jim is always quick to reply to any requests for help or information, and he is always willing to share whatever material he has uncovered. Please visit ThemeParkPress.com to see some of the Disney-related books Jim has authored.

Michael, Debbie, Mitchell, and Madison Sturba. Michael was involved with the first edition of this book. I met Michael in 1987 while working at the Canadian exhibit at World Showcase in EPCOT Center in Florida, and while Michael and his family live on the other side of the country, we maintain a solid friendship.

Travis Getz for creating the cover art for this second, revised edition of my book. Travis creates artwork and morale-supporting products for modern-day combat units. Travis draws some of his inspiration from the art created by Disney artists in WW II. He can be reached through his website, SquadronStore.com.

Dana Tye Rally, the "English schoolmarm". Thank you, Dana, for answering all of my syntax and punctuation questions.

Dave R. Smith and Robert Tieman, retired Walt Disney Company Archivists. I first started corresponding with Dave back in the mid-1980s. He was always generous with his time and always found research material for me to view in person, during treks to the Archives whenever I found myself in southern California. Robert was instrumental in answering the many insignia-related questions I posed over the years, often digging through original correspondence files in order to provide me with background material on the various designs I queried him about.

Dave Kaufman for providing images of Disney-designed insignia patches from his own collection. Dave is one of many fellow collectors I've had the pleasure to come to know over the many years I've been involved with this hobby. Other Disney friends include Gunnar Andreassen, Walt Blanchard, Michael Bowling, Robert Cowan, Matt Crandall, William DePiazza, Patrick and Karen Engle, Janet Ehli Fairchild, John Fawcett, Russell Flores, Lance Fontenot, David Gerstein, Keith Gluck, Violet Groves, Ted Hake, Carol and Jim Hansen, Greg and Carolyn Heberlein, Lynn Henderson, Leo Holzer, Jane and Tim Jinks, JB Kaufman, Jeff Kurtti, Kevin Lanagan, Howard Lowery, Paula Sigman Lowery, Sam Mah, Bob Molinari, Don Morin, Don Peri, Hans Perk, Gordon Porter, Maxine Porter, Bob and Claire Raymond, Phil Sears, Mark Sonntag, Paul Sorokowski, Ken Stigen, Timothy Susanin, Jeff and Annette Usall, John Vargo, Arthur Vassar, and Doug and Pat Wengle.

Thank you to historians Ron Williamson for sharing information about the Jacksonville Naval Air Station, Wayne Weiss for material related to war ace Jimmy Thach, Bernard Lutz and his staff at the National Film Board of Canada Archives, Les Hughes for his information on the Disney-designed OSS insignia, and Richard Nelson for the photo of the Group Automatic Flight Control Equipment Department patch.

I have had the honor of meeting and recording the biographies of many WW II veterans. Five in particular had a Disney connection: Emmet Cook (Prisoner of War, Stalag Luft III, I Wanted Wings, Donald Duck), Dan Sjodin (831st Bombardment Squadron, Timothy Mouse), Virgil Grier (USS *Escambia*, Jose Carioca), John Howard Davis (PT RON 11, Mosquito Fleet), and Walter Kundis (PT RON 36, boxing mosquito).

In 2007, I was asked by Walt Disney's daughter, Diane Disney Miller, to be a Consultant, Special Projects, at The Walt Disney Family Museum in San Francisco. I eventually loaned the Museum 48 items from my own collection for display in Gallery 6, which covers the war years. I have also conducted personal research for Diane, and I've been a guest speaker in the Museum's beautiful *Fantasia*-inspired theater. Being able to contribute to The Walt Disney Family Museum has been a fantastic experience for me thanks to the kindness and generosity of Diane, her husband Ron, and Museum staffers including Michael Labrie, Mary Beth Culler, Anel Muller, and Martin Salazar. A huge thank you is also due Diane who gave me permission to use any and all of the audio from the Pete Martin interviews as I saw fit. This series of interviews revealed many interesting stories related to Walt Disney's career—many of these stories were included in the book *The Story of Walt Disney*, by journalist Pete Martin and Diane Disney Miller. The interviews provide amazing insight into the life and times of Walt Disney.

A special thank you to Bob McLain and his company, Theme Park Press, for expressing an interest in this project and for publishing the second edition of my book.

And finally, to my wife Sandra, and my children Samantha, Daniel, and Adam—thank you for allowing me the time to spend on this project. I love you all very much.

All of the collectible items associated with this book are from my personal collection, unless otherwise credited. All images featured in the e-book or shown on the associated website compendium are used with the permission of the person owning the collectible.

One housekeeping note: where dimensions are given, width precedes height, and all measurements are in inches.

I hope you enjoy reading this book as much as I enjoyed researching and writing about this little-known chapter of Walt Disney's legacy. If you have any questions or comments about this book, the related collectibles or The Walt Disney Studios' involvement in World War II, you can reach me through ServiceWithCharacter@yahoo.com.

David Lesjak
Langley, British Columbia
May 2014

About the Author

David Lesjak has been writing about the history of Walt Disney and his Studio since the mid-1980s. He has had numerous Disney-related articles published in a variety of magazines and newspapers.

In 1987, Walt Disney's daughter, Diane Disney Miller, asked David to join the staff of The Walt Disney Family Museum as a Consultant, Special Projects. He loaned the Museum 48 war-related items from his collection for display in the Museum's Gallery 6, conducted personal research for Diane, and he has lectured at the Museum's Fantasia-inspired theater.

David owns one of the largest collections of Disney WW II-related material as well as a large collection of vintage 1930s Disney memorabilia. He maintains an extensive archive of original Disney research material from the 30s and 40s including period photographs, newspaper, magazine, and journal articles, as well as audio material.

He is the administrator or co-administrator of two blogs and two Facebook groups: vintagedisneymemorabilia.blogspot.com; toonsatwar.blogspot.com; The Friends of the Walt Disney Family Museum; and Disney and the War.

His other hobby is interviewing and writing about World War II veterans and their experiences.

About the Publisher

Theme Park Press is the largest independent publisher of Disney and Disney-related pop culture books in the world.

Established in November 2012 by Bob McLain, Theme Park Press has released best-selling print and digital books about such topics as Disney films and animation, the Disney theme parks, Disney historical and cultural studies, park touring guides, autobiographies, fiction, and more.

For more information, and a list of forthcoming titles, please visit:

ThemeParkPress.com

More Books from Theme Park Press

To see all our books, visit ThemeParkPress.com

Made in United States
Orlando, FL
20 July 2024